"American culture too often 'unites' around only division and shouting. Happily, Rick Lints's Uncommon Unity provides something different, something better—hope for thinking and acting 'differently with our differences,' both inside and outside the church, as we consider how to live out our witness more faithfully. This book is chock full of wisdom, ably reminding us that worldly power isn't the center of life, and thus we can't let disagreements about temporal politics define who we are. Uncommon Unity is filled beginning to end with biblical theology and thoughtful historical reflection. Buy, read, savor, act."

—BEN SASSE,
United States senator, Nebraska

"With scholarly precision and rigor, Rick Lints offers a Christian vision for true pluralism that allows for a healthier understanding of faith in public life. He demonstrates how the scriptural models of marriage, Trinity, and redemptive history can—and indeed must—confidently advance a vision for unity-in-diversity. This book is a gift to all Christians who find the cultural engagement that has characterized evangelicalism inadequate and who seek to become, in the words of Rabbi Jonathan Sacks, a 'creative minority' within our nation."

—TISH HARRISON WARREN,
Anglican priest; author of *Liturgy of the Ordinary* and
Prayer in the Night

"The writings of Richard Lints invariably display, within the contours of orthodoxy, fresh thought and analysis. This book is no exception. At a time when the siren demands of both unity and diversity are threatening to destroy the credibility of democracy itself, Lints outlines the patterns of unity and diversity within Scripture, and argues convincingly that these patterns ought to undergo some adaptation as they confront the complexities of our broken world. Nevertheless, it is the gospel itself that lays down the approaches to these tensions that our hearts desire. Highly recommended."

—D. A. CARSON,
Distinguished Emeritus Professor of New Testament,
Trinity Evangelical Divinity School;
president and cofounder of The Gospel Coalition

"Confident that Christ's kingdom out-narrates the distorted narratives of our age, Lints nevertheless recognizes that how we envision, tell, and practice that story is conditioned by other stories we often just assume. Identifying and analyzing these different takes on unity and diversity for many years, he at last shares the fruit of his labors! Diving beneath the tiresome and polarizing rhetoric of the culture wars, this book gives us deeply informed, well-considered, and timely insights that we desperately need."

—MICHAEL HORTON,
professor of theology and apologetics,
Westminster Seminary California

"Lints covers a breathtaking sweep of history in this short, elegant book. He takes a hard look at the contradictions woven into secular ideals of tolerance and self-determination and makes a strong case that Christianity in general, and evangelicalism in particular, holds the keys to intellectually honest pluralism and a renewed sense of common good in the modern world."

—MOLLY WORTHEN,
associate professor of history,
University of North Carolina, Chapel Hill

"When Christians think about diversity in the church, they likely go to the apostle Paul's teaching about the variety of gifts that church members possess. But what if differences among Christians go beyond spiritual gifts to ethnic, political, geographical, and economic circumstances? Richard Lints tackles this kind of variety without relying on the social sciences. Instead, he brings biblical and theological wisdom to bear on the human variations among Christians. It will provide an invaluable framework for Christians trying to sort out and answer the challenges of unity and diversity in the church."

—D. G. Hart,
Distinguished Associate Professor of History, Hillsdale College;
author *Benjamin Franklin: Cultural Protestant*

"Richard Lints proves a masterful guide in directing followers of Jesus Christ to rise above the seemingly endless division that has come to typify both American society and the church. Part historian, sociologist, biblical scholar, philosopher, psychologist, and theologian, yet always and fully pastoral, he provides a valuable map that helps make sense of our current moral and political maze. He exhorts Christ's people to see and live with one another as the God who made us intended, navigating our earthly citizenship by bringing to bear upon it the reality of our heavenly one. As a shepherd of Christ's sheep, I am grateful and commend his tutelage to all who seek to follow in Jesus's steps."

—LAURA MIGUÉLEZ QUAY,

senior pastor, Linebrook Church;

adjunct theology professor, Gordon-Conwell Theological Seminary

"The evangelical world is desperate for a new imagination of what it means to be a people of different ethnicities, nationaliities, and cultures in a society that rejects Christian assumptions. Uncommon Unity is the beginning of the imagination needed to carry the application of God's redemptive mission deep into the twenty-first century."

—ANTHONY B. BRADLEY,

professor of religious studies, The King's College

UNCOMMON UNITY

Wisdom for the Church
in an Age of Division

UNCOMMON UNITY

Wisdom for the Church in an Age of Division

RICHARD LINTS

LEXHAM PRESS

Uncommon Unity: Wisdom for the Church in an Age of Division

Copyright 2022 Richard Lints

Lexham Press, 1313 Commercial St., Bellingham, WA 98225
LexhamPress.com

Print ISBN 9781683596417
Digital ISBN 9781683596424
Library of Congress Control Number 2022937649

Lexham Editorial: Elliot Ritzema, Jeff Reimer, Allie Boman, Mandi Newell
Cover Design: Jim LePage, Brittany Schrock
Typesetting: Justin Marr

To Brannin and Tanya, whose lives exemplify
the gracious and generous wisdom of the gospel
at the heart of this book

CONTENTS

CONTENTS

FOREWORD

by Timothy Keller

The US church today stands in the midst of a maelstrom of conflict over *e pluribus unum*—unity and diversity. How can people who have been historically excluded and marginalized be genuinely included? How can the disempowered be empowered?

The great paradox is that the very motto, "out of many, one," is judged now to have been a failure. And indeed, how could that slogan, which was the nation's unofficial motto from the time it was put on the Great Seal of the United States in 1782, have ever been taken seriously when over 15 percent of its entire population was enslaved at the time?

Nevertheless, what Rick Lints here calls "the inclusion narrative of democracy" is still the only instrument our secular society has with which to address this problem. This narrative was quite radical in its day, because it held that governing authority did not flow from the governing to the governed, but the other way around—government by common consent.

But while statements in our founding documents—such as all persons being "created equal"—gestured toward belief in moral norms and absolutes that were to be honored by all, the reality on the ground was that women, slaves, and others were excluded. Why? Because at bottom the inclusion narrative of democracy is exactly that—the only way it can adjudicate competing claims and values is by majority rule. If government is by common consent, why can't a majority disenfranchise groups of people if the majority believe it is in the best

interest of the whole polity? "Democracy provides no built-in guarantees against immoral behavior" (49).

The inclusion narrative of democracy had another unintended
consequence. Americans wanted to escape the inherited privilege of
European class society. The great cry was for freedom of opportunity and therefore for a free market, but that led to a new American
version of class society based on economic success or failure rather
than on aristocratic rank. Robert Bellah in *Habits of the Heart* shows
how the religious nature of the majority of the population somewhat
cushioned people from the effect of business based on a pure, exclusive profit motive. But as religion has declined in society, increasing
numbers of people are excluded economically.

Lints, like Bellah, argues here that the democracy narrative alone
does not produce an inclusive society. We need other robust moral
and religious narratives out there in the public square, supplementing
and complementing the democracy narrative. This will be necessary
to create a society in which unity and diversity are held together in
balance, without one devouring the other.

This book shows how the gospel inclusion narrative can be a
resource for our society. The gospel is that we were "excluded" from
God's people and promises but now we "who once were far away
have been brought near by the blood of Christ" (Eph 2:12–13, NIV).
Because Jesus was excluded for us, we have been included. The gospel
inclusion narrative is neither identical with nor totally contradictory
to all parts of the democracy narrative. For example, the modern
idea of freedom is to be liberated from slavery in order to live as we
choose as long as we do not harm, but the biblical theme of exodus
is to be liberated from slavery in order to serve the living God and
thereby come to serve those around us. The two narratives are overlapping but not identical.

Like the democracy narrative, the gospel recognizes the reality
of the *imago Dei*, the absolute equal dignity of all individuals, but
unlike the democracy narrative, the gospel assumes human sinfulness, namely, that "there is an intrinsic human tendency to diminish

the dignity of others as a means of increasing one's own sense of significance" (49).

Like the democracy narrative, the gospel recognizes the importance of human personal identity to finding the balance between unity and diversity. But the gospel rejects the reductionism of modern identities—both those that reduce us to our social group and those that insist we can be radically self-defined.

Lints does a marvelous job of drilling down on the rich resources Christianity provides for this social challenge. Perhaps the greatest of all is the doctrine of the Trinity itself—God is neither more One than Three nor more Three than One. Then there is the teaching of the church as a body—made up of diverse parts but each comprising a crucial part of the whole. Then there is the biblical teaching on marriage, which again is a strong unity across profound diversity.

Some will ask how Christianity can really be able to take a servant stance to a pluralistic society. Doesn't all religion—and Christianity in particular—impose a monolithic social straitjacket on a culture if it gets the chance? In chapters 9 and 10 Lints shows how Christianity is different. It has been made, as it were, for cultural flexibility, and there is no recipe in the New Testament for a Christian culture.

Uncommon Unity is a crucial book. It will serve as a kind of "prolegomena" to the many discussions we are about to have on injustice, unity-in-diversity, and the relationship of religion to public life. There is great wisdom here for all of those projects.

PREFACE

It is an all-too-obvious truth that we live in polarized times. If one were to choose a cultural moment to best exhibit how to "get along with others," ours would definitely not be that time. Our disagreements run deep and by most accounts are getting worse rather than better. Into this nexus, a work both defending and describing the unity of the church may seem a hopeless task. It surely runs against the grain of our ordinary experiences of life together. Ours is a time that thinks far more about what makes us different from each other than what binds us together. We privilege opinions that emphasize the ways we disagree. We are drawn to media that promote a chasm alienating us from "the other side." We are inveterately suspicious of motives that do not align with ours.

At a personal level, we remember moments in our past of deep disagreements that broke apart valued relationships. We play over in our minds the recording of that long-standing argument with our spouse or our sibling or our boss or our former friend. The wounds of those disagreements do not seem to go away. We rehearse the argument again and again—too often only from our perspective. The fracturing of our significant relationships stays with us for a very long time; it is part of our hardwiring.

The pain of these conflicts, however, is a pungent reminder that this is not the way things are supposed to be. As much as we stumble into conflicts, we yearn for an end to them. The sweetness of reconciliation, when it does occur, serves as a reminder that conflict is not final or ultimate. It also provides a unique snapshot of the paradoxical unity-in-diversity for which we have been created. It is paradoxical in the sense that a certain difference is required for the kind of unity that is richer and more satisfying than mere uniformity. This is played out in obvious ways, as with a symphony of diverse instruments blending into a complex unity or a construction team building a house. The apostle Paul's words in Ephesians 4 and 1 Corinthians 12 frame the issue of the unity of the church in precisely these ways as well. Different gifts but one body. Different offices but one church.

Historical discussions on the unity of the church have often focused on the doctrinal or structural ties binding the church together—or binding churches to each other. In what follows, I will be turning this argument upside down. To think more carefully about the unity of the church, we must first reflect on the nature of difference as it stands in relation to the theological constructs of unity. That, in turn, requires us to examine our ordinary intuitions and experiences of difference and the manner in which they both help and hinder us from getting a clearer grasp on the fabric of the church in its unity-in-difference.

Diversity is part of the air we breathe today and a complex overlay on all our lives. It seems conjoined to the polarization of our times and also to the sheer variety of differences that we confront by virtue of the omnipresence of modern technology. We bump into a hundred different kinds of ketchup on grocery store shelves. We traverse the diverse cultures of the globe daily through the media. Our Twitter accounts put us in touch with an incredible array of voices. Diversity, with all its complex layers, is one of those taken-for-granted realities in which our lives are played out. There are many ways to discuss the complexity of difference, and part of the challenge of navigating through the web of differences today is knowing the implicit and explicit meanings of the different kinds of differences.

I intend to examine the ways in which committed and confessionally oriented Christians should think and live in a deeply pluralistic context largely interpreted through the constraints of a late-modern democracy. I am less concerned with the cultural contexts of diversity than how these contexts influence our experience of the unity-in-diversity of the church and the church's relation to these cultural contexts. I will also examine the ways the canon of Scripture itself thinks about diversity and the wisdom it offers for living in a thickly plural-ized culture, both inside the church and outside its walls.

Part 1 of the book (chapters 1–4) deals with the cultural and con-textual influences on how we understand and deal with difference. In chapter 1, I open by explaining why difference is important and why it matters for sustainable constructs of unity. I also consider the current cultural moment and the deep polarizations through which our differences are too often interpreted. In chapter 2, I look at the history of democracy in America and the peculiar impact it has had on the ways we think about difference and the kinds of difference that have been brought to the forefront of our consciousness. The dis-tinctive emphasis on inclusion and exclusion at the heart of modern democratic polity has profoundly shaped, for good and ill, the ways we relate to others across our differences. Chapter 3 turns to the dis-tinctively religious character of these issues, considering the sacred and secular roots of our instincts about constructive and destructive forms of difference. In that context, I ask whether a secular age has the moral resources to sustain the ties that bind us together across our differences. In the final chapter of part 1, I examine the social-cultural conditions of modernity as a window to the connections between plu-ralism and diversity. Those conditions include the movement from fate to choice represented in the power of the tools of modernity, which helps us understand the way in which our fascination with freedom has led to a much greater fracturing and fragmentation of our body politic, inside and outside the church.

In part 2 (chapters 5–8), I consider biblical resources for think-ing more clearly and navigating more faithfully the way in which difference relates to unity and the way in which unity relates to dif-ference. Chapter 5 argues for a biblical anthropology rooted in the early chapters of Genesis. The peculiar relational character of the persons depicted at the outset of creation serves as a template for human identity across the remainder of the canon. A person's iden-tity is found in relationships—first and foremost in their relationship to the God who made them, and derivatively in their relationships with other persons. This anthropology stands in opposition to the modern intuition that people's identity lies solely within themselves as individuals. In chapter 6, I examine three different biblical models of unity-in-diversity: marriage, the Trinity, and redemptive history. In each of these models, there is an overarching conceptual framework of difference-within-unity that may seem obvious at first glance but is often difficult to apply to other areas of our human experience. Recognizing the complex relationship of difference to unity in each of these models helps illuminate the fabric of the created order regarding human relations more generally. In chapter 7, I explore the history of the church's actual experience of unity-in-diversity and contrast it with the church's teaching about its unity. How the church lives out its sense of unity and how it doctrinally construes that unity have not always been closely aligned. Following the narrative of the lived experiences of the church across the ages may provide clues as to how one might think more carefully about the unity-in-diversity of the church in our own time. In the final chapter of part 2, I examine the relationship between the mission of the church and the unity of the church. The recent surge in missiological understandings of the church's identity has opened a new conversation regarding the movement dynamics of the church and the institutional dynamics of the church. This conversation in turn may provide a richer way to think about the church's unity-in-diversity. From this angle, the history of evangelical churches in particular can be viewed in a very different light. These sorts of churches are often far more interested in their evangelistic mission than in their institutional unity with other churches, and so tend to display a different kind of unity—what I call a missiological unity—than traditional ecclesiological analyses consider.

In part 3 (chapters 9–10), I explore the category of "wisdom" as the intended mechanism for engaging the issues of unity and difference. In chapter 9, the question of how the church is to live out its mission in different contexts (the theological issue of contextualization) comes to the forefront. The wisdom of the gospel strongly argues for the church to look differently in different contexts—but how different?

And how does the context influence the identity of the church? There is no mechanical way to provide answers to these questions. Wisdom, though messy, is the most appropriate tool to work through the complex issues surrounding the contextualization of the church.

In the concluding chapter, I explore the nature of wisdom at greater length. Wisdom is situational without being relativistic. It is grounded in the nature of reality while recognizing the complexities of human reality. It can hold in tension apparently contrasting convictions while keeping a clear eye on that which is final and ultimate. The clearest model of wisdom is found in the story of the gospel, which stands as a strong rebuke to human pretensions and a strong encouragement to courage and humility. These are essential to achieve the reconciliation required for a genuine experience of unity-in-difference in the life of the church.

In a time when the cultural patterns of fragmentation and polarization spill over into the church, it is important to remember that we were created for the experience of unity-in-difference and that our yearnings for it are themselves pointers in the right direction. Wisdom would suggest that seeking forgiveness and granting forgiveness are the surest routes for the journey. This is counterintuitive in a time like ours, since forgiveness is not grounded in natural rights but in the display of mercy both extended and received. The way of reconciliation does not stand in opposition to our natural rights but rather is the means to complete them. The violation of natural rights explains why the fracturing and fragmentation of human relations takes place. The grace of forgiveness explains why they may be put back together. This is the journey of the gospel as well, and my hope is that this gospel journey will help us to live more into the grace of forgiveness with each other.

Life is not like a river but like a tree. It does not move towards unity but away from it and the creatures grow further apart as they increase across time.

—C. S. Lewis, The Great Divorce

1

MAKING SENSE OF OUR DIFFERENCES

The worship service was as unusual as the surroundings of this small village in southern Zimbabwe. It began slowly, as families made their way to the village center following their leisurely Saturday-evening dinner. The men gathered on the right side of the structure, with the women and children meandering toward the left. I was helped through the local dialect by a gentle-souled translator. Then came the sudden banging of the drums, calling all to rise. The women and children began dancing in a large circle as a familiar hymn was sung. As the singing faded, the first preacher entered the pulpit to deliver what would be an hour-long sermon on the story of the exodus. Smaller children began falling asleep in their mothers' arms. Another song was followed by a second preacher and another hour-long sermon—this time on the book of Daniel. As the night wore on, older children and mothers were now sleeping. As the sun began to rise, the preaching came to a close after the twelfth sermon. Everyone had drifted to sleep at some point during the long, hot evening. At daybreak, there was a march to the local river for baptisms before we dispersed for Sunday lunch. With the heat of the day rising, the twelve preaching elders sat with me under a large shade tree. I had to ask, "Do you do this every Saturday night/Sunday morning?" Without hesitancy, the reply came, "Sometimes Tuesday nights as well!"

Throughout my stay, I struggled to make sense of these dear Christian brothers and sisters worshiping in a fashion *very* different from anything I had ever experienced. As a young church planter in the Boston suburbs, I had wrestled at great length over the precise details needed to conduct the most appealing worship service to attract folks as a congregation. How could I make sense of a world of differences from those Zimbabwean Christians? What about those neighbors in "my own backyard" whose cultural assumptions also seemed a world apart? Which differences mattered, and which ones could I affirm as diverse expressions of an equally genuine Christianity?

We are ever more conscious of diversity—not only in terms of Christian worship but across a broad array of factors: we encounter diverse political communities, ethnic and racial communities, vocational and economic communities, even communities with passionate diversity of sports loyalties. Our social contexts are pluralized in countless directions and experienced at many levels. The "contemporary" is often marked out from the "traditional" purely by the plurality of experience, with the contemporary connoting a much higher volume of diversity—diversity of music, of religion, of vocation, of culture, of language.[1] Tension in each of these spheres arises as different communities bump into each other.

Another factor contributing to our sense of living inside of deep differences is the technology in which our lives are embedded. Technology gives voice to everyone while also narrowing the range of voices influencing us. Consider how many individuals fill your email address book or the number of your friends on Facebook. Consider how many television channels compete for diverse niches of interest. Consider the vast number of locations we are transported to every day via the internet and the vast number of cultures we bump into

---

1. Peter Berger says, "Modernity is not necessarily secularizing; it is necessarily pluralizing. Modernity is characterized by an increasing plurality, within the same society, of different beliefs, values, and worldviews." Berger, "Secularization Falsified," *First Things* (February 2008): 23. One may argue that secularization is, at least in part, a consequence of certain kinds of pluralization. That question is tackled at greater length in chapters 3 and 4.

as a result. These varieties of experience in our lives have the consequence of privileging diversity over unity in our collective consciousness, even if they also produce an instinctive backlash against dealing with so many emotional differences.[2]

Certain kinds of difference elicit sharp reactions; other kinds may be shrugged off as inconsequential. There are many kinds of differences; some matter and others do not. The contexts in which differences are experienced often determine how those differences are interpreted. In the small community church, the pastor's relational investment and willingness to personally disciple is not only noticed but often analyzed, especially in the case of missteps or unintended slights. By contrast, for the megachurch pastor who has gained celebrity status, any relational awkwardness is excused in exchange for their platform presence. Churches deeply rooted in their denominational heritage take denominational differences seriously in all manner of budget matters—missionary sending and supporting, for example, are closely linked to a common denominational identity. In a nondenominational church, though, mission giving and other funding isn't allocated on this basis at all—denominational differences are inconsequential.

The costliness of difference is apparent when it becomes concrete. Differences of taste may not matter until it comes to deciding what the family will eat for dinner—together. Differences of fashion seem harmless enough until it's time for a family photo. Different habits of cleanliness may not seem significant until husband and wife must learn to live with these habits day in and day out. Differences matter when they serve as occasions for divisions and disagreements.

In a modern democracy, the freedom to express different opinions prevents a community or nation from becoming ideologically captive to any one partisan interest. On the other hand, most of us are wary

---

2. It also can create emotional exhaustion for individuals who feel as if they must disperse themselves among so many other people. See Jonathan Haidt, "The Age of Outrage," *City Journal*, December 17, 2017, https://www.city-journal.org/html/age-outrage-15608.html.

of disagreement when it becomes polarizing and interminable. We intuitively want others to agree with us. When we bump into differences of opinion too concretely and not merely in an abstract conversation about the body politic, it makes us uncomfortable. Certain kinds of differences hit too close to home. Uncovering genuine and deep disagreement can be so sharp as to paralyze us. When it breeds conflict, families, churches, communities, and even companies can be destroyed. People with whom we disagree may appear to threaten not merely beliefs but our sense of the common, overarching good.[3]

An important irony is the ever-growing disparity between the descriptive diversity of contemporary culture and the actual homogeneity of the communities in which we experience day-to-day life. We are conscious of the conflicts between Red Sox fans and Yankee fans, but part of what animates great sports rivalries is the unity of the respective rival communities. Under the pressures of pluralization, we tend to socially migrate to safe havens of unity. Social conservatives tend to listen to socially conservative commentators. Social radicals tend to read other social radicals. We migrate toward homogeneous communities as a response to the increase of diversity around us.[4] Our experience in the church can be similar. Baptists tend to congregate with Baptists and Lutherans with Lutherans, and so on. However, as I will note in later chapters, the lines of demarcation between traditional denominations appear to be blurring. Individuals now identify less with a particular denomination and are more likely to feel comfortable associating with a wide array of church traditions. There are still social styles and internal church cultures that largely

3. James Skillen, "Pluralism as a Matter of Principle," in *The Many and the One: Religious and Secular Perspectives on Ethical Pluralism in the Modern World*, ed. Richard Masden and Tracy B. Strong (Princeton: Princeton University Press, 2003), notes that not all differences present as one side being right and the other side wrong.

4. Chris Bale, *Breaking the Social Media Prism: How to Make Our Platforms Less Polarizing* (Princeton: Princeton University Press, 2021), challenges the assumption that social media is the primary contemporary polarizing force. In a counterintuitive way, when persons are exposed to significant differences of opinion on social media, it simply reinforces their own in-built biases and tribal identities.

determine who is attracted to certain churches and not others. The unique doctrines of a church may be less important compared to the music or the style of preaching, but there remains a distinctive ethos that attracts some and repels others. The loss of denominational identities is part of the larger story of the loss of a sense of belonging to particular local communities in our time. The experience of living in deep diversities exerts pressure on our natural sense we have of belonging to others. Many sociologists, following Robert Putnam's work, have noticed the significant increase in isolation and loneliness in the modern world.[5] There appears to be an ever-decreasing amount of social glue binding people together in genuine relationships in late modernity. The symptoms of social isolation are manifest and appear to be increasing. It is not simply that we are divided more and more by our differences, but also there are more and more obstacles to maintaining enduring relational connections of significance, even within our own local communities.[6]

It might appear hopeless at the outset to address the church's call to unity in the face of such overwhelming differences, especially given the virtually infinite number of them. But thinking clearly about difference will help us think more wisely about unity, the unity of the church in particular, and thus enable Christians to live more nimbly in a world of deep, embedded polarization. Some differences do matter and often create conflicts that are not easily resolved. It is also true that differences sometimes mask our commonalities and keep us from the tasks we are called to work on together as Christians.

---

5. The literature on this is vast (and somewhat contested) and centers on Robert Putnam, *Bowling Alone: The Collapse and Revival of American Community* (New York: Simon & Schuster, 2001). Mention could also be made of more recent treatments dealing with the consequences of social fragmentation and contemporary loneliness. See Timothy Carney, *Alienated America: Why Some Places Thrive While Other Places Collapse* (New York: Harper, 2019); and Ben Sasse, *The Vanishing American Adult* (New York: St. Martin's, 2017).

6. Sasse notes that the average American adult has gone in the span of twenty years from having three close friends to having only two close friends. Sasse, *Vanishing American Adult*, 124. Most of us know that if you ask the typical baby-boomer father whether he has bared his soul with anyone in the last year, the overwhelming (honest) reply is no.

In this work I want to investigate the differences between as well as inside churches, discerning which ones are complementary and which ones are divisive. Discussions about the unity of the church have traditionally bypassed this concern in favor of a doctrinal account of essential beliefs necessary for church unity. These doctrinal issues are not inconsequential; however, they often miss the social realities in which most individuals in late modernity experience church unity or disunity.

OUR PRESENT DIVERSITIES

In the early decades of the twenty-first century in the West, the concept of difference is increasingly attached to the categories of race, ethnicity, gender, and sexuality.[7] When universities employ a "diversity officer," it is for the purpose of increasing racial and ethnic diversity in the student body. "Diversity training" within companies, likewise, is directed primarily at racial and ethnic differences among employees. When the US Census attempts to take a snapshot of the population every ten years, it is also prominently concerned with the ethnic and racial makeup of the population. In these and many other ways, "diversity" is a term loaded with connotations that draw attention to certain kinds of differences while avoiding others. Unfortunately, the language of diversity in some circles defines a person's identity solely in terms of ethnicity or race (and to some extent gender and sexuality as well). In later chapters I argue that, while these identity markers are important, they are not the sole basis by which identity is secured. Humans are far too complex to be reducible to a single identity marker.

---

7. These are discussed at much greater length in later chapters. The emergence of this set of difference is helpfully charted by David A. Hollinger, *Postethnic America* (New York: Basic Books, 2005), who suggests that, when these categories emerged on the US Census form in the late 1970s, they thereby began to serve as the interpretive categories for understanding the different "kinds" of American citizens. Robert Putnam refers to the four canonical ethno-racial categories: white, African American, Latino, and Asian, also as prescribed by the US Census. See his "E Pluribus Unum: Diversity and Community in the Twenty-First Century," *Scandinavian Political Studies* 30, no. 2 (2007): 137–74. One of the difficulties with these categories, as many have pointed out, is the complexity of children (and grandchildren) of "mixed" marriages. Do children born to parents of different ethnicities belong to one category, two categories, or neither?

Further, these identity markers are not sufficiently cohesive as to mean the same for everyone under their umbrella.[8]

This emphasis on racial identity has emerged from reconstructing the history of modern democracy as primarily a history of discrimination. On this reading, the differences that matter historically arose in the cultural systems of inclusion and exclusion.[9] Though we must take seriously the story of democracy's bent toward inclusion and exclusion, it would be a mistake to view this narrative as the *only* story worth telling, or that this story captures everything important about inclusion and exclusion.[10] The story of the gospel is also a narrative of inclusion and exclusion, but it has far greater implications and explanatory power, and it does so without minimizing the significance of the cultural systems of democracy that bend toward exclusion. The main thing I want to do in this book is to view the gospel story as the interpretive lens through which we best understand the telos of creation as a rich, deep, and complex unity-in-difference. Insofar as our cultural moment has come to emphasize diversity in certain ways, it is also appropriate for those of us who confess the gospel to think through how we relate to this wider cultural conversation as well as how the contemporary categories of diversity influence the ways we navigate differences in the church and outside the church.[11] We should

---

8. Emerging out of the movement we now refer to as postmodernism, there is a sizeable group of intellectuals who have argued that *all* of human experience must be interpreted through the lens of race, ethnicity, and sexuality. These movements range from critical race theory to fourth-wave feminism to whiteness studies to intersectionality. The common core to these movements is the claim that systemic bias related to race, ethnicity, and sexuality is the primary window through which to interpret human behavior.

9. This is often referred to the "politics of identity." Jonathan Rauch defines it as a "political mobilization organized around group characteristics such as race, gender, and sexuality, as opposed to party, ideology, or pecuniary interest." Rauch, "Speaking as a … ," *New York Review of Books*, November 9, 2017, http://www.nybooks.com/articles/2017/11/09/mark-lilla-liberal-speaking. Identity politics is ably defended by Amy Gutman, *Identity in Politics* (Princeton: Princeton University Press, 2003), and ably criticized by Jean Bethke Elshtain, *Democracy on Trial* (New York: Basic Books, 1995).

10. Chapter 2 is devoted in its entirety to this peculiar story.

11. Francis Fukuyama, "Why National Identity Matters," *Journal of Democracy* 29, no. 4 (2018): 5–17, makes the point that politics on the Right and the Left both read the narrative of discrimination as a way to leverage political power. He writes, "The left has focused less

not forget that there are other differences among us (family systems, personality types, experiences, language, education, economic conditions, neighborhoods, peer groups, and so on), all of which serve to bind us together with certain persons while distinguishing us from others. We all yearn for unity-in-the-midst-of-our-differences. This unity seems elusive today, in our cultural discourse and in our ecclesial discourse.[12] Thinking more clearly and wisely about that unity-in-difference is the challenge before us.

It is important to understand what gave rise to the current categories by which we understand the differences that our cultural moment emphasizes. A significant part of that historical narrative indicates that the nebulous construct of "diversity" became a much more pronounced positive after the cultural revolutions of the 1960s.[13] It was an era of protest against certain kinds of exclusionary practices in the modern democratic state and an ever-increasing sense of alienation from older structures of political power and political authority. It was a radical decade rooted both in a yearning for greater democratization and in a revolt against the history of democracy. The 1960s called into question the melting-pot narrative that saw cultural uniformity as the highest social good. The decade served as a pungent reminder

---

on broad economic equality and more on promoting the interests of a wide variety of groups perceived as being marginalized—Blacks, immigrants, women, Hispanics, the LGBT community, refugees, and the like. The ight, meanwhile, is redefining itself as a collection of patriots who seek to protect traditional national identity, an identity that is often explicitly connected to race, ethnicity, or religion." On both the Right and the Left, "political leaders have mobilized followers around the perception that a group's dignity has been affronted, disparaged, or otherwise disregarded. This resentment engenders demands for public recognition of the dignity of the group in question. A humiliated group seeking restitution of its dignity carries far more emotional weight than people simply pursuing their economic advantage" (5).

12. Martha Nussbaum reminds us that there are significantly different models among the diverse countries in the West as to what is "common" and thereby how to deal with differences. She highlights in particular the differences between many European countries where genealogy and religious identity (not religious practice) serve as the framework of commonality, whereas in North America genealogy is far less significant as an overarching commonality. See Nussbaum, *The New Religious Intolerance: Overcoming the Politics of Fear in an Anxious Age* (Cambridge, MA: Harvard University Press, 2012).

13. See Richard Lints, *Progressive and Conservative Religious Ideologies: The Tumultuous Decade of the 1960s* (London: Routledge, 2010).

that "democratic unity" is somewhat of an oxymoron, since democracy is a social polity that grants protections for diverse opinions.[14] It permits and even encourages differences of opinion; therefore, social unity in democracy will always be tentative and fragile.[15] In Steven Pinker's apt phrase, "democracy is essentially based on giving people the right to complain."[16]

The framework for engaging with certain kinds of diversity in our time has been sketched out by our secular democracy. (We might also call this democratic secularism.)[17] There is much lament in conservative religious circles about the moral emptiness of a secular democracy loosed from religious convictions, while at other times Christians have ardently defended this social polity because it provides for a wide religious freedom that enables them to speak into the public moral issues of the day.[18] Yet while Christians remain remarkably free (historically speaking) to express their convictions openly, their voice remains one among a myriad of other voices clamoring for attention in the contemporary public square. In American democracy, persons are

14. See Gordon Wood, "The American Enlightenment," in *America and Enlightenment Constitutionalism*, ed. Gary McDowell and Jonathan O'Neill (New York: Palgrave, 2006), 159–78.

15. Joseph Ellis suggests that the founding of democracy in America carried within it two central conflicting intuitions—namely, that sovereignty is to be located in the individual (thereby depicting government as an alien force, making rebellion against it a natural act) and that sovereignty is located in that collective called the "people" (thereby making government an essential protector of liberty rather than its enemy). American history is essentially the constant and conflicting interaction of these two cultural intuitions. See Ellis, *American Creation: Triumphs and Tragedies at the Founding of the Republic* (New York: Knopf, 2007).

16. Steven Pinker, *Enlightenment Now* (New York: Viking, 2018), 205. Jeffrey Stout refers to democracy in less pejorative terms but aims in the same direction when he refers to it as an "endless conversation" without fixed points. See Stout, *Democracy and Tradition* (Princeton: Princeton University Press, 2003), 12.

17. Charles Taylor asserts that democracy and secularism are products uniquely owing their origins to the Christian West. It seems clear enough that secularism does not demand democracy (e.g., the Soviet Union and modern China), but whether democracy can survive apart from some form of civil religion is an open-ended question. Taylor, "Can Secularism Travel?," in *Beyond the Secular West*, ed. Akeel Bilgrami (New York: Columbia University Press, 2016), 1–27.

18. Christopher Wolfe sketches out this divided spectrum accurately in historical perspective. See Wolfe, "Free Exercise, Religious Conscience and the Common Good," in *Challenges to Religious Liberty in the Twenty-First Century*, ed. Gerard V. Bradley (Cambridge: Cambridge University Press, 2012), 93–111.

protected from the intrusion of others by virtue of possessing certain rights enunciated in the Constitution. Tolerance is one way to frame those rights and is a primary political manner of dealing with difference, but it should not be the only way Christians respond to those with whom they disagree—inside or outside the church. Tolerance as the sole or primary democratic mechanism for dealing with diversity often pushes us toward a shallow way of engaging with each other honestly and generously. Merely being tolerant of others may mean we do not take them seriously enough as persons made in God's image.

We have embraced a social polity that encourages freedom of opinion largely for two reasons. First, freedom of opinion serves as a check on impositions of power. And second, those protected freedoms allow one's convictions even when in the minority. We aim at these goals but rarely ever fully achieve them in practice.[19] But values are always aspirational by nature, and it is dangerous when we assume that any form of politics will solve our deep disagreements. A contemporary political theorist and politician puts it this way:

> It seems clear that in America today, we're facing problems that feel too big for us, so we're lashing out at each other, often over less important matters. ... Fortunately, we can avoid addressing the big problems as long as someone else—some nearer target— is standing in the way of our securing the political power even to try. It's easier to shriek at the people on the other side of the street. ... At least our contempt unites us with other Americans who think like we do. At least *we* are not like *them*.[20]

Utopian political projects, whether on the Right or the Left, always founder on the rock of reality. Human nature is fragile and flawed,

---

19. Patrick Deneen, Introduction to *Augustine and the Limits of Politics*, by Jean Bethke Elshtain (Notre Dame: University of Notre Dame Press, 2018), writes, "Democracy is more a cultural ethos than it is a set of solutions. It acknowledges the pervasiveness of conflict and the fact that our loyalties are not one; our wills are not single; our opinions are not uniform; our ideals are not from the same cloth."

20. Ben Sasse, *Them: Why We Hate Each Other and How We Can Heal* (New York: St. Martin's, 2018), 9.

and human communities will always manifest those flaws and that fragility. We should not suppose there is a set of political arrangements looming in the future that would resolve all our disagreements. The Puritan vision of a "city on a hill" appeared to promise a stable moral order, but it was an illusion to suppose human brokenness (individually and communally) could be overcome by any political arrangement. Every couple of generations, that vision of a utopian political framework comes to life again among groups of conservative Christians.[21] In our time, outsiders to the Christian faith (or outsiders to the particular tradition of Christianity manifest in the political order) often view that dream as a moral imposition on their own human rights. Christians of all stripes should recognize that a prophetic presence in politics rather than a new political order more nearly captures the missionary task of Christians in their own culture. Christians will flourish only as they learn better how to live in a religiously plural and deeply diverse secular age and how best to work for appropriate kinds of unity.[22]

Listening to the Echoes
from Ancient Contexts

Christians also have much to learn from the ancients, who remind us that unity and diversity have been perennial concerns that unveil assumptions about the nature of reality itself. Under the rubric of the "one and the many," we learn from Plato that these issues animated

---

21. See D. G. Hart, *A Secular Faith: Why Christianity Favors the Separation of Church and State* (Chicago: Ivan R. Dee, 2006).

22. Roger Finke and Rodney Stark offer a minority opinion that religious belief and practice thrive far better in more diverse settings than in less diverse settings. They use rates of religious participation to make the case that when a religious monopoly takes hold (e.g., in Puritan Massachusetts in the 1690s or in Roman Catholic France throughout the modern period), religious participation is very low. When religious diversity is introduced on a larger scale, religious participation increases significantly. See Finke and Stark, *The Churching of America, 1776–2005: Winners and Losers in Our Religious Economy*, 2nd ed. (New Brunswick, NJ: Rutgers University Press, 2005).

discussion well before his time.[23] Was the world in which humans lived essentially unified, or was it made up of an infinite number of discrete parts in a state of constant flux? The issue was not a scientific or empirical question in the modern sense of those terms, but rather a question of meaning and purpose. Did the world have one defining purpose or meaning, or was the world constantly changing without any fixed meaning or purpose? It is unlikely that the average person in the ancient world was concerned with such abstract questions, but we do know that these matters became significant as ancient empires rose and fell, and historians interpreted the flow of history as having (or lacking) purpose. The ruling elites of the ancient world wrestled with their own convictions on what held empires together and what divided them, leading to their downfall.

In contrast, ancient Israelites believed that Yahweh moved history with an inexorable purpose, and that he exercised oversight of all diverse nations in the created order. Yahweh was no local deity. Yahweh consistently reminded Israel they were to have no other gods (Exod 20). The underlying premise was that Israel's identity would inevitably be formed by what and whom they worshiped. If they would worship the living God, Israel would be "alive" to justice and compassion. Worship dead idols, and they, like the golden calf (Exod 32), would have eyes but would not see, would have ears but would not hear, and their hearts would grow stone cold to justice and compassion. The unity of their worship was underwritten in part by the cultural separation from the nations that surrounded them. Though similarities existed between the moral codes of ancient Israel and some of the larger surrounding empires, Israel's law book displays far more distinctive elements than similarities—the most distinctive difference being the command to worship the one and only living God.

With the radical call to go out into the nations with the good news of Jesus, the early church found itself in uncharted waters. If

---

23. See Colin Gunton, *The One, The Three and the Many: God, Creation and the Culture of Modernity* (Cambridge: Cambridge University Press, 1993).

it was to be "all things to all people" (1 Cor 9:22) by adapting to the various languages and cultural habits throughout the gentile world, in what would their unity consist, and how would it be sustained? Underscoring this concern was the conundrum of abiding by the command of Israel to worship only the *one* true God while also affirming the full deity of Jesus. How was the early church to understand the unity of God, and in what manner would it frame the relationships of the persons in the Triune God?

The early church emerged in the age of empires that contained within their boundaries smaller local tribal cultures. In the Mediterranean world, Roman authority over its colonies vacillated between ambivalence and tyranny. History remembers the latter most vividly, and this has often provided an argument for a countercultural understanding of the Christian faith. The ruling authorities viewed Christianity as an alternative to Roman paganism with its local and imperial deities, including the emperor himself. The persecution of the early church in the latter half of the first century resulted in the dispersion of Christians out of Jerusalem and into many other cities and towns of the empire. Early Christians in the volatile and violent world of the late Roman Empire developed a sense of their fundamental difference from all things Roman, but they also, by virtue of being culturally scattered, developed a sense of being "at home" in many diverse cultures. As historian Mark Noll notes, "The great turning point represented by the destruction of Jerusalem (in AD 70) was to move Christianity outward, to transform it from a religion shaped in nearly every particular by its early Jewish environment into a religion advancing toward universal significance in the broader reaches of the Mediterranean world, and then beyond."[24]

Christians soon learned they would have to survive outside the cultural homogeneity of first-century Judaism, speak the languages of the gentiles, and adapt to their customs and cultural habits. By the early

---

24. Mark A. Noll, *Turning Points: Decisive Moments in the History of Christianity*, 3rd ed. (Grand Rapids: Baker Academic, 2012), 42.

second century, Christians had become at home speaking Latin in Italy, North Africa, and Spain. They spoke Greek in the eastern Mediterranean and eastern Europe and learned Syriac in the Middle East. They were a people who belonged nowhere and everywhere at the same time.

The move from the Jewish world into the pagan gentile cultures represented the gravest challenge to the early Christians.[25] In almost every letter of the New Testament, the challenge of taking the gospel to the gentiles was of supreme importance. The book of Acts charts this journey beginning with the ascension of Jesus (his final climactic encounter with his disciples) through the first preaching of the gospel in Jerusalem to its initial foray to the Samaritans and then full bore into gentile lands at Athens before culminating with Paul's proclamation of the gospel at Rome. In the space of Luke's narrative, Christianity made the massive cultural leap from its origins in the Jewish world to a much wider and diverse set of gentile destinations. This cultural journey forced early Christians to wrestle with being a minority religion within the Roman Empire, as both a sect of Judaism and increasingly a set of communities embedded in many diverse gentile cities.[26] Not only did they have to wrestle with the variety of settings they found themselves in, but they also had to wrestle with the variety of ways the Christian faith would look in those different settings. How much of the Jewish law was to be observed? How was church discipline to be administered?

---

25. There was a Jewish diaspora that had been underway in the long centuries before Jesus. There were significant Jewish communities in Babylon (modern-day Iraq) as well as Egypt and elsewhere along the coast of North Africa. However, wherever Jewish communities were sustained, there was a cultural continuity with the Jewish communities of Judea. When the early Christian communities scattered from Judea, by contrast, the development of multiple cultural assimilations took place. See Michael J. Kruger, *Christianity at the Crossroads: How the Second Century Shaped the Future of the Church* (Downers Grove, IL: IVP Academic, 2018).

26. Robert Louis Wilken summarizes the journey: "Early in the second century there were Aramaic-speaking Christians in Adiabene (modern Arbil) in northern Iraq. … The gospel was brought to Central Asia and to China by Syriac-speaking missionaries. [They entered into] other linguistic worlds, those of the Copts up the Nile River in Egypt, the Nubians (in present-day Sudan), the Ethiopians farther south, the Armenians east of Asia Minor, and the Georgians between the Black and Caspian Seas." Wilken, *The First Thousand Years: A Global History of Christianity* (New Haven: Yale University Press, 2012), 26.

What were appropriate Sabbath practices? How were Christians to relate to the variety of pagan festivals? In what did their unity consist, and in what ways did Christian communities adapt differently to different settings?

Overlaid on the significant cultural diversity of the first century, the early Christian communities learned to speak into a Mediterranean world that had consolidated power into the hands of one person—the emperor. In the century before Jesus, Rome had extended its imperial rule over most of modern-day France, Spain, Italy, and Greece, as well as over much of North Africa and large swaths of the eastern Mediterranean world.[27] Travel and trade were largely unrestricted within the empire. Consequently, local cultures were interacting with each other while the conflicts between them were held in check by the heavy hand of the Roman military. By the end of the third century AD, the empire became so large it was necessary for it to be divided into four administrative districts.

We cannot draw a straight line from the religiously pluralistic world in which Christianity first emerged and the religiously pluralistic world of the early twenty-first century. The Roman Empire with its multiculturalism, both genuine and fragile, was the primary globalizing force of the world into which Christianity entered. In the empire, there was no sharp conceptual difference between the political powers and the religion of the state.[28] The *pax Romana* (the peace of the Roman Empire) was conceptualized in a hierarchy of deities—local deities exercising influence over cities and towns, and imperial deities exercising influence across the empire—culminating in the rule of the emperor himself. The unitary rule of the emperor

---

27. Wilken notes, "By the first century Rome's empire reached from the Euphrates River in the east to the Atlantic Ocean in the west, from the olive groves and vineyards of North Africa on the southern coast of the Mediterranean to the great rivers of the north, the Danube flowing into the Black Sea and the Rhine into the North Sea." Wilken, *The First Thousand Years*, 7.

28. Robert Joustra, following the lead of many others, makes the point that there would have been no way to distinguish the "religious" from the "non-religious" in the ancient world. The consequence is that we must recognize that the sacred-secular distinction is peculiarly modern. See his *The Religious Problem with Religious Freedom* (London: Routledge, 2018).

was the means by which the remarkable cultural diversity across the empire was kept in check.

It is fair to say that early Christian communities had little interest in political affairs, in all likelihood because of the imperial nature of politics—that is, until one of the emperors converted to Christianity in the early fourth century. Constantine's conversion changed the political dynamic for Christian communities across the empire. Late in the fourth century, Christianity was declared the official religion of the empire under Emperor Theodosius. This action set in motion a strange alliance between political powers and Christian authorities that would last nearly fifteen hundred years in parts of the West. Whatever else may be said of those fifteen hundred years, the days in which the church was the central organizing institution of the culture are long gone in these early decades of the twenty-first century. Through its first centuries of existence, Christianity emerged as a fast-growing minority religion often granted considerable social tolerance, though sometimes (as under Emperor Diocletian in the late third century) suffering significant official persecution owing to its rejection of the pantheon of Roman gods. But there is abundant evidence that many of the early Christian communities earned the trust of their pagan neighbors by their commitment to the social virtues of compassion, generosity, kindness, and gentleness, and thereby resisted being treated as cultural miscreants leading an insurgency intending to overthrow imperial rule.[29]

FROM FATE TO CHOICE TO FRAGMENTATION

Ours is a vastly different world than the world of the early church. The two are separated not merely by enormous technological, economic, and political differences but also by how difference itself is experienced. In the ancient world, religions, cities, and cultures were

29. See Alan Kreider, *The Patient Ferment of the Early Church: The Improbable Rise of Christianity in the Roman Empire* (Grand Rapids: Baker Academic, 2016), and Larry Hurtado, *Why on Earth Did Anyone Become a Christian in the First Three Centuries?* (Milwaukee: Marquette University Press, 2016).

experienced objectively—arranged in a hierarchy of cultures and deities that was a taken-for-granted fact of the world and was also experienced in and through other taken-for-granted realities such as the homogeneity of the local culture, the universality of military might, and the permanence of economic hierarchies. There was a certain "fixed" nature to the way the ancient world was, and it was not malleable to one's own desires.

By contrast, our world has moved from *fate* to *choice*.[30] There are few fixed points in how we experience the world. In a democracy, our choices determine the future, which would have been an alien intuition in the ancient world. We are also witnessing the victory of the particular over the universal. We give our attention to fragments and individual interests. We are faced every day with virtually infinite options with an infinite number of details within those options. Think of how many different kinds of ketchup or soft drinks or breads fill our grocery shelves. The monarchs of the medieval world could not have dreamed of so many trivial choices. Condemned to fragmentary details, we seem all too comfortable with the loss of a universal context—regrettably content to relinquish an overarching purpose to life. Former President Barack Obama put it this way in 2006: "Each day, it seems, thousands of Americans are going about their daily rounds—dropping off the kids at school, driving to the office, flying to a business meeting, shopping at the mall, trying to stay on their diets—and they're coming to the realization that something is missing. They are deciding that their work, their possessions, their diversions, their sheer busyness, is not enough. They want a sense of purpose, a narrative arc to their lives."[31]

The modern truism that "change is the only constant" also points at the underlying reality that modern democracies have very few

---

30. This is Peter Berger's phrase from his work *The Heretical Imperative* (New York: Anchor, 1979).

31. Barack Obama, "Faith in the Public Square," January 2006, reprinted as "Obama's 2006 Speech on Faith and Politics," *New York Times*, June 28, 2006, https://www.nytimes.com/2006/06/28/us/politics/2006obamaspeech.html.

fixed points. Freedom of conscience and opinion are elusive grounds on which to build enduring cultural unity. So we should not be surprised that modern democracies tend toward disorder and fragmentation, if also in an orderly, prescribed fashion. Social commentators are mixed on this point, but the preponderance of evidence today suggests that the initial interaction between diverse ethnic and racial groups produces greater negative engagement, decreases interethnic tolerance, and makes social solidarity more fragile.[32] But there is also evidence suggesting younger generations are more at home with cultural and religious diversity over time, even if the initial interactions tend to be negative. One further bit of conflicting evidence suggests that though religious conviction is actually more important to most people than their ethnic or racial identity, the more contentious and more public conflicts of our times focus on ethnicity and race.[33] We tend to care more about our personal religious convictions but seem to be bothered more by the ethnic and racial differences that surround us. However, on neither religious nor racial matters is there evidence that a sustainable unity-in-diversity is within our grasp.

Modern political liberalism is built on the bare notions of individual rights and freedoms. For a time, certain kinds of cultural variety allied with these freedoms may have stimulated innovation and entrepreneurship, but they also generated considerable social friction and often downright hostility between the diverse subgroups within the culture. That social friction and those hostilities have not vanished in the present, nor are they any longer interpreted by an overarching moral vision that could, in part, inspire initiatives to overcome those

---

32. This is Robert Putnam's thesis in his "E Pluribus Unum." Putnam nonetheless holds out the hope that societies that are culturally diverse over the long run are in fact more creative and stable.

33. In "E Pluribus Unum," Putnam writes, "In fact, our own survey evidence suggests that for most Americans their religious identity is actually more important to them than their ethnic identity, but the salience of religious differences as lines of social identity has sharply diminished" (162).

frictions and hostilities.[34] It is a common intuition that we have now entered a stage of such significant social polarization that no strategy exists to overcome it.

Our social lives are deeply fractured not only by diverse religious convictions but also by (and primarily by) a system wherein individuals are free to pursue whatever they desire as long as it does not conflict with others in their pursuits. This is as true inside the church as outside the church. This freedom to determine one's own identity is the hallmark of modern democratic liberalism. As Mark Lilla puts it, "Personal choice. Individual rights. Self-definition. We speak these words as if a wedding vow. We hear them in school, we hear them on television, we hear them in stuffy Wall Street boardrooms, in Silicon Valley playpens, we hear them in church, we even hear them in bed. We hear them so often it's hard for us to think or talk about any subject except in these self-regarding terms."[35] But we also realize that human decisions are often subverted by the commercial pressures of the marketplace; we are not nearly as "free" as public discourse would suggest. The desires that motivate our "free choices" are subtly undermined by consumer pressures. As Jeffrey Stout comments, "We obviously fall far short of the democratic ideals we espouse, on any reasonable interpretation of their substance. The ideal of equal voice, in particular, is hardly consistent with the dominant role that big money now plays."[36]

Freedom of self-determination carries with it an unintended license for greed and power. Democracy is supposed to check this very sort of behavior, but it is easily exploited by powerful economic

---

34. Fukuyama, "Identity," notes that cultural diversity is not an unalloyed good: "Syria and Afghanistan are very diverse places, but their diversity has yielded violence and conflict rather than creativity and resilience. In Kenya, where there are sharp divisions between ethnic groups, diversity feeds an inward-looking political corruption based on ethnic ties" (9).

35. Mark Lilla, *The Once and Future Liberal: After Identity Politics* (New York: Harper, 2017), 29. It should be noted that Lilla is not yearning for a return to a golden era when Americans were less selfish. He is simply highlighting the social forces at work in late modern liberal democracies—the sort of forces that late modern liberal democracies were intended to blunt.

36. Stout, *Democracy and Tradition*, 4.

entities. Late modern democracy lacks a common moral tradition
that would give it the convictions to keep these sorts of behaviors restrained. The distinction between virtue and vice may not
have relieved earlier times of moral decay, but the absence of any
agreed-on distinction between them today makes it all the more difficult to sustain a commitment to anything resembling the "common
good." The polarization of our contemporary cultural conversation
has resulted in the loss of confidence in democratic liberalism even
as democratic liberalism provides the structures by which it is possible to complain about the polarization. Without a common civic
morality to restrain large consumer forces, the public square is not
only empty but also alienating. People tend to look for social rein-
forcement of their own self-identity in homogeneous communities
when there is not a set of shared goals promoting the common good.
Ironically, the greater the yearning for a common good, the more
suspicion there is about any one group imposing its sense of the
common good on others. The fracturing of the sense of belonging to
others becomes the dominant paradigm. "If you are not for me, on
my terms, then you are against me." But the more tribal the search
for self-identity is, the more polarized our common life becomes and
the greater our tendency toward conflict. Without a larger perception of the common good, or at least of some form of commonality
among all our differences, our social polity is doomed to failure.[37]
It is not an accident that democracy itself seems tenuous in an age
of global capitalism, corporate corruption, identity politics, and
theocratic terrorism.[38]

Church life is likewise polarized. Though the church has been
freed from state control, it remains downstream from culture and has

---

37. I am here concurring with Jean Bethke Elshtain, *Augustine and the Limits of Politics*
(Notre Dame: University of Notre Dame Press, 2018): "There is something like a common
nature and it is this thread of commonality that supports both individuality and plurality, and
that helps us preserve the spaces between us. Out of one, many ones, each a new beginning;
yet these many ones share a nature in common" (104).

38. Stout, *Democracy and Tradition*, 7.

imbibed the same celebration of self-defining freedom as the wider public square. There are surely notable exceptions, but as in many eras, the church reflects the world it lives in even as it struggles to speak prophetically to that world.

In the 1940s and 1950s, a vigorous discussion arose among public intellectuals regarding the emergence and increasing danger of "mass culture." This was a reference to the rise of a consumer economy and the end of the subsistence economy.[39] People were able to spend their income not simply on matters of survival but on matters of convenience as well—consumer goods as diverse as the automobile, the dishwasher, the television, and the fast-food industry. The transformation into a consumer culture was alarming to a small but significant number of public voices, predominantly on the political Left. The concern they raised was that consumer culture numbed people's moral sensibilities to the crises of the times.[40] By the 1990s and early 2000s, the criticism of consumerism had become a cottage industry. Commentators on both the Right and the Left expressed a fear that it had eliminated thoughtful discussion of the big issues of the time and removed the ethical dimension to our life together.[41]

---

39. Mass culture is not the same as political populism. The latter points at movements that see themselves largely as a protest movement against the cultural elites, many of whom are instrumental in the creation of mass culture. One thinks of the populist disdain for the barons of Hollywood or for the boardrooms of corporations controlling a variety of consumer industries.

40. Maurice Isserman representatively wrote, "If mass culture as portrayed in the 1950s, was not the cold dark dungeon of Stalinist-style totalitarianism, it offered only the dubious advantages of being stuck between floors in a brightly lit elevator with piped-in muzak. Americans were being psychologically manipulated in ways they could not understand, their deepest anxieties deliberately exploited by politicians, propagandists, and advertisers." Isserman, *If I Had a Hammer: The Death of the Old Left and the Birth of the New Left* (New York: Basic Books, 1987), 100.

41. A small sampling of this literature noticeably includes many religiously conservative authors: Craig Bartholomew and Thorsten Moritz, eds., *Christ and Consumerism* (Carlisle: Paternoster, 2000); Zygmunt Bauman, *Liquid Modernity* (London: Polity Press, 2000); Teresa Brennan, *Exhausting Modernity: Grounds for a New Economy* (London: Routledge, 2000); Rodney Clapp, ed., *The Consuming Passion: Christianity and the Consumer Culture* (Downers Grove, IL: InterVarsity Press, 1998); Mike Featherston, *Consumer Culture and Postmodernism* (London: Sage, 1991); Stephen Fjellman, *Vinyl Leaves: Walt Disney World and America* (Boulder, CO: Westview Press, 1992); Rob Kroes, *If You've Seen One, You've Seen the Mall: Europeans and American Mass Culture* (Urbana: University of Illinois Press, 1996); Conrad Lodziak, *The Myth*

Looking back on those discussions, it is fair to say that mass culture morphed in ways not imagined at midcentury and diminished
our ability to deal with our differences and disagreements in local and
practical ways. Mass culture in the West transformed us into a global
consumer culture. It created the illusion of heightened individuality
while implicitly demanding conformity. Mass culture tends toward
homogeneity—a McDonald's hamburger is the same whether you
buy it in Maine or Montana or Moscow; so too with Starbucks or
Coke or any of the other vehicles of mass culture. And with the rise
of social media as the primary platform of communication in mass
culture, this homogeneity is now hyper-localized and creates little
room for deep deliberative conversation across differences.[42] With
consumer culture comes the danger that individual freedoms will
crowd out the duty to care for anything other than their own material
well-being.[43] Mass culture also tends to remove us from the concrete
relations of ordinary life, making it appear we belong everywhere and
nowhere at the same time. The significance of local mediating structures like churches and neighborhood associations diminished under
the pressure of the national and the global.[44] It is not an uncommon
experience in a congregation for a "celebrity pastor" to be of greater

---

of Consumerism (London: Pluto Press, 2002); Vincent Miller, *Consuming Religion: Christian
Faith and Practice in a Consumer Culture* (New York: Continuum, 2004); Laurence Moore,
Selling God (New York: Oxford University Press, 1994); David Myers, *The American Paradox:
Spiritual Hunger in an Age of Plenty* (New Haven: Yale University Press, 2000); George Ritzer,
Explorations in the Sociology of Consumption: Fast Food, Credit Cards and Casinos (London:
Sage, 2001); Tyler Wigg-Stevenson, *Brand Jesus: Christianity in a Consumerist Age* (New York:
Seabury, 2007); Sam Van Eman, *On Earth as It Is in Advertising: Moving from Commercial Hype
to Gospel Hope* (Grand Rapids: Brazos, 2005); Robert Wuthnow, *God and Mammon* (New
York: Free Press, 1994).

42. It should also be noted that evangelicals have been especially prone to the temptations
of mass culture. Evangelical celebrities transcend all local realities, and as many of them became
overtly political (and partisan), they damaged the ability to speak across cultural differences. On
this see D. G. Hart, *From Billy Graham to Sarah Palin: Evangelicals and the Betrayal of American
Conservativism* (Grand Rapids: Eerdmans, 2011).

43. See Elshtain, *Democracy on Trial*.

44. See Peter Berger, Brigitte Berger, and Hansfried Kellner, *The Homeless Mind:
Modernization and Consciousness* (New York: Random House, 1973).

significance than the local pastor, though that celebrity pastor has never once appeared in person to the congregation.

The Logic of the Gospel

How do we heal this fracturing and fragmentation, so deeply entrenched in our social polity and seemingly so arbitrary in its emotional attachments? The first step is to recognize that our task as Christians is to live as faithful witnesses in it. It is not realistic to suppose that fundamental social conflicts are going to be resolved anytime soon, whether nationally, globally, or within the church. We must begin to cultivate the desire to live together in, with, and through our differences. As philosopher Nicholas Wolterstorff writes, "We must live together. It is to politics and not to epistemology that we shall have to look for an answer as to how to do that. 'Liberal' politics has fallen on bad days recently. But to its animating vision of a society in which persons of diverse traditions live together in justice and friendship, conversing with each other and slowly altering their traditions in response to the conversation—to that, there is no viable alternative."[45]

This need is as true in the church as it is in the culture at large. Besides oppression, accepting the reality of our differences is the only social option available to us today. As Christians, we can retreat from this social polity, seek to dominate it, or learn to live with it wisely. Undoubtedly, many Christians today are wary of the fracturing of our social cohesion. They are wary of its effects on their children. They are wary of engaging yet another generation of culture wars. They are also wary of the pretensions of "neutrality" so often articulated by the most ardent defenders of tolerance and diversity.

It is unlikely that any grand social strategy will alleviate the polarization. However, as a minority voice within our entrenched polarized communities, we Christians must ponder the internal logic of

---

45. Nicholas Wolterstorff, *John Locke and the Ethics of Belief* (New York: Cambridge University Press, 1996), 246.

the gospel itself as a social strategy to pursue. This gospel affirms that human differences are given by our Creator in order to manifest the interdependence of the body as the very means to honor God with a deeper unity. The unique vocation of Christians is to express a commitment to justice and mercy, grace and truth, to our diverse neighbors inside the church and outside of it.[46] Living this out rather than giving in to despair is our unique calling today, and is desperately needed for the church to flourish.

Much has been written in the recent past on the theological significance of the "other"—other nations, other communities, other people.[47] In a time of increased scrutiny and anxiety about our polarizations, the language of the other has focused attention on the immensely important work of reconciliation in the context of these conflicts—a theme near the very heart of the gospel. The language of the other has provided us a way to think more clearly about the intensely personal nature of conflict and the impact of core disagreements about our own identity. Love of neighbor (the other) is a consistent theme in the teaching of Jesus. Loving our neighbors also entails that we hear the truth from our neighbors, even when we find it uncomfortable.

"Neighborliness" is just the name we give to the divine intention that humans are created to live together in communities. A community of people, such as a family, a neighborhood, or a church, is a nexus of relationships whose corporate identity requires cooperation in the face of differences. Communities, small or large, survive to the extent that collaboration and cooperation are naturally woven into the fabric of the community. Marriages often disintegrate in the face of the loss of a child's life—a crisis that requires collaboration and yet where the stress seems so great that collaboration is no longer possible. When the cooperation required is significant enough, differences

---

46. See Patrick Deneen, "The Ignoble Lie," *First Things* (April 2018), https://www.firstthings.com/article/2018/04/the-ignoble-lie.

47. One of the most powerful and poignant theological treatments of the "other" is Miroslav Volf, *Exclusion and Embrace: A Theological Exploration of Identity, Otherness, and Reconciliation* (Nashville: Abingdon, 1996).

can quickly turn into disagreements, and significant disagreements are often the stress points that threaten the well-being of communities. Churches go into wilderness periods when pastoral leadership is absent and a cacophony of voices arise with no discernible strategy for settling the disagreements. Disagreements are also constraints on the individual's own self-will in a community. They are also a threat to that self-will.

The logic of communal life is straightforward. The greater the collaboration, the greater the opportunity for conflict unless there is a constraint on the self-interest of individuals in the community. But what could constrain self-interest? The gospel is the story in which Jesus sacrifices his human self-interest for the greater good— the greater good of his Father's glory, and the greater good of those who would be reconciled to God by that act of sacrifice. It is the logic of the gospel that constrains self-interest.

Christians, who confess a large narrative moral arc from creation to redemption to consummation, have a unique opportunity for a humble prophetic witness to our late modern democratic secular culture. The difference of differences has to do with the nature of the communities in which those differences are played out and the constraints on self-interest imposed by the community or the goals to which the community aspires. The more significant the community, the more likely disagreement will be threatening, and the more important it will be to learn how to deal with the disagreement. Absent a larger narrative or moral arc that constrains self-interest, communities will inevitably lurch toward disorder.

The mission of God as manifest in Christ does not seek the homogenization of the public square with the goal that everyone be the same, but rather the opportunity to speak about our disagreements in the public square honestly, graciously, and humbly. Dealing with disagreements as Christians requires humility and wisdom. It requires a more thorough reckoning with the relationships in which God has placed us and coming to peace with the communities in which those relationships are embedded. It also requires a vigilance against resentment and cynicism—resentment against others and cynicism toward the present depth of the problems. It requires faith, hope, and charity. Why should we suppose this is different for us when it has been the norm for Christians in every age of the church's life? As Christians, we must engage the social world of polarizations on its own God-given terms rather than the terms being dictated by elites or culture warriors or even our own fears. The church ought not lose sight of its confession nor of its peculiar call to reflect the character of God in this world. Grace is more powerful than sin, and God's grace is far more powerful than the principalities and powers of this age.

According to the Christian story, in the beginning there were two persons. They were quite different from each other, yet they belonged together. In retrospect, the union of the man and the woman seems almost counterintuitive given such undeniable differences. But in the beautiful final passage of Genesis 2, the two are united (literally "put back together") while still retaining their own voice. As the story progresses in Genesis 3, their union deteriorates into disunion, their differences turn into disagreements. Eventually, across generations, those disagreements fostered systemic conflicts. The two were created for a relationship of unity-in-diversity, which was effectively destroyed by the pursuit of their own self-interest. The template of a unity-in-diversity at the end of Genesis 2 would, however, remain as a promissory note, not simply for marriages but for a broad array of relationships across redemptive history, awaiting its fulfillment in the gospel and experienced in fits and starts in the life of the church. The trajectory of that narrative remains true today. In one sense, there is nothing new under the sun. The deep divisions that surround us weigh heavily on our conscience, tugging at our hearts and reminding us there must be a better way. We yearn for a genuine unity across our disagreements and rarely fathom how it could happen. But still we hope, and still we are called not to abandon the goal of a genuine unity-in-diversity.

Learning to live with differences large and small, local and global, is part and parcel of the Christian calling today. There is no emperor who will impose unity on our cultural conversations (thankfully). There is no longer even the echo of an older common culture that binds us together. Ours is a time loosed from the politically artificial frameworks of cultural unity, a time when we are reminded of how much work is required to get along with our neighbors.

In the next chapter, I tell the story of the emergence of the racial and ethnic differences that serve as the interpretive key to every other kind of difference in late modern times. It begins with the story of the birth of democracy and the categories intrinsic to that political polity. It is not a set of abstractions, but a concrete narrative rooted in actual events in our past that continue to echo into the present. It is a narrative neither identical to the story of the gospel, nor one entirely absent the echoes of the gospel—if we listen carefully to hear it.

We have frequently printed the word Democracy. Yet I cannot too often repeat that it is a word the gist of which still sleeps quite unawakened, notwithstanding the resonance and the many angry tempests out of which its syllables have come, from pen or tongue.

—WALT WHITMAN, DEMOCRATIC VISTAS (1870)

2

THE INCLUSION NARRATIVE
OF DEMOCRACY

INSIDERS AND OUTSIDERS

The rhetoric of democracy and the lived reality of democracy have not always coincided across American history. While everyone is promised an equal voice, the history of our democracy has often brought attention to those whose voices apparently are not equal. Recent controversies surrounding voting rights have brought back memories of the early twentieth century, when access to the ballot was restricted by poll taxes or literacy tests. The military draft during the Vietnam War brought to the surface the tension of being required to serve as an eighteen-year-old without the corresponding right to vote. The experience of being a Republican in a deep blue state or a Democrat in a deep red state often causes doubts about the significance of one's voice as a political minority. In the 1940s, by federal regulation, the voices of fundamentalists were excluded from national radio during the "religious broadcasting" window; instead, these slots were made available solely to mainline Protestant denominations. An especially egregious example of the tension between the rhetoric and lived realities of democracy was the Alien and Sedition Acts of 1798, which made it a crime to publicly dissent from any federal government policy, effectively removing voices who disagreed with any policy decision of the Adams administration. In these and many other ways, democracy, while fostering a sense of respect for all voices, has at various times and in various ways ironically excluded voices from the democratic process.

This exclusion process has proved influential for how we have understood our differences across American history. When you feel your voice is not heard in the political process, you inevitably sense that you are different from those whose opinions are politically powerful. Almost everyone at one time or another has been on the losing end of a democratically decided issue, finding themselves to be outsiders. As outsiders, they notice how different they are from the insiders and begin to frame their identity in terms of those differences. This insider-outsider dynamic creates the tendency to stereotype others, which in turn creates the opportunity for partisan divisions. Democracy is intended to protect diverse points of view, but in so doing it becomes fertile soil for emphasizing the very diversity of our points of view, strangely accentuating our differences. Stranger still is the fact that the majority voice in one era may well become a minority voice in the next era. Recognizing that democracy is not simply a set of political procedures, but a framework of cultural values that seeps into the fabric of everyday human experience, means that our notions of political difference will themselves also eventually seep into everyday life.[1]

Christians have paid too little attention to this side of democracy, often failing to recognize how the social context of democracy influences the ways in which the church understands and relates to differences and why unity has come to be conceived in the way it is. In addition, the church's paradoxical relationship to politics has been shaped by two contrasting intuitions: the belief that politics can be corrupting, and the belief that politics is the key to cultural influence and change. This has produced an uneasy alliance across American history between the church and the state, often predicated on which

---

1. Nathan O. Hatch's now-classic work *The Democratization of American Christianity* (New Haven: Yale University Press, 1989) makes a compelling case for the profound influence of democracy on the way Christianity has been lived out in American history.

side of the difference equation the church finds itself. Sometimes the church has been the insider, and other times it has found itself very much on the outside. Democracy has granted to Christians the right of dissent when legislative matters do not go their way, but the church's belief in the settled nature of ultimate truth has meant that Christians have not always felt comfortable as dissenters.[2] Before embarking on an exploration of appropriate ways to express differences of ultimate matters in the context of democracy, I turn first to the story of democracy—and specifically the unfolding of its history of inclusion and exclusion as an interpretive guide for our dominant categories of difference.

THE STORY OF DEMOCRACY AND THE INCLUSION NARRATIVE

From the beginning, the American experiment was revolutionary not because it invested political authority in every person (which it did not) but rather because it granted political voice to a larger group of citizens than any previous governing polity.[3] The principle was established from the outset that governing authority would flow from the governed to those who govern. However, at its inception the "governed" excluded women, slaves, Native Americans, and all nonlandowning persons. The notion of universal suffrage or genuine direct democracy was not even on the table for discussion during the last half of the eighteenth century.[4] The move from the rule by a few

---

2. These tensions are spelled out in a clear and thoughtful way by D. G. Hart in *A Secular Faith*.

3. In ancient Athens, direct democracy included a greater percentage of persons within the city-state. However, ancient Athens was demographically much more homogeneous and much smaller. See James Miller, *Can Democracy Work? A Short History of a Radical Idea, from Ancient Athens to Our World* (New York: Farrar, Straus and Giroux, 2018). Along with many others, Jean Bethke Elshtain notes the relatively low percentage of actual persons in Athens who had political voice. "By our contemporary reckoning, it was a rather peculiar democracy, of course: the vast majority of the populace of Athens could not vote, deliberate in assembly, or indeed fight in a war—the signal responsibility and privilege of the citizen. Slaves, laborers and women were excluded from its sphere." Elshtain, *Democracy on Trial* (New York: Basic Books, 1995), 92.

4. As most historians of this period recognize, the founders conceived of the new nation as a republic rather than a democracy. Ancient Rome, rather than ancient Athens, was the model

(the English monarch or a ruling elite) to the rule by many was radical in its own right, and it surely began a trajectory toward universal suffrage, which would come much later in American history.

The conceptual transition from the rule by a few to the rule by the many was initially grounded in the claim that all persons had "natural rights" given by their Creator by which the equality and dignity of all persons was guaranteed. A major parenthesis to this claim, however, was the tragic compromise applying natural rights only to landowning white males.[5] Most of the founders understood that universal equality was the only logical ground for a democratic polity, but also that chattel slavery would have to be tolerated if the federation of the colonies was to be united into one nation. Equality was affirmed while being catastrophically and absolutely denied at the same time.[6] The enduring nature of "equality within limits" would shape the discussion of "appropriate diversity" across the rest of American history.

Early in the American republic, equality and dignity were spelled out by affirming the freedom of speech, the freedom of conscience, the freedom of assembly, the freedom of protest, and the freedom of religion, each of which was integrally connected to the other freedoms. As many have noticed, however, liberty and equality stand in tension with each other.[7] The more liberty is granted to citizens, the greater

---

in the minds of the founders, with the possible exception of Thomas Paine. See Sean Wilentz, *The Rise of American Democracy: Jefferson to Lincoln* (New York: Norton, 2005).

5. The colonies were following the practice in England of granting the vote to landowning males on the assumption that they had a stake in the governance over the land by virtue of their property. Alexander Keyssar, in *The Right to Vote: The Contested History of Democracy in the United States* (New York: Basic Books, 2005), charts this practice and uses the lens of voting rights to interpret democracy across American history. Wilentz, in *The Rise of American Democracy*, describes the fears of the founders in extending the vote to non-landowning males, lest they be disproportionately swayed by those to whom they were fiscally indebted.

6. It is worth noting that voting rights, though extremely limited by contemporary standards at the end of the eighteenth century, did greatly expand over the first fifty years of the nineteenth century. Expansion rather than contraction was the clear trajectory of voting rights, even if many persons were still excluded. See Keyssar, *Right to Vote*, chapter 2.

7. The humorist Roger Price put the point aptly: "Democracy demands that all of its citizens *begin* the race even. Egalitarianism insists that they all *finish* the race evenly." Price, *The Great Roob Revolution* (1970), cited in Paul Fussell, *Class: A Guide through the American Status System* (New York: Simon & Schuster, 1983), 20.

the likelihood of inequality emerging. The more equality is enforced, the less liberty can be granted.[8]

Protecting these "natural rights" proved complex.[9] The rhetoric of "no taxation without representation" echoed more strongly through some of the colonies than others as the questions of limits on voting rights and the disestablishment of the church were hotly debated. Early in the American Revolution, controversy raged as to whether ordinary persons were sufficiently politically engaged to govern themselves or the country as a whole.[10] Most of the leaders of the American Revolution (e.g., Washington, Adams, Franklin, Madison, Hamilton) did not think direct rule by ordinary citizens was the appropriate means to secure the freedoms spelled out in the Bill of Rights. The founders feared that "mob rule" would prove too unstable to govern a nation.[11] There was a wide consensus regarding the flaws of human nature, which required a system of checks and balances but would also require a democratic aristocracy who would representatively rule on behalf of ordinary citizens. These citizens were not any more morally deficient than the governing class; they were simply not trained or

8. The freedom of the markets eventually also contributed to the waning of equality in the early American republic. Free enterprise was one of the founding rallying cries across the colonies, though it was little noticed at the time that this would lead inevitably to a new kind of class society—rooted not in heredity but in economic success or failure. See Mark A. Noll, ed., *God and Mammon: Protestants, Money, and the Markets, 1790–1860* (New York: Oxford University Press, 2001). A contemporary analysis that charts the manner in which the freedom of markets has undermined a wider moral framework is Michael Sandel, *What Money Can't Buy: The Moral Limits of Markets* (New York: Farrar, Straus and Giroux, 2013).

9. There were debates in revolutionary America prior to 1789 as to whether these were "rights" or "privileges." If they were privileges, they could be limited in their application. If they were natural rights, then every person (not just every citizen) must own them. See Rosemarie Zaggari, "Suffrage and Representation," in *A Companion to the American Revolution*, ed. Jack P. Greene and J. R. Pole (London: Blackwell, 2000), 661–67.

10. Primary documents surrounding this early colonial controversy can be found in *The Essential Federalist and Anti-Federalist Papers*, ed. David Wootton (Indianapolis: Hackett, 2003). The historical context for the controversy is well described by Gordon Wood, *The Idea of America: Reflections on the Birth of the United States* (New York: Penguin, 2012). For a helpful overview of the recurring echoes of the controversy in American history, see Bruce Cain, *Democracy More or Less: America's Political Reform Quandary* (Cambridge: Cambridge University Press, 2014).

11. See Wilentz, *Rise of American Democracy*.

skilled in politics.[12] Ordinary citizens could select those from among their number to rule in periodic elections, but it was those elected to rule who would serve as a quasi-natural aristocracy. Differences of opinion were expressed passionately within the democratic aristocracy, but the important differences were the differences that mattered to the political class.

America lived with these tensions in the early days of the republic not because they were unnoticed but because all the presidents of the first two generations were men of aristocratic background—highly educated, possessing significant administrative experience, often having served in the military—and were themselves a strong enough political glue to keep the cultural tensions at bay.[13] They were the sort of public-minded aristocrats who were groomed in the English system to govern with strength of conviction and administrative acumen.[14] They were part of an elite class, but they were enculturated to think primarily of their responsibilities toward those of ordinary means. They believed in a shared moral order, though there was no

---

12. There were considerable discussions about the character of the checks and balances required in a democratically oriented government by virtue of the flaws in human nature. These flaws, however, did not separate the governed from those who govern. The contrasting moral traditions that swirled during this early phase of the nation framed these flaws in diverse ways, and often stood in contrast to the minority of Enlightenment-inspired secular voices expressing far more optimism in human nature. For the classic description of these controversies, see Henry May, *The Enlightenment in America* (New York: Oxford University Press, 1976). The diverse ways Americans interpreted the Enlightenment are spelled out in complex ways by Caroline Winterer, *American Enlightenments: Pursuing Happiness in the Age of Reason* (New Haven: Yale University Press, 2018).

13. Many of the founders had served in political positions in the colonies under British rule. Most of them were also rooted in the nitty-gritty of local politics in their own colony (Franklin in Pennsylvania, Hamilton in New York, Adams in Massachusetts, Jefferson and Madison in Virginia, etc.). Franklin actually served at one time at three different levels of the colonial government—as a representative from Pennsylvania to the Second Continental Congress, as president of the Pennsylvania State Convention (which drew up the new state constitution), and as a delegate to the Pennsylvania Provincial Congress (which replaced the British colonial assembly). See Walter Isaacson, *Benjamin Franklin: An American Life* (New York: Simon & Schuster, 2004).

14. Historians have long argued that Washington was the paradigm of a benevolent aristocratic ruler, and by the sheer power of his persona kept the political tensions of the early republic from boiling over. See Ron Chernow, *Washington: A Life* (New York: Penguin, 2011), and Joseph Ellis, *His Excellency: George Washington* (New York: Vintage, 2005).

single Christian tradition that brought that order.[15] They still stood with a foot in the old (Christian) world and the noblesse oblige of the ruling class, even if they firmly believed in the future of the new nation unencumbered by the structures of monarchy and aristocracy and a single established religion.

The central controversy at the time of the revolution was the authority of the federal government relative to the individual colonies/states. Great was the fear of an all-powerful central government in the minds of many of the colonists. They remembered all too clearly the abuses of a governing monarch whose power was unlimited. At the time of the Declaration of Independence, in 1776, it was by no means clear there would be a single nation composed of all the states/colonies. That matter was not settled until it became clear that the individual colonies would be helpless against the European powers unless they stood together, and that a strong federal government was necessary to sustain their common interests against external foes.[16]

The sentiment in many of the colonies throughout the latter half of the eighteenth century was the fear of rule by a few, as they had experienced with the colonial rule of Britain. This also translated into fear of the emergence of a new federal aristocracy that would erode the independence of the respective colonies. In light of these fears, it was decided that elected representatives from each of the colonies would serve in a proportional manner, and that the representatives would serve limited terms.[17] Looking back, we can see how radi-

---

15. It seems clear enough that there was a shared moral order among the founders of the American republic. The generic morality they shared undoubtedly had Christian origins, but the distinctive doctrinal elements of the Christian faith were not part of the shared inheritance among the founders. An accessible and fair reading of the history on these matters can be found in Mark A. Noll, Nathan O. Hatch, and George M. Marsden, *The Search for Christian America*, 2nd ed. (Colorado Springs: Helmers and Howard, 1989).

16. Joseph Ellis, *The Quartet: Orchestrating the Second American Revolution* (New York: Vintage, 2016), makes a compelling case that a strong central government only came to pass with the passage of the Bill of Rights in the 1790s.

17. On the contested issue of proportional representation, the compromise reached was to allow each state/colony to appoint two senators regardless of the size of the respective

cal a move it was to suppose that ordinary citizens could elect (and remove) those who would exercise political authority. Again, it's true that far more people were excluded than included, but far more were included than had ever been included previously. The seeds of the "inclusion narrative" at the heart of modern liberal democracies had been planted, and they had been planted in a world that had never known or experienced such a thing. We do well to remember how radical this inclusion narrative was, even in its earliest phase.

The conceptual distance from rule by many to rule by all, however, is short indeed—except where vested interests keep political voices from expanding.[18] The move toward greater and greater inclusion of the population was implicit in the move away from monarchy. The movement was not predetermined, and it came with no guarantees, but over the long arc of American history, there can be little doubt that the inclusion narrative exercised significant emotional energy toward expansion rather than contraction of who was to be included as "ordinary citizens." This inclusion narrative was central to the advent of American democracy, and it continues to exercise significant cultural force. It has also shaped the fundamental ways that Americans have thought about difference—through the lens of those who have been included and those who have been excluded. Exclusion from the political process has come to define how Americans have understood their differences. Race, gender, and ethnicity have a peculiar resonance in the present public square because of their peculiar place in the history of American democracy.

population of the state/colony and a proportion of congressmen based on the size of the population of the state/colony. This bicameral arrangement of the federal legislature mirrored in some ways the upper and lower houses of the British Parliament—with the notable exception that both houses of Congress would be composed of members elected indirectly by their respective states. Isaacson, *Benjamin Franklin*, notes that Franklin was the primary advocate of a unicameral arrangement, which had been in place prior to 1789.

18. Keyssar comments, "If the legitimacy of a government depended on the consent of the governed, then limitations on suffrage were intrinsically problematic, since voting was the primary instrument through which a populace could express or withhold consent." Keyssar, *Right to Vote*, 8.

THE STORY OF DEMOCRACY AND
THE EXCLUSION NARRATIVE

One of the great tragedies at the founding of the republic was the decision to delay the legislative status of slavery until 1808.[19] The permission granted to the Southern colonies to maintain slavery happened in spite of the deep misgivings of many of the founding fathers, even among those who owned slaves themselves.[20] There was an obvious gap between theory and practice at the beginning of America when the Second Continental Congress deleted Thomas Jefferson's denunciation of slavery from the Declaration of Independence but kept his universal declaration of equality. There can be little doubt that this decision was reached as a compromise to bring the Southern colonies into a united front against the British, but the enigma of resisting the "enslavement" of their colonial rulers while affirming the enslavement of a huge swath of their own population seems almost too stark to believe.[21] The Declaration of Independence expressed the daring political demand that "all men are created equal" and should have the right

---

19. According to section 1, article 9 of the Constitution, this was the earliest date at which the Atlantic slave trade could be legislatively addressed.

20. Thomas Jefferson, a Southern plantation farmer, remains the greatest of the enigmas among the founding fathers in this regard. See Jon Meacham, *Thomas Jefferson: The Art of Power* (New York: Random House, 2013). In Jefferson's *Notes on the State of Virginia* (1782), he gives expression to a hierarchy of "races" owing to physical distinctions, and in large measure defends the treatment of Africans in the colonies based on this hierarchy. How he understood this in relation to his defense of the universal-equality claim in the Declaration of Independence is a puzzle about which historians continue to conjecture. It is also worth noting that Washington came to the realization within less than a decade after the Constitution that his own slaves ought to be freed. According to the terms of his will, all his slaves were freed in 1799, when he died. As late as 1781, Benjamin Franklin owned a slave, but by 1787 he had accepted the presidency of the Pennsylvania Society for the Promotion of the Abolition of Slavery. Even George Mason, a Virginia planter who owned slaves, referred to the system of slavery as "pernicious" at the Constitutional Convention in 1791 and said that "every master of slaves is a petty tyrant: they bring the judgement of heaven on a country." Isaacson, *Benjamin Franklin*, 464.

21. It should also be clear that the controversy over slavery at the Constitutional Convention in 1787 was not a minor matter, but of gravest significance to the creation of a new government. By 1787, Massachusetts, Rhode Island, Connecticut, and Pennsylvania had abolished slavery, and New Hampshire was on the verge of a formal declaration of emancipation. It was the representatives of South Carolina and Georgia, in particular, who were adamant that slavery would not be a matter of federal legislation in the new Constitution. See Wilentz, *Rise of American Democracy*.

of self-determination. But as a historian of democracy notes, "The efforts to realize this demand would be played out in counterpoint to chattel slavery, the most extreme form of servitude. The equality of political rights which is the first mark of American citizenship was proclaimed in the accepted presence of its absolute denial."[22]

Democracy carries with it a certain logic of inclusion—all ordinary citizens are to have a voice in their governance. But American democracy also carries with it a procedural impulse for compromise—in this instance, to keep the diverse constituencies of the nation together. The rough-and-tumble nature of democratic politics requires the consent of the majority, which inevitably means no side in a political debate is likely to get everything they want. In the 1770s, the founders realized that many of the Southern colonies would not join the union if slavery was outlawed. That political compromise would eventually tear the country apart—a union the compromise had been intended to protect. As with monarchy or aristocracy, so with democracy, there were no moral guarantees that the "system" would produce the right outcome. History has shown that democracy does not move inexorably or predictably toward its goals. It does move with an internal momentum to include rather than exclude, but it also gives ordinary citizens the freedom to exclude rather than include.

Slavery had a long history prior to modern times and was by no means unique to the English-speaking world.[23] Slavery was a common reality in ancient Greece and continued throughout much of the Roman Empire and in most of its neighboring empires in the first millennium AD. The Muslim conquest across much of the Middle East and North Africa resulted in the enslavement of conquered peoples from the eighth through the fifteenth centuries. The slave trade was quite active across many of the African kingdoms of the thirteenth through the sixteenth centuries as well. What made the Atlantic slave

---

22. Miller, *Can Democracy Work?*, 92.

23. Joseph C. Miller, *The Problem of Slavery as History: A Global Approach* (New Haven: Yale University Press, 2012).

trade unique in the long and tragic history of slavery was its racial justification. The growth of the Atlantic slave trade in the fifteenth century was primarily economic in its orientation but became legitimated in the minds of many Europeans because of its racial character.[24]

It is a tragic irony that a British high court ruled that slaves could not be held against their will in 1772—four years before the American colonies declared independence from Britain—on the grounds that humans were meant to be free and not slaves within the empire.[25] Slavery's exclusively racial (that is, African) character made its modern version historically unique and all the more tragic that it was embedded in a political polity oriented to expand rather than limit the claims of equality and dignity. The enduring result was that race would continue to be the Achilles's heel of American democracy throughout its history. Alexis de Tocqueville would prophetically write in 1840, "If ever America undergoes great revolutions, they will be brought about by the presence of the Black race on the soil of the United States, that is to say, they will owe their origin, not to the equality, but to the inequality, of conditions."[26] Only twenty years

---

24. The central colonial powers, England, Holland, and Portugal, controlled the sea lanes and therefore controlled international trade. Cotton and sugar were the two dominant commodities of international trade and were labor-intensive crops. The new colonial economies based on the international trade of sugar and later cotton called for a greatly expanded labor force, which in turn provided the economic justification of the slave trade. Native Americans were first tried as slaves on the emerging cotton and sugar plantations of North and South America. However, they had family structures intact in the Americas, which made enslavement far more difficult and escape far easier. It was also not unimportant that European diseases decimated Native Americans. It soon became apparent to the colonial powers, and especially to the elite class of the new agrarian economies of the Americas, that the residents of African kingdoms were easier prey, more willing to trade off each other, and, dislodged from their social base, were economically more efficient as laborers on the plantations.

25. Historians generally date the abolition of slavery in Britain to 1833, when the slave trade was (mostly) abolished throughout the British Empire by an official act of Parliament. See Seymour Drescher, *Abolition: A History of Slavery and Antislavery* (Cambridge: Cambridge University Press, 2010). It is also worth mentioning that William Wilberforce's persistent campaign for abolition was rooted in his evangelical faith. On the relationship between John Newton, the former slave-ship captain, and Wilberforce, see Jonathan Aitken, *John Newton: From Disgrace to Amazing Grace* (Wheaton: Crossway, 2013).

26. Alexis de Tocqueville, *Democracy in America*, cited in Cornel West, *Race Matters* (Boston: Beacon, 2001), 95.

after de Tocqueville wrote those words, the nation's last war fought on its own soil, and also its deadliest, would rage for four long years over the issue of slavery. Presidents Lincoln and then Grant attempted to reconstruct race relations more equitably, but the cultural forces defending discrimination proved too strong, and the era of Jim Crow, segregation, and lynchings would be launched in the 1880s and legally last for nearly eighty years.[27]

In the short interval between the Civil War and the end of Reconstruction, all former slaves were granted full citizenship rights and all Black males were granted the right to vote. During the decade of the 1870s, Blacks were represented at the local, state, and federal level in numbers that are unmatched even to this day. With the end of Ulysses S. Grant's administration in 1877, the era of reconstruction effectively came to an end, and the era of legal segregation emerged.[28] For a short time, the logic of democracy had been enacted by force, only to be stopped in its tracks by the very same logic from another angle—the freedom of self-determination granted to a majority.

As former male slaves were given the right to vote, another voice emerged from a large cohort that had also been excluded from the vote—namely, that of women. The women's rights movement, which started as early as the 1830s and became intertwined with the struggle to abolish slavery, gained early public notoriety at the Seneca Falls Convention of 1848.[29] Elizabeth Cady Stanton and Lucretia Mott,

27. It is important to note that the Black church under Jim Crow was the primary institution voicing concern for universal equality and dignity—though it was little heard in the wider political square at the time. Religion more generally was being marginalized politically in this era, even as religious affiliation increased significantly. W. E. B. Dubois was the most prominent of the Black churchmen arguing for a greater commitment to the founding ideals of democracy, even as he lamented the present realities of American democracy. See Curtis Evans, "W. E. B. Du Bois: Interpreting Religion and the Problem of the Negro Church," *Journal of the American Academy of Religion* 75, no. 2 (2007): 268–97; and Elvira Basevich, "W. E. B. Du Bois' Critique of American Democracy during the Jim Crow Era," *The Journal of Political Philosophy* 27, no. 3 (2019): 1–23.

28. On President Grant's role in reconstruction, see Ron Chernow, *Grant* (New York: Penguin, 2018).

29. See Ellen Carol Dubois, *Feminism and Suffrage: The Emergence of an Independent Women's Movement in America, 1848–1869* (Ithaca, NY: Cornell University Press, 1999).

who had previously met as abolitionists working against slavery, convened a two-day meeting of three hundred women and men to call for the elimination of public discrimination against women and demand their enfranchisement. A Declaration of Sentiments was adopted by a significant majority, but the proposal for women's suffrage met with great resistance. The key figure urging the suffrage issue was, quite significantly, the African American abolitionist, Frederick Douglass. On that basis, the conference was historically significant for intertwining race and gender issues. But, as in the twentieth century, so in the nineteenth century, the movement for racial equality would precede that for gender equality.[30]

With the passage of the Nineteenth Amendment in 1920, women were granted the vote.[31] In many ways, the women's movement mirrored the abolitionist movements but was never as culturally explosive; there was nothing comparable to the Civil War to settle the issue.[32] It was quite clear, however, that the movement for women's suffrage followed similar conceptual lines as that for abolition. The original restriction on voting rights applied to slaves, women, Native Americans, and recent immigrants. These groups gained a political identity by virtue of their exclusion rather than any common cultural association either across the groups or within the groups. More than a century after the Civil War, these excluded groups gained a distinctly political identity by virtue of their connection to the exclusion narrative of American democracy. The historical narratives of exclusion

30. The civil rights movement of the 1950s and 1960s preceded the second wave of the feminist movement of the 1960s and 1970s. The proximity of the #MeToo movement and Black Lives Matter in the recent past have again reminded us of the interweaving of race and gender concerns.

31. Earlier, in 1869, a rift had developed among feminists over the proposed Fifteenth Amendment, which gave the vote to Black men. Susan B. Anthony, Elizabeth Cady Stanton, and others refused to endorse the amendment because it did not give women the ballot. Other suffragists, however, including Lucy Stone and Julia Ward Howe, argued that once Black men were enfranchised, women would inevitably achieve their goal.

32. In 1872, Anthony went to the polls in Rochester, New York, and cast a ballot in the presidential election, citing her citizenship under the Fourteenth Amendment. She was arrested, tried, convicted, and fined $100, which she refused to pay.

tied them together and were the generative forces that eventually produced the identity politics of our time.

Another tragedy at the founding of the republic was the exclusion of Native Americans, though on very different grounds from those of Africans or women. Native Americans had already been culturally established in the land long before the Americans revolted against the British. The colonial settlers originally developed a mostly peaceable strategy for dealing with the three large Native American groups they encountered (the Algonquins in New England, the Iroquois nations in the Adirondacks, and the Muskogean group of tribes in the Southeast), though the clash of cultures was everywhere a point of tension.[33] Trade between the tribes and the settlers proved to be a bridge between the cultures, but it was always tenuous given the contrasting sympathies with the other large trading partners in the background—the British and the French. After the American Revolution, the colonists' desire to expand into territories to the west made coexistence increasingly difficult. Federal treaties established terms of peace, though the frequent alliances between the tribes and the British or the French or the Spanish served to undermine confidence in the treaties and increased the suspicion between the colonists and the tribes, as did the colonists' willingness to violate the treaties when it suited them. As immigration across the Atlantic increased, the land itself became the primary point of conflict and led, tragically, to many bloody wars. As with the colonists' use of chattel slavery, so their treatment of Native Americans carried with it a terrible irony—having fled authoritarian rule, they exercised that same authoritarian rule over populations in their own midst. The height of that tragedy occurred during the Andrew Jackson presidency (1829–1837), when most of the federal treaties with the Native Americans were abrogated unilaterally and Native Americans were

---

33. Rough estimates of the total Native American population prior to 1776 put the total between 100,000 and 200,000. See Peter Marshall, "The West and the Amerindians: 1756–1776," in *A Companion to the American Revolution*, ed. Jack P. Greene and J. R. Pole (Oxford: Blackwell, 2000), 157–64.

pushed forcibly beyond the Mississippi River against their will.[34] With his own personal instincts, Jackson represented the two contrasting sides of the narrative of democracy. His rhetoric strongly suggested that ordinary people needed to be more directly heard in the corridors of power in Washington but also excluded as part of the "people" every Native American, all of whom had been on American shores long before the Europeans arrived.[35]

THE STORY OF DEMOCRACY AND
THE ETHNO-RACIAL PENTAGON

Ethnicity entered the political lexicon in more ambiguous and diffuse ways than either race or gender: through diverse waves of immigration. As immigrants came to America, many brought customs and languages that appeared strange to those who had come in earlier generations. America has always been a nation of immigrants that nonetheless has a long history of suspicion toward immigrants.[36] Newer immigrants have always brought new challenges as to what it means to be "American." If there is such a thing as a national ideology in America, it is nonethnic by virtue of the universalist commitment proclaimed in the Constitution to provide the benefits of citizenship irrespective of ancestral affiliations. American history, however, has been defined by a predominantly ethnic ideology determined by ancestral-derived distinctions.[37] The Constitution declares that ethnic

---

34. Jackson simply ignored the 1832 Supreme Court decision granting the Cherokee Indians sovereign rights as a nation and removed the Cherokee forcibly from their ancestral lands. Miller, *Can Democracy Work?*, 111.

35. Jon Meacham's magisterial biography of Jackson captures well both sides of Jackson's character. See his *American Lion: Andrew Jackson in the White House* (New York: Random House, 2008).

36. The polling on this issue has been relatively consistent since the beginning of polling on the question. The percentage of Americans in favor of less immigration has always hovered near 50 percent. Only a small percentage, normally less than 10 percent, favor increasing immigration. The remaining are content with the status quo.

37. David A. Hollinger sets up his argument for a "post-ethnic America" in this fashion. In the immediate aftermath of 9/11, he laments, "Ethnic affiliations should not be taken as primordial but American history has too often suggested they were" (*Postethnic America*, 21).

affiliations should not be taken as primordial, but American history has too often suggested they were.

Through the diverse waves of immigration in the nineteenth and early twentieth centuries, populations came to the United States largely in search of economic opportunities in contrast to the economic hardships they faced in their own countries of origin.[38] The pattern of immigration prior to the 1960s was not largely motivated by the attraction of American democracy or by political persecution elsewhere.[39] On a large scale, the massive migration movements of the nineteenth century were motivated by the job market, the rise of commercial agriculture, and industrialization near large urban areas. Increase in global trade throughout the nineteenth and twentieth centuries also made migration to economically vital regions much more viable.

The waves of immigrants coming to America would not have seen themselves as coming from a general region of the world, but rather from a specific town or village in a particular part of a particular country. As one commentator notes of the Italian immigration at the turn of the twentieth century, "Italians did not think of themselves as Italians at all but as Sicilians, Calabrese, Abruzzi, Romans, Venetians, and so forth: to some extent they still do."[40] Group identities existed, but they were almost always local rather than national, what we refer to today as "ethnic." Retaining the home culture after coming to America meant retaining the language and networks of kinship and friendship derived from their ancestral roots.

The melting-pot image has always failed to do justice to the realities of immigration in America. After passing through immigration

---

38. There is considerable evidence that most immigrants who came to America throughout its history have been people of means in their country of origin. Two helpful introductions to the history of immigration in America are Roger Daniels, *Coming to America: A History of Immigration and Ethnicity in American Life* (New York: Harper Perennial, 2002); and David Gerber, *American Immigration: A Very Short Introduction* (New York: Oxford University Press, 2011).

39. Asylum seekers did not become a significant percentage of immigrants until the 1980s and 1990s. Peter Schuck, *Diversity in America: Keeping Government at a Safe Distance* (Cambridge, MA: Harvard University Press, 2003), 86.

40. Schuck, *Diversity in America*, 7.

control, most immigrants settled in parts of America where they could join relatives or friends. In that sense, immigration was radically different from the forced migration of Africans in the slave trade. But like Africans, immigrant populations were treated with scorn and often legal forms of discrimination, especially where the language differences were stark. Given how fragile and experimental American democracy was in the world throughout much of the nineteenth century, there was widespread fear that foreigners represented strange political realities that would threaten core democratic values.[41] Because immigrants brought unusual customs, or did not speak English, or did not assimilate quickly to the "American" way, stereotypes formed about them that were not unique or peculiar to America, but were often expressed in uniquely and peculiarly American ways.

In spite of this, immigrant groups, though they were stereotyped and initially bore the brunt of discrimination, quickly learned how to treat later immigrant groups with the same scorn as they had been treated. These stereotypes were socially constructed and frequently the origin of our later categories of ethnicity. It is important to note that not only was ethnic identity socially constructed and significantly pliable, but it rarely arose from the "national culture of origin" as such. Immigrants' senses of social identity were rooted in local culture but later absorbed into a "national culture" as a result of the stereotyping they endured upon settling in America. Italian immigrants became "Italian Americans" though they initially self-identified as Venetians, Romans, and so on. Immigrants from Sicily did not think of themselves as having common cultural ties to Venetians, but

---

41. The Alien and Sedition Acts of 1798 (passed by a Federalist congress fearful of a war with France) placed into law limits on recent immigrants, as well as limits on the constitutional rights of free speech and press. The fear of foreigners had a basis in facts: France and Britain were consistently violating the integrity of US boundaries. It also had a basis in stereotypes: only "dangerous" people would criticize the government, and therefore dissent from government policy was viewed as criminal behavior. The acts were repealed shortly after President John Adams's term expired in 1801. See Charles Slack, *Liberty's First Crisis: Adams, Jefferson, and the Misfits Who Saved Free Speech* (New York: Grove, 2016), for a description of the historical context of the controversy.

once stereotyped as "Italians" upon arrival in the United States, they gradually lost their sense of culturally belonging to Sicily—eventually becoming Italian, then Italian American, and then several generations later simply American. Along the course of that historical trajectory, they endured many discriminatory slights. The trajectory from a local identity rooted in their ancestral home, to a national stereotyped identity on American shores, to an assimilated "American" identity did not happen in mechanical or predictable fashion. The length of the trajectory was dependent on a host of other variables: the job market, the religious subculture, the political environment, and the customs, habits, and language of the immigrants.[42]

There have been two large waves of immigration to America since 1890. The first wave, which lasted until 1920, brought large numbers of diverse European immigrants (Irish and Polish Catholics, Russian Jews, German Lutherans, and so on) to the United States. Many of them experienced discrimination by virtue of their religious as well as their cultural habits. They entered into what we now refer to as a culture dominated by WASPs (White Anglo-Saxon Protestants). The second wave of immigration, from 1965 to 1990, began as the result of the Hart-Celler Immigration Act of 1965. Though significant numbers of European immigrants were a part of this second wave, it also included large numbers of immigrants from many other parts of the globe.

It was this second wave that introduced the division of immigrants into large generic ethnic categories. The Hart-Celler Act officially removed the 1924 quotas that had limited immigration from countries outside of northern Europe. Though it continued to reference immigrants by country, it set in motion federal classifications based on regions of the globe, which were then formally endorsed in the census of 1970. With this census form, the "ethno-racial pentagon"

---

42. The impact of first-generation immigrants on the "elite" end of American culture has been often overlooked. Since 1965, first-generation immigrants have accounted for three to four times as many of America's Nobel Laureates, National Academy of Sciences members, Academy Award-winning film directors, and winners of Kennedy Center awards in the performing arts as native-born Americans. See Robert Putnam, "E Pluribus Unum," 140.

became the de facto set of categories in thinking about race and eth-nicity in America.[43] Cultures were divided into five categories—Asian American, Latino, African American, Native American, and white. No significant political discussion led to these categories, nor was there any serious social-scientific data that identified these broad types as descriptively significant.[44] They were simply developed to enable leg-islative discussion around the issue of discrimination without having to deal with a global country-by-country analysis.[45]

However, a large-scale movement in both the academy and pop-ular culture developed around the ethno-racial pentagon whose pri-mary goal was to encourage greater demographic diversity within every sphere of American culture. Unfortunately, the categories of the movement were derived from a largely bureaucratic decision (the census) that homogenized the population into five generic catego-ries. When we now refer to ethnicity or race, we are addressing the historical narrative of people groups that were previously excluded on the basis of biology (skin color) or stereotypes. While categories of race or ethnicity rooted in biology or stereotypes have long been discredited, the narratives of exclusion are very much a part of their present identity.[46]

---

43. It was only during the second wave of immigration that the first wave of immigrants became Euro-Americans and eventually classified as "white." See Hollinger, *Postethnic America*.

44. Hollinger notes with considerable irony, "The ethno-racial pentagon essentially erased much of the cultural diversity within the European American block. The category of European and American as it concerned Irish American identity had accomplished in short order a task that centuries a British Imperial Power could not complete making the Irish indistinguishable from the English." Hollinger, *Postethnic America*, 25.

45. The single event most responsible for marking out the lines that separate one "ethnic" block from another was the issuing of a directive by the Office of Management and Budget in 1977 that the budget be designed to enable government workers to gather information to prove whether the Civil Rights Act of 1964 was being enforced as a protection against racial and ethnic discrimination. Thereafter, all federal collection of information used the ethno-racial pentagon as the de facto categories of classification.

46. Jews had once widely been thought of as a race. The "racial" category was rooted in the deep prejudices against Jews in many parts of American culture and was socially constructed to make sense of that reality. When their exclusion was judged not to be as extreme as Blacks or Latinos, the category of Jews as a race dropped out of our lexicon.

When we consider people of mixed race or mixed ethnicity, it quickly becomes evident how artificial the categories of the ethno-racial pentagon actually are.[47] Most individuals live in many social circles simultaneously, and they live their lives shifting identities among the various groups of which they are a part. Individual identity, in other words, is wrapped up in many overlapping communities. The broad ethno-racial categories also homogenized diverse cultures within the pentagon—for example, supposing that folks from Mexico, Argentina, and Puerto Rico share a common culture simply because they speak a common language.

The history of political exclusion and discrimination still struck a chord in popular culture, even if the categories defining the excluded populations did not do justice to the cultural complexities of the populations themselves. Doing justice both to the history of discrimination and the complexity of cultural formation has been the challenge of American democracy's public discourse on diversity. Glossing over the complexity of cultural formation simply leaves stereotypes of cultural groups in place and doesn't allow for genuine identities to form outside of those stereotypes. However, the existence of stereotypes undoubtedly forms the conceptual backbone in the narrative of discrimination across America's history. A fine line has formed between recognizing the reality of stereotypes that have been placed on others and accepting those stereotypes as defining their key identity markers. Turning generic ethnic or racial categories into defining cultural

---

47. Putnam records the following anecdote in support of this reality: "Several of my grandchildren were raised in Costa Rica, the children of an American mother (my daughter) and a Costa Rican father. A few years ago, they moved to Pittsburgh and at the end of the first week of school, my granddaughter Miriam came home and asked my daughter: 'People keep calling me "Hispanic." What do they mean? I tell them "No, I'm Costa Rican."' My daughter, a social historian by profession, but also a mom, knew she had to answer the question seriously, and she replied: '"Hispanic" is how North Americans refer to people whose parents came from Latin America.' 'Oh,' asked Miriam, 'is Daddy Hispanic?' 'Yes,' replied my daughter. After a pause, Miriam asked: 'Are you Hispanic?' and my daughter replied 'No.' After a much longer pause came Miriam's inevitable question: 'Am I Hispanic?' 'That's a difficult question, isn't it?' replied my daughter. Miriam was learning about the complicated way in which Americans today divide up the world, and in the process, she was reconstructing her own social identity." Putnam, "E Pluribus Unum," 160.

frameworks pigeonholes individuals and communities into the very stereotypes that created the problems in the first place. It also imposes undue obstacles to the emergence of transethnic and transracial communities, and thereby makes it more difficult to fully engage the work of reconciliation across these differences.[48]

Democracy is hardwired to be supersensitive to the inclusion narrative—and susceptible at the same time to large-scale discrimination and exclusion. Majorities are no less prone to discriminatory actions toward minorities than self-interested monarchs might have been. Democracy provides no built-in guarantees against immoral behavior. It is a polity containing the seeds of self-criticism, since it permits a diversity of opinion in the public square, and in particular the self-criticism of limiting the diversity of voices in the public square.[49] There is an intrinsic human tendency to diminish the dignity of others as a means of increasing one's own sense of significance.[50] This tendency is not uniquely manifest in a democracy; it is simply given unique political space to operate.

Movements to bring more voices into the political process may well appear to solve one set of divisions within the culture, yet they have also created larger and larger diversities of opinions in the public square. The movements for inclusion fostered a different kind of tension that has long festered in modern liberal democracies: Granting individuals (and communities) the freedom of self-expression also

---

48. Putnam and others have argued that the mediating institutions that are not under direct government oversight provide the best avenues to construct cross-ethnic identities. "Community centers, athletic fields, and schools were among the most efficacious instruments for incorporating new immigrants a century ago, and we need to reinvest in such places and activities once again, enabling us all to become comfortable with diversity." Putnam, "E Pluribus Unum," 164.

49. Democratic egalitarian ideals derive from European origins. If group identity is deterministically connected to countries of descent, then only a portion of the American population would have a "right" to those egalitarian ideals, but this is manifestly not the case. It is the irony of the inclusion narrative that those who have been excluded may nonetheless claim as their own the natural rights of the inclusion narrative. See Hollinger, *Postethnic America*, 125.

50. The heresy of nationalism in Nazi Germany or Soviet Russia was the notion that ethnicity was the only proper foundation of a nation. Separating "us" from "them" was the backbone of politics—a tendency that can be found in various forms of American nationalism on the Right and identity politics on the Left.

created the platforms for deep polarization of conviction to come to the surface. The only cultural traffic police at the political intersection was the consent of the majority. At one level, this was simply a procedural way of dealing with conflict. The result has been that we have fewer and fewer substantive means of dealing with conflict as the common cultural bonds of a generic religious faith fade from view. The demise of a quasi-cohesive civil religion provided by mainline Protestantism during the middle decades of the twentieth century has meant there is precious little moral glue left to bind the nation together.[51] The only "common bond" in a secular democracy has been the existence of a common procedure. The question before us is whether our current cultural moment will move toward greater polarization, or whether there are resources for thinking differently about difference. We turn in the next chapter to the complexity of dealing with difference in a culture without a common moral framework.

---

51. See George M. Marsden, *The Twilight of the American Enlightenment: The 1950s and the Crisis of Liberal Belief* (New York: Basic Books, 2014).

Modern culture, in breaking with the structures and beliefs of Christendom, also carried certain facets of Christian life further than they ever were taken or could have been taken with Christendom.

—CHARLES TAYLOR, "A CATHOLIC MODERNITY?"

3

THE SACRED AND SECULAR DIMENSIONS OF DIVERSITY

THE END OF CHRISTENDOM?

"Christendom" is the term for when Christianity is the exclusively sanctioned religion of the land. In the West, the crumbling of Christendom gained steam legally in the aftermath of the American Bill of Rights privileging no form of the Christian church. This marked the beginning of the end of a politically established religion governing all the citizens. With the freedom-of-religion clause in the Bill of Rights and the abolishing of religious tests for office in the early decades of the nineteenth century, churches were forced to reflect quite differently on their cultural presence. They were left without an official voice in the corridors of political power, but they were also freed from state control. The public and political squares were officially open to many diverse and competing religious views. On the positive side, this meant the Christian faith would no longer be coerced by the state and persons would be free to live out their faith according to their own conscience.[1]

---

1. Charles Taylor remarks in wry fashion, "So a vote of thanks to Voltaire and others for (not necessarily wittingly) showing us this and for allowing us to live the gospel in a purer way, free of that continual and often bloody forcing of conscience which was the sin and blight of those 'Christian' centuries. The gospel was always meant to stand out, unencumbered by arms." Taylor, "A Catholic Modernity?," in *A Catholic Modernity? Charles Taylor's Marianist Award Lecture*, ed. James L. Heft (New York: Oxford University Press, 1999), 18.

Over the next century and a half, the church's presence remained
pervasive despite disestablishment. To the surprise of many
Europeans, churches in America actually gained greater vitality as
a result of being disestablished, and also gained a greater public
platform, even though they no longer had direct political sanction.[2] Churches cast not a weaker but a stronger moral shadow
across politics—seen nowhere more prophetically and tragically
than in the debates over slavery in the antebellum period.[3] The
generic Christian tradition remained dominant in the minds of most
Americans even if a large majority of them did not regularly attend a
church.[4] The Puritan vision of America as a shining city set on a hill
was not representative of the religious condition of most American
cities at the founding of the republic, but it did nonetheless cast a
large shadow over the nation.

The absence of ecclesiastical establishment did not usher in
the end of Christendom; a generally ambiguous Christianity persisted. Though most states quickly moved toward disestablishment
by the beginning of the nineteenth century, Protestant Christianity
retained many public privileges.[5] Most states had blue laws outlaw-

---

2. The best single volume on the history of religion in America surrounding the early
republic is Mark A. Noll, *America's God: From Jonathan Edwards to Abraham Lincoln* (New York:
Oxford University Press, 2005). Noll captures well the intrinsic tension between the disestablishment of churches in the century and the all-pervasive influence of a generic Christianity
between 1760 and 1860.

3. Mark Noll makes the case that abolitionists in New England and defenders of slavery
in the South were identical in many respects regarding their evangelical convictions. Though
they appealed to the Bible to defend their contrasting views of slavery, their respective social
settings are far more determinative of their views on slavery than their commitment to evangelical doctrine. See Noll, *God and Race in American Politics: A Short History* (Princeton: Princeton
University Press, 2008), especially chapter 1. Noll offers a lengthier examination of the issue
in his *The Civil War as a Theological Crisis* (Chapel Hill: University of North Carolina Press,
2006), 31–50.

4. Church attendance in the early republic hovered near 20 percent of the population. See
Finke and Stark, *The Churching of America*, chapter 2.

5. One must be careful to distinguish the claim that there was a moral shadow cast by
Christian churches from the claim that America was a Christian nation at its founding. The
latter claim has virtually no sustainable evidence in its favor. See Noll, Hatch, and Marsden,
The Search for Christian America.

ing certain activities on the Sabbath, as well as official ceremonies of remembrance of God's providential oversight of historical events. Education, which in Christendom had always had a conspicuous religious component, continued to include Protestant teachings. In the mid-nineteenth century, many state universities still required chapel attendance and were likely to have clergymen as presidents. Legally established Christendom may have been nearing its end, but cultural Christendom remained everywhere present.[6]

Well into the 1950s, mainline Protestant churches, predominantly Northern and white, regarded themselves as constituting an informal religious establishment. Mainline Protestant leaders were part of the liberal moderate cultural mainstream, and distinctive Christians like Reinhold Niebuhr were viewed as important public statesmen. The last great manifestation of public Protestant influence was in the Prohibition movement, culminating in the Eighteenth Amendment in 1919.

The moral shadow of cultural Christendom vanished almost completely in the cultural revolutions of the 1960s and early 1970s. By 1976, which *Time* magazine declared the "Year of the Evangelical" on its front cover, it was evident to most cultural observers that America was no longer even a culturally Protestant nation. Religion still seemed to thrive in places, but the animating forces of media, technology, education, and politics instilled a secular ethos. There were no public declarations now proclaiming a secular nation, but in the culture-shaping megacities, advancing secularity was taken for granted—and with that reality came a distinctive way to think about diversity. It is to that story we now turn.

---

6. George M. Marsden, in *The Twilight of the American Enlightenment*, argues that the 1950s represented the last episode of a culturally influential (though not legally established) Protestant liberalism in America, which succumbed to the revolutionary decade of the 1960s. When the leaders of the Christian Right arose in the late 1970s, they gained a following by appealing to their "outsider" status, but quickly were tarnished with the "establishment" brush as they sought political influence by virtue of the increasing numbers of their movement.

The Social Imaginary of Our Time

The modern social consciousness, what Charles Taylor refers to as the "social imaginary," has altered the way in which inclusion and exclusion narratives are viewed. The social imaginary refers to the implicit assumptions of the way the world works, including what is normal and normative.[7] It is not always conscious, nor is it identical to an explicit worldview. The social imaginary of our time may be described at an abstract level with the language of "late secular modernity," but this label lacks the specificity of any particular person's identity.[8] A straight line from a large social context to an individual's identity simply does not exist. Nonetheless, it is appropriate to describe the patterns of social identity across significant swaths of a population. Survey data captures broad patterns of social identity while failing to do justice to the unique identities of individuals within the large cohort being surveyed. The uniqueness of each individual rarely matches the large-scale stereotypes, but inevitably similar influences appear even on a small-scale individual level. We need self-awareness to see those large patterns in our own lives even if they do not correspond precisely.

With these qualifications in mind, it is appropriate to say that the social imaginary of a large number of people in our times may be described as: late, secular, and modern.

---

7. Charles Taylor, *Modern Social Imaginaries* (Durham, NC: Duke University Press, 2003): "By social imaginary ... I am thinking of the ways people imagine their social existence, how they fit together with others, how things go on between them and their fellows, the expectations that are normally met, and the deeper normative notions and images underlying these expectations" (23).

8. Peter Berger, *The Sacred Canopy: Elements of a Sociological Theory of Religion* (Garden City, NY: Doubleday, 1967), writes, "Every individual biography is an episode within the history of society, which both precedes and survives it. Society was there before the individual was born and it will be there after they have died. What is more, it is within society, and as a result of social processes, that the individual becomes a person, that he attains and holds onto an identity, and that he carries out the various projects that constitute his life. Persons cannot exist apart from society. The two statements that society is the product of persons and that persons are the product of society, are not contradictory" (3).

OUR SOCIAL IMAGINARY: *LATE* SECULAR MODERNITY

The adjective "late" refers to the duration of social changes that have been underway for a very long time (and should not be taken to infer that this age is nearly over). Though current intuitions regarding issues of sexual identity, globalization, and genetics may seem recent and revolutionary, the cultural conditions that give rise to them are the result of a long process of technological, economic, and political change. This process dates back to the Protestant Reformation in the sixteenth century, gained considerable momentum in the Enlightenment of the seventeenth century, acquired political currency with the rise of democracies in the eighteenth century, and exponentially progressed with the Industrial Revolution of the nineteenth century. Nevertheless, the complexity of history makes it hard to adjudicate exactly when modernity began. Time periods are not cleanly marked by precise signage. More often they are marked by significant events that make demands that cannot be conveniently dismissed—events that "jump off the pages" of history. The Reformation and the American Revolution are cases in point. Revolutionary historical events resist the normal narrative structure of a society's life and thereby alter its own self-perception.[9] Thus it is appropriate to say that, whenever modernity actually began, it has lasted a long time.

One of the difficulties in the contemporary use of the term "modern" is the divorce that has taken place in peoples' minds between the recent past and the more distant past. The horizon of our social consciousness often supposes that most events of significance happened in the last twenty years. "Modern" technology is not a reference to the printing press or the steam engine but to the iPhone and Snapchat. The result is the illusion that the modern era began in the recent past. The speed with which the information revolution

---

9. I have argued at length in *Progressive and Conservative Religious Ideologies* that the 1960s was one of the revolutionary decades in American history.

occurred in the lifetime of the millennial generation blurs the ability to conceptually connect the past to the present. The information revolution is surely a very different stage of modernity than the age of the printing press or the steam engine. However, the rise of technologies that transformed the sense of place and time in the era of the printing press and the era of Netflix and Instagram share important similarities. Adding the adjective "late" is simply to remind us that though the information revolution may appear to be an entirely different era, closer inspection suggests it is a stage of an age that began several centuries ago.

The intuitions surrounding the present technological conditions are fed by another stream. The thoroughly modern (and liberal) concern for being freed from tradition has given the mistaken impression that the present is unrelated to the past. The present may have a limitless future, but freedom from the past is built into these cultural intuitions. This disconnect of the present from the past gains rhetorical force by the enduring fascination with the idea of "progress" during the entire period of modernity.[10] The greater the perception of progress a culture experiences, the greater will be the conceptual distance between past and present. This inclination—that the past lacked substantive progress and thereby offers few lessons for the present—wrongly assumes that human dysfunction is also going the way of the horse and buggy. In reverse, some people's nostalgia for a simpler and safer past is grounded in the misguided perception that earlier times were not embedded in the new technologies of their era, in turn masking the reality that the past was experienced as every bit as complex as the present is to us.

OUR SOCIAL IMAGINARY: LATE SECULAR *MODERNITY*

What then characterizes the "modern"? At its most basic level, modernity may be construed as the production of technologically induced ways of thinking and living in the world.[11] In this regard, the

---

10. See Christopher Lasch, *The True and Only Heaven: Progress and Its Critics* (New York: Norton, 1991), for a careful expression of this sentiment. A helpful historical overview may be found in Robert Nisbet, *The History of the Idea of Progress* (New York: Basic Books, 1980).

11. The debates about modernity are legion and far beyond the scope of adequate characterization here. I am essentially following the work of Peter Berger in what follows. See Berger,

Reformation and the Enlightenment created the conceptual and cultural environments in which the scientific and technological advances of the Industrial Revolution not only took hold but also created a different social consciousness about the nature of the world. The democratization of religion (Reformation) and ideas (Enlightenment) spilled out into the empirical observation and exploitation of the natural world (Industrial Revolution). By this means, a new century of expansion and globalization emerged. New forms of economic exchange sprang up, as did entirely new forms of social and political organizations, inspired by the inventions and innovations of the era. These were not all experienced in the same way around the globe, but the "before" and "after" of these revolutions marked out a new era in cultural formation.

In traditional societies, significance and security were largely centered on class and function, and these did not change from generation to generation. If you were born into the lower classes, there was little expectation that you would ascend any higher. If your father was a blacksmith in a medieval village, you would most likely follow him into that vocation.

With the rise of modern liberal democracies, these traditional and stable mechanisms of significance and security disappeared. In their place came the ideal of freedom of social movement, as well as the notion of equality across all class divisions. The democratic ideal of every person being equal in dignity and rights rarely matched people's experience, but the ideal nonetheless stood as an implicit value. The advent of liberal democracies was a primary push toward greater equality across a diverse population, but the forces of modernity, broadly construed, also increased the diversity of people rubbing shoulders with each other visually and now virtually, appearing to eliminate older class distinctions.[12] The massive rise in specialization

---

Rumor of Angels (Garden City, NY: Doubleday, 1970), and Berger and Thomas Luckmann, *Modernity, Pluralism and the Crisis of Meaning: The Orientation of Modern Man* (Gütersloh: Bertelsmann, 1995).

12. Peter Berger says, "Modernity generates social pluralism, which in turn generates voluntary associations which then function as a school of democracy. Eventually something

and the diversity of labor in modern technological societies has also meant that social sympathies began to reside within broad vocational groupings rather than with kinship and family. Software engineers closely identify with peers in their field. Faculty in a specialized discipline emotionally connect best with other like-minded faculty. It is rare now for people to "inherit" their vocation from their parents or be limited in social interactions by the networks of their parents' and grandparents' families. Growing up in a pastor's home no longer increases the likelihood of becoming a pastor. A schoolteacher's children are not more likely to become schoolteachers themselves. The disruption of previously stable social identities across generations has brought with it renewed thinking about how identity and social location are related, and also how those social identities influence the constant interaction of diverse social identities.

The Industrial Revolution of the eighteenth and nineteenth centuries introduced major changes to transportation (coal-fired engines, steam-powered trains and ships) and created new economies of scale within the Western world.[13] Exploration continued at a furious pace across North America. Western culture spread its tentacles with the new industrial empires taming the "uncivilized" world by virtue of the sophistication of their tools and technologies.[14] Monopolies were built within the new empires by the acquisition of new tools and the expansion of capital markets. Limits on human achievement seemed to recede in proportion to the increase in technological advances.

---

like the New England town meeting became a universal social and political norm." Berger, "Pluralism, Protestantization and the Voluntary Principle," in *Democracy and the New Religious Pluralism*, ed. Thomas Banchoff (New York: Oxford University Press, 2007), 25.

13. Albert Borgmann argues in compelling fashion that modernity was the era of domination, most clearly characterized in the building of the American railroads in the nineteenth century. See Borgmann, *Crossing the Postmodern Divide* (Chicago: University of Chicago Press, 1992).

14. The language of "civilization" has taken on negative connotations in the postcolonial period of the past fifty years. However, the original positive connotations associated with the term were attached because of its association with cultural changes wrought by the Industrial Revolution. However one views the imperial dimensions of that language, underlying it was a way to refer to the massive changes that took place because of the scientific discoveries and industrial inventions of the era.

The formation of these new economic empires was a function of the power of the tools, tragically manifested also in the domination of whole people groups for economic and political ends. The plantation economies of cotton and sugar in the Southern United States were the most notable evidence of this domination and have been the most persistent in the postcolonial imagination in America.[15]

The transportation revolutions of the twentieth century (automobile and plane) reordered population patterns into suburban/urban frameworks and deepened the economic divide between the first and third worlds. The tools of transportation helped to modify central assumptions about time and space. Westerners were less likely to think of themselves as "tied down" to a place or time. A trip across America took nearly eight months at the beginning of the eighteenth century, and two weeks by the end of the nineteenth century. By the middle of the twentieth century, it could be accomplished in less than a day. In that same time period, Americans were becoming citizens of the world, flying to Cape Town or Calcutta with the same ease as traveling to California. Global events were now unfolding before their very eyes with the widespread distribution of televisions in the mid-twentieth century. The narrative of progress served to legitimate this brave new world where the old boundaries and limitations were melting away into thin air.[16] Anything seemed possible—and fast.

The spirit of optimism and triumph at the beginning of the twentieth century dissipated as the century wore on. Two world wars brought devastation across the European continent. The Holocaust, along with the Russian gulags and China's Cultural Revolution, killed populations on a scale never before imagined. The second half of the twentieth century unfolded in America with the global tensions

---

15. America was functionally different from the colonial empires of the British, the French, the Dutch, and the Portuguese, not having any distant colonies of its own. However, the early American thirst for lands to explore and conquer eventually pushed the boundaries of the country from its origins on the East Coast all the way to the Pacific. See Wolfgang Reinhard, *A Short History of Colonialism* (Manchester: Manchester University Press, 2011).

16. Marshall Berman reflects this imaginary in his cultural history of the late twentieth century, *All That Is Solid Melts into Air* (New: York: Simon & Schuster, 1982).

of the Cold War, the tragedies of Vietnam and Watergate, and the assassinations of John F. Kennedy and Martin Luther King Jr., each challenging the narrative of progress.[17] The demise of the European colonial empires in the 1960s also signaled a waning of the triumphal spirit of the West, even if television extended the West's commercial and cultural influence more pervasively than any colonial empire.[18] The new superpowers of the twentieth century had held out hope of a new world order but eventually fell under moral suspicion in the rest of the world because of their military might. Great modern military tyrannies came crashing down before the twentieth century was over, but not before the world realized the danger of weapons of mass destruction and those who controlled them. As the globe grew ever smaller, so did the fragility of human coexistence. The spirit of modernity framed a protest against the (dangerous) powers that be while also concluding there were no realistic alternatives. The result: a culture bordering on the cynical, vacillating awkwardly between naive optimism in the tools of technology and profound pessimism about the use of those tools.[19]

The more life changed, and the quicker those changes occurred, the more precarious personal security and significance seemed to be. Convictions about who "we" were also changed as the melting pot of American culture added new ingredients. America was becoming less distinctive with the blending of so many cultures and the increasing awareness of cultural differences. Identity seemed deeply rooted in the strangeness of this new set of cultural interactions, increasingly highlighting the differences of race, ethnicity, and gender because of their peculiar history in the exclusion narrative of American democracy. In the aftermath of the civil rights movement of the 1960s, race

---

17. See Lasch, *True and Only Heaven*.

18. Harold MacMillan the British prime minister gave his famous "Winds of Change" speech in 1960 in Cape Town, South Africa, announcing the beginning of independence for the African colonies of Britain. By the end of the decade, most of the African nations were free from colonial rule.

19. See Dick Keyes, *Seeing through Cynicism: A Reconsideration of the Power of Suspicion* (Downers Grove, IL: InterVarsity Press, 2006).

came to dominate the discourse on difference even as it subdued many other important diversity variables. In the post-1960s period, race has been the interpretive key to understanding difference and has routinely been stretched to bring other differences into its orbit. The pervasive intuition of equality in modernity fostered a counter-reaction of inequality by anyone and everyone who self-identified as a cultural "outsider." By making one's outsider status analogous to the exclusion narrative of race, one could also gain cultural status. Nearly anyone could be an outsider by defining themselves over against whoever they believed had discriminated against them.

In the latter half of the twentieth century, Americans became citizens of the globe, which was both decreasing in size (owing to the power of technology) and increasing in size (with awareness of vast numbers of diverse cultures). In a time of self-definition, what were Americans to think of themselves? Who were they supposed to be? How were individuals to relate to others who did not share their cultural context within the larger construct of late modernity?[20] As the twenty-first century dawned, the multiplicity of cultural intersections underscored the difficulty of knowing how to think of the unity of any sustainable variety and made diversity virtually omnipresent in our consciousness.

OUR SOCIAL IMAGINARY: LATE *SECULAR* MODERNITY

What does it mean to be "secular"? Boiled down to its most basic elements, secularization refers to life that is carried on without an abiding sense of a transcendent reality invading ordinary events. It should be clearly distinguished from "secularism," which refers to an ideology supposing there are no transcendent realities outside the material world. A secular age is an age in which God may still be on people's mental landscape but makes little practical difference to the ordinary

---

20. The most influential Christian to write on these tensions has been Volf in *Exclusion and Embrace*.

affairs of life.[21] The cultural forces shaping life's intuitions make God an absentee landlord at best. A secular age have many religious believers, but those believers exert minimal influence on public morality or on the discourse in the public square. Secular nonreligious people live within what Charles Taylor refers to as the "immanent frame." They have developed means and methods that appear to secure a sense of significance without any reference to a transcendent deity. They may be acquainted with a few religious people, but the religious folk seem strangely out of place in their world, veritable aliens from another planet. There remains a sense in a secular age (as opposed to a secular worldview) that there must be more to ordinary life, but without any great impulse to discover what that might be.

It was not an uncommon prophecy through the first half of the twentieth century that religious belief of any substance would soon go the way of the horse-drawn buggy and the oil-burning lantern.[22] This was not primarily a statement of intellectual confidence by atheists but more often grounded in the fact that religious conviction was slowly eroding under the forces of secularization. It was not that the problem of evil proved God could not exist; it was simply that believing in God seemed irrelevant to modern life. Until the mid-nineteenth century, the differences between theism and atheism were conceived largely in metaphysical terms and the debate centered on the requisite evidence for the best explanation of competing metaphysical claims. On this score, David Hume's arguments in the eighteenth century against theism looked similar to the arguments batted back and forth by sophisticated skeptics in the third and fourth centuries. By the second half of the twentieth century, arguments for and against God's existence appeared quaint. The evidence for theism or atheism

---

21. The literature on secularity is enormous. One of the most influential and significant treatments is Charles Taylor, *A Secular Age* (Cambridge, MA: Belknap Press of Harvard University Press, 2007). A helpful summary treatment of Taylor is James K. A. Smith, *How (Not) to Be Secular: Reading Charles Taylor* (Grand Rapids: Eerdmans, 2014).

22. This was a core assumption of the Death of God movement of the 1960s. See Lints, *Progressive and Conservative Religious Ideologies*, chapter 7, "The Death beyond the Death of God."

no longer mattered, at least on the surface of the mental landscape for ordinary persons in the developed West.[23]

RECONCILING DIFFERENCES WITHOUT A RELIGIOUS FRAMEWORK?

How does late secular modernity think about difference? In particular, how does it think about resolving conflicts arising from naturally occurring differences of opinion? The modern solution has been democracy, but in late secular modernity the defenders of liberal democracy have largely eschewed reference to any moral social consensus. The early modern defenders of liberal democracies either implicitly or explicitly appealed to a moral framework rooted in a generic Christian theism. In late secular modernity, appeal to that moral framework has largely been lost. In what follows, I ask whether a moral framework without a religious basis is a viable strategy—and what the lessons are for Christians in reconciling their own differences.

Most late modern liberal democracies work on the assumption that individuals have the right to pursue their own conception of the good without collective interference. In this era, politics simply prescribes a set of procedures for adjudicating conflicts between different conceptions of the good without reference to anything beyond the competing desires of individuals. Those procedures appear to grant to each citizen the apparent freedom to do as they please as long as they do not harm others.[24] This fundamental moral principle

---

23. The question of whether secularity is only a by-product of modernity in the West or is also descriptive of other global locations is taken up by Charles Taylor, "Can Secularism Travel?" and "A Secular Age outside Latin Christendom," in *Beyond the Secular West*, ed. Akeel Bilgrami (New York: Columbia University Press, 2016), 1–27 and 246–60, respectively.

24. Defining good for oneself in a consumer culture leads to the desire for more than what one needs, which in turn runs the consumer engine. The broader market works on the assumption that the market will morally police itself. The encouragement of virtue or the restraint of vice has largely been absent from the language of markets. The language of morality was reinterpreted into the language of markets. Americans adapted to this reality by reimagining religion and morality as commodities that could be placed into markets. See Laurence Moore, *Selling God: American Religion in the Marketplace of Culture* (New York: Oxford University Press, 1995), and Kathryn Lofton, *Consuming Religion* (Chicago: University of Chicago Press, 2017).

triumphs over all other moral principles in a liberal democracy, but where does the principle come from? The principle is either connected to a conception of the good or it is not. If it is connected to a moral conception of the good, it would appear to be a very odd morality with no prescription other than to do what is right in one's own eyes. If it is not connected to a moral conception of the good, it would be an arbitrary principle arising simply from a majoritarian assertion of will. Neither end of this dilemma does justice to our ordinary instincts of the good and the adjudicating of conflicts. Without a wider moral framework, justice will always appear arbitrary. This dilemma illustrates the intrinsic problem of defining human freedom (determining one's own good) as the highest of virtues, and democracy as the procedural framework for protecting that unconstrained freedom—absent any purpose or goals at which freedom aims. For a season, this problem was hidden from view under the cultural cover of a (disestablished) generic Christianity.

That borrowed moral capital went unnoticed by the early Enlightenment figures. For them, religion posed a problem to be solved rather than a framework for promoting virtuous behavior. Religious conflict was the primary source of cultural difficulties, the resolution of which was to grant freedom to individuals to determine the good for themselves. This strategy sought to dissolve the problem of religious conflict. In the mind of Enlightenment figures such as Thomas Hobbes and David Hume, modernity was born in part out of the fracturing of European religious communities, and the only viable alternative was to build political boundaries to keep the public space free from church interference. The "religious wars" of the sixteenth and seventeenth centuries provided ample grounds for securing public safety by restraining the role religion could play in modern societies.[25] Religious traditions left unfettered would always

---

25. The "religious wars" of the seventeenth century were not in fact distinctively religious. They were largely fought between imperial dynasties, the central differences not being religious but contrasting views of civil powers. The mythology that Catholics were killing Protestants and vice versa just does not fit the historical facts on most occasions. In contrast

be tempted to (violently) dominate others—so it seemed to many Enlightenment intellectuals.[26] In the competition between competing religious claims, empirical evidence that implied religious conflicts were irresolvable became irrelevant. The only viable political solution was to remove religion from the public square. The consensus of a majority, independent of religious beliefs, emerged as the unique Enlightenment solution to the problem of social fragmentation.

In modern times, this principle's most prominent spokesperson has been the Harvard political theorist John Rawls. He argued that liberal democracy should resist a religious framework in order to avoid repeating the religious wars of seventeenth-century Europe.[27] For Rawls, justice should be rooted in what all citizens have in common. In other words, justice should be interpreted as fairness. Conflicts in the political sphere could or should only be solved by appeal to "public reason"—namely, the marshaling of evidence accessible to all persons independent of their religious or metaphysical beliefs. Fairness is granting to others the free right to do as they see appropriate without harming others. In his early work, Rawls believed fairness was discovered by means of a thought experiment in which individuals behind a "veil of ignorance," without knowledge of their present circumstances, would decide how the laws of the land should be written. Behind this veil of ignorance, they would not know how the laws would favor or disfavor them. Therefore, they could not opt for a set of laws out of self-interest. In this case, Rawls supposed everyone would choose fairness as the fundamental political principle. It was a secularized form of the golden rule—treat others

---

to the Enlightenment myth, there was no religiously neutral state that stepped in to resolve religious differences in this period. See William Cavanaugh, *The Myth of Religious Violence* (New York: Oxford University Press, 2009). For a broader and more nuanced consideration of the role of religion in the early modern European wars, see *The European Wars of Religion: An Interdisciplinary Reassessment of Sources, Interpretations, and Myths*, ed. Wolfgang Palaver, Harriet Rudolph, and Dietmar Regensburger (London: Routledge, 2016).

26. This is classically formulated by Immanuel Kant in his *Religion within the Limits of Reason Alone*, trans. Theodore M. Greene and Hoyt H. Hudson (San Francisco: HarperOne, 2008 [original 1793]).

27. John Rawls, *A Theory of Justice* (Cambridge, MA: Harvard University Press, 1971).

as you want to be treated. The conclusion of the thought experiment went a step further: that you can do as you want as long as you do not harm others.

Rawls supposed that there was no need for a wider moral tradition to underwrite this fairness principle. In his later work, he downplayed the significance of the veil of ignorance, but still appealed to neutral, public reason as the only way to ground the legitimacy of liberal democracy. It was Rawls's conviction that citizens in their public capacity must engage one another only in terms of reasons whose status *as* reasons are shared among them. Since there are secular people in most modern democracies, as well as people with diverse religious views, religious people should not argue for political policies based on religious reasons. They should only argue on the basis of shared beliefs with secular people—what Rawls referred to as the overlapping consensus.[28] As a consequence, only secular reasons are appropriate in the political sphere. Religion is out of bounds.

Refusing to allow religious beliefs in the public square is quite illiberal. It denies people the right to bring their deepest convictions into the public square, save for those whose deepest convictions are secular. Putting religious convictions on the sidelines in the hope of avoiding religious conflict simply sets up other ideological conflicts arising from diverse secular claims to justice. Contrary to Rawls's claims, marginalizing religious conviction has not brought irresolvable conflict to an end. The twentieth century was witness to secular conflicts resulting in the bloodiest wars of the last two millennia. There can be little doubt that the secular turn has done little to diminish human conflict.

---

28. Rawls appears to significantly alter this "secular-reason" requirement in a later essay of his, "The Idea of Public Reason Revisited," *University of Chicago Law Review* 64, no. 3 (1997): 765–807. In his later work, he allows for a diversity of comprehensive claims in the public square and seems to suggest that it is the "overlapping consensus" between all the claims that will finally preserve the normative status of justice in a democracy. However, the overlapping consensus still reduces to a secular-public-reason requirement, since secular people in the public square will not have any overlapping consensus of a religious sort with any other viewpoint in the public square.

Rawls believed most people most of the time will come to accept liberal democracy because of what most people have in common—namely, a commitment to the fundamental fairness of the system ideally constructed. But in the aftermath of 9/11 and the attempt to plant the seeds of democracy across much of the Middle East, this intuition seems naive. Democracy requires a moral tradition rooted in a transcendent source of respect for others, a moral framework distinctive to Christianity. These words, penned by Nicholas Wolterstorff, are closer to the reality of the twenty-first century: "What's becoming clear to all of us as we look around the globe, is that that [democratic] ethos is much less transplantable than once it was thought to be. In fact, one begins to wonder whether it can only be successfully transplanted into soil rather like that in which it first grew: the soil of a fractured Christendom."[29]

Rawls worked under the assumption that modern democratic societies were becoming increasingly secular and that it was appropriate to devise a theory of justice on secular grounds. The older (pre-1990s) secularization thesis, so prominent among academics in the West, supposed that modern industrial cultures would eventually see the withering and fading away of religious beliefs and religious institutions. That older thesis has by and large now died.[30] In spite of predictions that late modernity would see the end of organized religion, the opposite has happened. The last decades of the twentieth century and first decades of the twenty-first century have seen a remarkable resurgence of religion globally. Religion in late modernity is actually

---

29. Nicholas Wolterstorff, "From Liberal to Plural," in *Christian Philosophy at the Close of the Twentieth Century: Assessment and Perspective*, ed. Sander Griffioen and Bert Balk (Kampen: Kok, 1995), 209.

30. Conceptual critiques of the secularization thesis include David Martin, *On Secularization: Toward a Revised General Theory* (London: Ashgate, 2005); Peter Berger, *The Desecularization of the World* (Grand Rapids: Eerdmans, 1999); Rodney Stark, *The Triumph of Faith: Why the World Is More Religious Than Ever* (Wilmington, DE: ISI Books, 2015). An important proviso is needed at this point. Though the demise of religion has not happened, the increasing tentacles of secularization continue to increase, running side by side with the resurgence of global religious movements. For a nuanced explication and implicit criticism of the secular age, see Taylor, *A Secular Age*.

on the rise, rather than in decline.[31] Late modernity has brought not a universal secularity devoid of religion, but a deepening experience of religious, cultural, and economic diversity.[32] How then shall we deal with so much diversity in a democracy if a secular worldview is actually not the tie that binds us all together?

Jeffrey Stout, another secular political theorist, has expressed significant doubts about the "naked public square" represented by Rawls and those theorists who believe there is no appropriate place for religious or moral conviction in dealing with our differences.[33] Stout believes irresolvable religious differences were the original impetus toward secularizing the public square, which simply implied the need for neutral procedures to settle our differences. The result has been a public square where arguments are increasingly secured by secular reasons rather than religious reasons, only because religious reasons are no longer shared by all.

In contrast to Rawls, Stout does allow for religious arguments in the public square but supposes they will be mostly irrelevant to the majority of citizens who have no religious convictions. According to Stout, all citizens in a democracy ought to be free to express whatever premises actually serve as a reason for their claims about justice. The ability to persuade others of one's views will determine whether their arguments are sufficient. No determination should or could be made in advance as to what will be persuasive. The constant and persistent conversation in a democracy is the key to its viability—and therefore, there can only be pragmatic criteria of

31. Religious demographers have charted the incredible increase of religious believers around the globe in the twentieth century. Their results reached the public conscience through the work of, among others, Philip Jenkins, *The Next Christendom*, 3rd ed. (New York: Oxford University Press, 2011 [original 2002]). The best demographic data charting the resurgence of global Christianity is to be found in Todd Johnson and Gino Zurlo, *The World Christian Encyclopedia*, 3rd ed. (New York: Oxford University Press, 2019).

32. Steven Pinker, *Enlightenment Now: The Case for Reason, Science, Humanism and Progress* (New York: Viking, 2018), defends the primacy of secular science as the cause of progress in the modern world while affirming that religion, though not dying, has nonetheless a very peripheral role to play in the modern world.

33. See Jeffrey Stout, *Democracy and Tradition*.

persuasion in the public domain of a democracy. For Stout, "ethical norms are creatures of discursive social practice."[34] The norms that govern the public square are simply the norms to which we consent as the governed.

There are many problems here. Moral judgments are and must be conceptually separate from social consensus. The persuasiveness of an argument may be grounded by appeal to moral or immoral motives. The moral nature of a claim is intuitively different from its persuasiveness. Social consensus is not the same as moral norms.[35] Ad campaigns for new cars often appeal to the baser motives of consumers, such as the lust for power or the sexual appeal of a new car, or the lure of belonging to the class of haves rather than have-nots. Whether or not persuasion is successful is irrelevant to the question of whether it is morally appropriate, and so with social consensus. A confederation of slaveholding states does not imbue the practice with moral commendation merely because of the consensus of a wide swath of its states. Most of us have the gut instinct that successful persuasion in a technologically advanced consumer culture can be as dangerous as the dictates of a self-centered monarch of early modern Europe—though we all (wrongly) suppose that only others (not us) are susceptible to illegitimate forms of persuasion. Pragmatic procedures in a democracy alone will not satisfy the human longing for a moral framework to make sense of life. Moral norms reside outside of human experience, rooted in a transcendent source. It is on this basis that human actions are accountable to a standard not simply relative to social consensus or private desires.

Theologian Stanley Hauerwas is one of the sharpest critics of the Rawlsian defense of a morally neutral democracy.[36] He has objected

---

34. Stout, *Democracy and Tradition*, 246.

35. Nicholas Wolterstorff comments at this point, "The rabbit of moral obligation cannot be pulled out from the hat of social practice." Wolterstorff, "Jeffrey Stout on Democracy and Its Contemporary Christian Critics," *Journal of Religious Ethics* 33, no. 4 (Dec 2005): 641.

36. See especially Stanley Hauerwas, *After Christendom: How the Church Is to Behave if Freedom, Justice, and a Christian Nation Are Bad Ideas* (Nashville: Abingdon, 1991).

strenuously to stripping political discourse of any notion of the "common good," as well as the corresponding loss of moral concepts of sin or vice. Religious diversity has been used as an excuse to vacate the public square of substantive notions of the good, in favor of privileging the rights of any individual or group to define the good for themselves. The result has been the hollowing out of political speech, making it a nuanced form of sophistry devoid of moral convictions. According to Hauerwas, this solution is far worse than the problem.

The critical question for Hauerwas is whether modern liberal democracies produce the kind of citizens for which we yearn. His answer is not simply no, but rather that we have produced the opposite—citizens whose primary concern is their own self-interest, who view any restraint on their freedom as intrinsically abhorrent. Modern secular democracies lack an organizing moral tradition that aims at producing virtuous citizens and settle instead for the chaos and polarization of each citizen defining virtue in his or her own self-interested way. But in a polity that privileges the diversity of opinion, what alternative is there? To Hauerwas, the answer is to lean more (not less) into those elements of a moral tradition that keeps its eyes on the common good by continually asking, What is the purpose of humans? As one might ask what makes a watch a good watch, so one should ask what makes a person a good person. It is the purpose for which things are made that determines the criteria by which they should be judged. A watch is a good watch if it tells time correctly. A person is a good person if he treats others with respect and generosity, if she acts justly and delights in beauty. These are the ends for which humans have been created. Obedience to authoritarian rule (that is, the whims of a monarchy) is not the purpose for which humans have been created. Freedom from arbitrary rule is part of what it means to be human, but freedom is not its own end. Human freedom is not morally boundless. It is grounded in the moral obligations to treat others with respect, to act justly, and to delight in the beautiful. Each of these in turn constrains human desire from simply doing whatever one wants. This is the fundamental intention (though often not practiced) of an ecclesial community defined by a thick moral framework. According to Hauerwas, the church ought to stand as an alternative community without regard for current political structures. There is no political structure the church may embrace.[37] For Hauerwas, it is to Christianity and not to politics that we should look to produce the kind of humans for which we yearn.

Unlike Hauerwas, Nicholas Wolterstorff has argued that a liberal democracy is the only realistic political option at present, and Christians should not abandon the democratic process in spite of the present moral chaos. In contrast to the secular optimism of Rawls and Stout, as well as the pessimism toward liberal democracies expressed by Hauerwas, Wolterstorff believes we must hold out for a liberal democracy possessing three core elements:

1. Those who govern should be accountable to those who are governed.

2. Every person who belongs to the governed ought to have an equal voice.

3. Everyone has an obligation not to violate others because everyone has worth.[38]

However, this third principle is at odds with a purely secular account of democracy. On these terms, a sustainable democracy cannot centrally be about the sheer expression of the human will. If there are natural rights, then there are also natural obligations that apply to human relationships arising from a claim of universal human dignity.[39] As a universal claim, human rights require a grounding outside of each individual and which provides a moral framework

---

37. Hauerwas calls these communities of character. See Stanley Hauerwas, *A Community of Character: Toward the Construction of a Christian Social Ethic* (Notre Dame: University of Notre Dame Press, 1991).

38. See Nicholas Wolterstorff, "Jeffrey Stout," 646.

39. For a defense of this claim, see Nicholas Wolterstorff, *Justice: Rights and Wrongs* (Princeton: Princeton University Press, 2008), and Oliver O'Donovan, *Desire of the Nations: Rediscovering the Roots of Political Theology* (Cambridge: Cambridge University Press, 1999).

of checks and balances necessary to limit individual self-interest.[40] The strength of democracy lies in the structures by which individual differences bump into each other and hinder purely selfish actions. Democracy's danger lies in the freedom of individuals not to negotiate those differences and thereby to dominate or separate from others. No polity can provide a complete hedge around that danger, but a polity that is morally serious about human dysfunction may more adequately treat human diversity constructively rather than merely defensively.[41]

As globalization and large-scale migration patterns continue, an increasing diversity will be the common experience in developed and developing democracies. The messy and at times chaotic politics of the United States and Europe will be the norm toward which other countries are headed. In this context, stereotyping others will continue to sustain group identities over against other groups, and thereby to differentiate insiders and outsiders, distinguishing "us" from "them" in damaging ways.[42] These patterns may run deep in the human psyche and are uniquely unleashed in democratically oriented cultures, but they are deeply unsatisfying options in the long run because they do not reflect the reality of the created order; they

---

40. From a very different vantage point than Wolterstorff, Martha Nussbaum has also argued that liberal democracies require a moral grounding. "Confrontation with the different in no way entails that there are no cross-cultural moral standards and that the only norms are those set by each local tradition. In other words, moral principles undergirding a democratic embrace of diversity cannot be equated with pragmatic local practices. There must be cross-cultural moral principles. The question remains—from whence do these principles come?" See Nussbaum, *Cultivating Humanity: A Classical Defense of Reform in Liberal Education* (Cambridge, MA: Harvard University Press, 1997), 30.

41. Wolterstorff writes, "Yet we must live together. It is to politics and not to epistemology that we shall have to look for an answer as to how to do that. 'Liberal' politics has fallen on bad days recently. But to its animating vision of a society in which persons of diverse traditions live together in justice and friendship, conversing with each other and slowly altering their traditions in response to the conversation—to that, there is no viable alternative." Nicholas Wolterstorff, *John Locke*, 246.

42. See Ben Sasse, *Them: Why We Hate Each Other and How We Can Heal* (New York: Griffin, 2019). Reaching similar conclusions about the "tribal" nature of human tendencies, but applied to the church, see Christena Cleveland, *Disunity in Christ* (Downers Grove, IL: InterVarsity Press, 2013).

work only by treating others as if "we" are better than "them." As Christians, we should know better (but often do not). In a world where God has created everyone with a sacred dignity, there are no grounds for claiming the superiority of some over others. Our diversity arises not because some are higher up the evolutionary scale, but because God has created an enormous diversity of persons, each of whom is always worthy of dignity and respect—and not only when they are "like us." Diversity and equality are not mutually exclusive.

WHOSE JUSTICE, WHICH NARRATIVE?

The American constitutional documents lay out procedures to protect a common commitment to civility and justice, but the procedures are not themselves the substance of the common moral tradition. Democracy in this sense is not opposed to moral traditions, but the question remains: Whose justice? And in the language I have used, Which narrative?[43]

There is no such notion as a universal or common "American" identity, let alone one that will dissolve the internal tensions connected to the long history of ethnic and racial stereotyping. "America" is simply a polity of procedural frameworks that permit and encourage these matters to be discussed in the public square. Procedure alone, however, will never deal with the entrenched nature of the problem, even if it provides a platform that enables a discussion of the entrenched nature of the problem.[44] This is as true in the church as it is in the wider culture.[45]

---

43. Alasdair MacIntyre raises these questions in the contemporary context. He has argued that it is not possible to have a civic morality without a moral tradition behind it. There is no such thing as "justice" without a moral framework. It is imperative, therefore, to recognize both the need for a moral framework and the need for a moral framework adequate to any satisfactory notion of justice. See MacIntyre, *Whose Justice? Which Rationality?* (Notre Dame: University of Notre Dame Press, 1988). As a result, he remains pessimistic about the American project as a secular liberal democracy that appears to provide virtually no moral resources to sustain robust notions of justice and virtue.

44. The analogy with marriage is appropriate here. Marriage therapy that emphasizes communication is surely on the right track, but communication alone will not address underlying pathologies. Yet without transparent communication, the underlying pathologies have no hope of being dealt with.

45. Books of church order are important, but by themselves they are futile in restraining conflict. A common commitment to a shared set of moral norms is requisite to sustaining a

The internal tensions between the Constitution's commitment
to the "inalienable rights" of all, and the tragic exclusion of whole
people groups, has meant America is vulnerable to the sharpest of
criticisms and also liable to be self-conscious of the need for criticism. Today, the response of many traditional Christians takes two
dominant forms. One is to support political leaders (even morally
dubious ones) who reinvigorate the flames of Christendom by reim-
posing an older religiosity. The second option has been a form of
cultural retreat and isolation from the public square.[46] Neither option
will be effective in dealing with the democratically infused diversity
of our time, nor does either option capture the Christian calling to
be faithfully present in our peculiar cultural context. The nostalgia
for a long-lost "America" instills a longing for an impossible utopia.
Abandoning civic responsibility in the time and place where God
has put us gives up the hope of God's future kingdom being brought
to bear on the present.

Democracy highlights the significance of diversity and encourages us to see more fully the splendor of God's diverse creation.
Democracy has also illuminated human brokenness and our long
history of stereotyping and exclusion. It has provided a minimal set
of procedures for dealing with our important differences, though it
is often more frustrating than fruitful. Neutral procedures by themselves will not right the wrongs of exclusionary practices. Righting
wrongs is a necessary moral project and thereby requires a moral
framework. Democracy has taken us on a journey, but when we have
reached a fork in the road its only counsel has been, "You are free
to choose whichever fork you prefer." When the fork in the road is
the choice between inclusion or exclusion, absolute freedom is not
an adequate grounding for making a responsible choice. Responsible

---

genuine unity-in-diversity within the church as it is in the wider culture.

46. See Elshtain, *Augustine*. These two mistaken options reflect the fallacies Augustine
points to in trying to bring the city of God into reality before its time, or in supposing that the
city of God and the city of man are entirely at odds with each other.

choices require morally responsible agents, and morally responsible agents require a moral framework to which they are accountable.

Where can we find the moral principles to deal with the underlying pathologies of discrimination and exclusion? It is not enough to say that we all know these actions are wrong. There must be a moral framework that explains why discrimination across certain kinds of differences is wrong. Defining ourselves outside of a moral tradition inevitably leads to arbitrary claims of victimhood or entitlement. Stripped of a moral tradition, biological or geographic or group identities will not satisfy the deep longings of the human heart for enduring significance and security.

THE GOSPEL'S INCLUSION NARRATIVE

Modern democracies require both a concern for immanent means (free exchange of diverse views) and transcendent ends (principles guarding the sacredness of life), but we must distinguish them from each other. Using the language of Augustine, when cultures seek to establish the city of God on earth, they inevitably confuse the immanent with the transcendent goals of life and thus develop their own idolatries. The result is always a dystopia rather than a utopia. On the other hand, when people suppose there is nothing over and above the city of man—that is, nothing beyond the immanent—there is little to stop tyrannical political authority.

The sheer amount of social diversity requires us to think afresh about human equality and dignity in communities. The human heart is tempted to suppose our dignity is most stable when it is part of a stable social tribe. However, the tendency of every social tribe to find ways to exclude those outside the tribe is opposed to the "universal equality" proposition rooted in the Christian claim that God has created everyone with significance and security.

Christians have many lessons to learn from the inclusion and exclusion narratives, though the gospel itself is a miraculous narrative of those who, having excluded themselves by virtue of their sin, are changed into those who have been included by God's grace. The gospel's inclusion narrative seems almost too good to be true. There can be little doubt that giving voice to this peculiar inclusion narrative is desperately needed to deal with the conflict of differences in our communities of late modern liberal democracy.

The inclusion narrative of the gospel is like marriage. This union is intended to bring two very different individuals into an enduring relationship precisely because their differences make each more fully human. As I will argue in a later chapter, marriage is a pervasive metaphor in Scripture by which God illustrates the intended relationship of unity and diversity. Wives and husbands are stronger by virtue of bumping into their differences. However, marriage also presents continuous opportunities to stereotype across gender and roles in ways that undermine the other's significance and security.

This means Christians ought to engage and not merely tolerate life in a democracy. Their voice in a liberal democracy is found in the radically counterintuitive claim that they are to show hospitality to those with whom they have deep disagreements inside the church as well as outside the church.[47] The moral framework Christians bring to bear extends not simply to the boundaries of the church but even to their neighbors outside the church. The dignity of persons that undergirds the responsibility to treat our neighbors with respect is not limited only to our Christian neighbors. It extends to all our neighbors, and it does so by virtue of the fact that God has created everyone with a sacred dignity. It ought to be a distinctive contribution of Christians in late modernity to graciously point at the universal character of human dignity and the attendant responsibility to treat others with respect. They should engage disagreements neither by seeking to dominate nor by being merely tolerant.[48]

---

47. Martin Marty, *When Faiths Collide* (Oxford: Blackwell, 2005), extends this suggestion at great length as a prophetic call to Christian churches to engage global diversity on distinctively Christian terms.

48. Tolerance effectively says, "Live and let live." It does not incentivize constructive relationships across significant differences. It shows little regard for the common good of both parties. And it still requires moral boundaries to depict intolerable actions, such as theft, rape, or embezzlement.

Christians should therefore invite the outsider into the common wisdom of this part of their tradition. The contemporary democratic ethos may look askance at evangelism and proselytizing in the public square because of past abuses. Changing the ethos with respect to evangelism may well require us to think of evangelism less in terms of defeating an enemy and more in terms of showing hospitality to the stranger—that is, showing respect in the face of our important differences. Another distinctive Christian contribution to late modern democracies should be the introduction of mercy and compassion as unifying virtues, reflective of the gospel we profess.

One of the great challenges facing Christians at this cultural moment is recognizing the gospel's inclusion narrative as distinct from democracy's inclusion narrative, but with many overlapping concerns. Christianity should play a critical role in the moral functioning of a liberal democracy, but we must be careful not to conflate Christianity and democracy. For a people to commit themselves to fully looking after the welfare of all—including the marginalized, the weak, and the powerless—we need grounds for believing in the universal dignity and sacredness of humankind.[49] Christians in our late secular modernity must recognize that the gospel provides the resources necessary for this task.

---

49. See Glenn Tinder, "Can We Be Good without God?," *The Atlantic*, December 1989, https://www.theatlantic.com/magazine/archive/1989/12/can-we-be-good-without-god/306721/.

The national airline of Indonesia calls itself by the name of Garuda, the mythological bird of the Ramayana. The name, which is emblazoned on its airplanes, is appropriate. The traveler flying over the Indonesian archipelago with its myriad islands may well feel himself to be borne on the wings of the original Garuda. Which makes him too a quasi-mythological being, a god perhaps, or at least a demigod, soaring through the sky with unimaginable speed and served by machines of unimaginable power. Down below are the mere mortals, in their small villages and fields. This jet traveler in the Third World is a pretty good metaphor of modernity.

—PETER BERGER, THE HERETICAL IMPERATIVE

4

THE PLURALIST IMPULSE
AND PLURAL IDENTITIES

TAKING RADICAL DIVERSITY FOR GRANTED

Peter Berger begins his most significant work on the relationship of modernity to religious faith, *The Heretical Imperative*, by drawing attention to the stark differences between the past and the present, which we simply take for granted. Berger argues that it is a fallacy to suppose the most significant change of the modern age has been the power of new technologies. The more profound revolution of the technological age has been the reordering of the inner consciousness of individuals. Undoubtedly, much more "work" can be accomplished with far less effort than was thought possible fifty or a hundred years ago—let alone a millennium ago.[1] The power of new tools has also brought a more widely distributed affluence than could have even been imagined in earlier eras.[2] The rulers of the

---

1. The downside of the revolution in productivity has been the loss of jobs replaced through automation. The scale of job loss is a matter of considerable controversy, but there can be little doubt that many job types (e.g., telephone switchboard operators, secretarial pools of typists) have disappeared under the weight of technological innovation. The projected job losses in the next generation seem far wider and at a much more threatening scale owing to advances in artificial intelligence.

2. A significant downside of widely distributed affluence has been the rise of social inequality. The numbers most often used to measure social inequality relate to income inequality. However, a question not often addressed in public discourse is whether raw income is an adequate measure of inequality or whether progressive taxation and social welfare entitlements should also be included in the analysis. See Steven Pinker, *Enlightenment Now*, for a detailed

ancient world or the kings and queens of the medieval era could not have dreamed of living in such luxury as is now taken for granted throughout much of the globe. However, more than the material affluence of our lifestyles, it is the taken-for-granted intuitions about the social world we inhabit that are more radically different from the Pharaohs and Caesars.

Producers (and users) of technology are mentally shaped by that technology while too often assuming the power of it is purely external to them. It is a naive intuition to suppose the world has changed while the categories of human thought remain unchanged. The world may be filled with technological innovations undreamed of fifty years ago, but the greater change has occurred in how persons relate to their world, what they think about themselves, and how they relate to the social contexts of their lives. They have contributed to a radically different social imaginary.

Changes of consciousness are not new to late modernity. It is the manner in which they have changed that is radically new. It has always been the case that the tools of a particular epoch have influenced the social contexts of human experience and influenced how meaning is attached to those experiences. The printing press profoundly reshaped European society (and European Christianity) in the fifteenth and sixteenth centuries.[3] The transportation revolutions associated with the Industrial Revolution transformed people's sense of time and space in the nineteenth century. Broadcast television brought new values through the vehicle of mass culture in the middle decades of the twentieth century.

When social forces change, assumptions about life are reshaped and human relationships are altered. The technology revolution of

analysis of the remarkable increase in global affluence in the latter part of the twentieth century, along with a chastened analysis of the issue of inequality.

3. See Elizabeth Eisenstein, *The Printing Revolution in Early Modern Europe* (Cambridge: Cambridge University Press, 2012). This is an abridged version of her earlier, massive, two-volume study, *The Printing Press as an Agent of Change* (Cambridge: Cambridge University Press, 1980). In the later work, Eisenstein draws comparisons between the printing revolution of the fifteenth century and the information revolution of the twentieth century.

the last two generations does not change this dynamic, but it accelerates it considerably. The trajectory is from a social imaginary in which one's direction is relatively fixed to a social imaginary in which one's direction can change at every moment of life. The vast array of current options made possible now through technology gives the illusion that an individual can travel in multiple different social directions. The power of our tools creates many more choices than could have been conceived in earlier times. The fates of history no longer appear to bind us.

If late modern democracy privileges certain kinds of diversity, it is because technological changes have introduced a strikingly new mental landscape that embraces cultural diversity at a much more tacit or intuitive level.

RELIGION AND THE PLURALIST IMPULSE

On the Boeing 767 operated by Garuda Airlines mentioned in the epigraph to this chapter, the travelers have a multitude of choices. They can change their ticket and fly to Hong Kong rather than Bangkok. They can use a credit card, that little plastic pearl of great price, as currency in any country they choose. Their cell phone connects them to the New York Stock Exchange or the Tokyo Stock Exchange or the London Stock Exchange. These choices, however, represent only a small slice of a larger array of choices, all part of the taken-for-granted fabric of life in late modernity. There are choices of occupation, choices of place of residence, choices of marriage, choices of the number of children, choices of vacation destination. The endless list of external options often veils the inner choices of consciousness. These are lifestyle choices, the choices of religious preference and choices of moral norms. The abortion debate is cast in the same terms as the contemporary controversy over sexual preferences. "Choice" has become a dominant mental category in modern life.

More choices require more reflection. When we reflect, we become more conscious of ourselves, turning attention from the objectively given outside world to our own subjectivity. Inevitably, two things happen simultaneously: the outside world becomes more questionable, while our own inner world becomes more complex. Any solution that appears as the "only" one is viewed with suspicion. The hegemony of truth itself comes under scrutiny. Our own personal narrative becomes the lens through which we see the virtually infinite number of data points in our experience. In a world of overabundant, technologically driven data in which no narrative could possibly account for all of it, our own "take" on the data is both privileged and fragile.[4]

The result is a much deeper pluralization—what we may call the *pluralist impulse* in modern life. The diverse cultures of the globe are no longer simply distant realities. Our awareness is now raised to unprecedented levels because of the tools of technology, mass communication, and transportation. Each day, the entire globe is brought into our lives via the internet. Faraway lands like Afghanistan and Iran are now no longer distant. American neighborhoods also manifest this global character—Indonesian Muslims and Sri Lankan Hindus are as likely to be neighbors as are Scotch Presbyterians and Irish Catholics.[5] Rabbi Jonathan Sacks writes,

> Life is encountering difference and diversity. Think about it. Walk down any city street in any western society and you will encounter in one hour more religious, cultural and

4. David Tracy has written of the relationship between the ambiguity of our primordial experiences of the world around us and the diverse interpretations of that reality by different individuals. The result of this relationship is turning everything from "fact" into "interpretation." See Tracy, *Plurality and Ambiguity* (New York: Crossroad, 1991).

5. Sanford Cloud, "Dealing with the Unfinished Business of America: Fighting Bias, Bigotry, and Racism in the Twenty-first Century," in *Democracy and Religion: Free Exercise and Diverse Visions*, ed. David Odell Scott (Kent, OH: Kent State University Press, 2004), 336–48, argues that the national survey data (TAP II) strongly suggests that the more contact a person has with different groups, the more likely they are to feel close to people who are different from them. By contrast Robert Putnam has argued that the short-term impact of increased contact with cultural diversity is a retreat into enclaves of cultural homogeneity. He nonetheless holds out hope that the long-term consequence of contact with cultural diversity would be greater understanding and tolerance. See Putnam, "E Pluribus Unum," 137–74.

ethnic diversity than an 18th century anthropologist would have encountered in an entire lifetime. This is an amazing thing. Every school I go into in London has between 40 and 60 ethnic groups within its student body. It is stunning. Never before have we been so close to so much difference.[6]

It is obvious that the vast diversity of cultures across the globe are interconnected as never before. What is not so obvious is that this "global village" is presented as a reality that does not require philosophical justification or reflection. When the experience of a global village becomes intuitive, the diverse religions of the world tend to be seen as simply one more dimension of a culture's subjective interpretation of the world.[7] In the hands of modern secular critics, religion is not seen as referencing something "out there" but rather reflects the inner experience of individuals, by means of which meaning is projected onto what's "out there" in culturally relevant ways.[8]

Religion, then, inevitably becomes "thin" in the context of the pluralist impulse. As modernity extended its pluralizing influence, the strategy of restraining any single religion from dominance was deepened by secularizing religious traditions. Christmas is less about Jesus than a consumer holiday of gift giving. Sunday is different from

---

6. Jonathan Sacks, "On the Dignity of Difference," The Rabbi Sacks Legacy Trust, February 10, 2017, http://rabbisacks.org/rabbi-sacks-national-prayer-breakfast/.

7. As I noted in chapter 1, the conceptual category of "religion" is a term of relatively recent vintage. Within the last century, scholars needed a concept to understand what was common among the diverse faiths of the world and what was distinctive to each of the traditions. The consequent secular study of religion supposes that the ordinary vantage point for reflection on the divine is outside of any particular faith community. In this regard, "religion" refers to the phenomenon of giving meaning to the world outside of ourselves by reference to something transcendent to the world. Since meaning is increasingly thought to be socially constructed, religion is often studied as if it is one among many ways of making meaning in the world.

8. The sheer diversity of religious accounts of the world may appear as a primary intellectual defeater for all religions. This is the implicit argument of William Hutchison, Religious Pluralism in America: The Contentious History of a Founding Ideal (New Haven: Yale University Press, 2004). It is the explicit argument of Peter Berger, The Heretical Imperative.

the other days of the week, not by virtue of attendance at a worship service, but rather by virtue of the NFL owning it—"The same day the church used to own," as it was memorably put in the 2015 movie *Concussion*. In a myriad of ways, religious conviction diminished as the twentieth century played out, becoming yet another sign of an acceptable, if also bland, cultural diversity.[9] Maintaining religious and social diversity in the latter half of the twentieth century became the outward expression of the pluralist impulse, and its guarantor. It allowed for multiple opinions without granting favored status to any of them.

Late secular modernity brought a cultural ethos wherein one chooses one's religious tradition rather than simply inheriting it.[10] As the twentieth century wore on, Americans shopped for a church as they might shop for groceries. When a religious tradition or a church is chosen for convenience, it ceases to have much traction in a person's life: the religious tradition can be abandoned as quickly as it was initially chosen. A massive Pew Landscape Survey in 2007 demonstrated that though church attendance has remained relatively stable for a generation, there was an exponential increase in the number of people who "crossed over" from one religious tradition to another during the previous fifty years.[11] There has also been a sharp increase in the frequency of people training their children in multiple religious traditions. Belonging to a religious tradition has

---

9. When President Dwight Eisenhower declared in 1954, "Our Government makes no sense unless it is founded on a deeply held religious faith, and I don't care what it is," many viewed it as an affirmation of religion so ambiguous and pluralized that it was no longer recognizable as genuine religion. Eisenhower's recognition of the civil religion of the political establishment at midcentury seemed hopelessly enamored of a religion so subjective as to undermine any concrete religious tradition speaking with conviction into the public square.

10. See Robert Putnam and David Campbell, *American Grace: How Religion Divides and Unites Us* (New York: Simon & Schuster, 2010), chapter 5. The notable exception, according to Putnam and Campbell, is African Americans. Anglos are far more prone to "lapse" or drift away from the faith of their parents. African Americans are twice as likely to remain in the tradition of their parents, where religion is more deeply tied to race.

11. Pew Research Center, "Religious Landscape Survey," 2007, https://www.pewforum.org/religious-landscape-study/.

become like wearing a particular set of clothes one day that could easily be switched the next day.

Over the period from 1960 to 1990, religious endogamy (the practice of marrying only within one's religious tradition) largely faded in America, at least among Protestants, Catholics, and Jews.[12] Mixed marriages across diverse religious traditions became as common as marriages within well-defined religious traditions.[13] In the 1960s, it was essential to keep track of potential mates' religious affiliations. By the 1990s, religion was hardly more important to romance than left- or right-handedness, an attribute that seldom matters to social status or social fit. Religion became a category of personal preference rather than an important criterion in choosing a mate. Similarly, though most Americans know their own religious affiliation, for younger Americans that affiliation is less significant as a social marker. Religious conviction remains more important to people than ethnic identity, though most experience greater social divisions along ethnic rather than religious lines.[14] None of these changes are the result of an intentional effort to change religion into a subjective aspect of culture; it simply succumbed to the pluralist impulse that people follow in late modernity.[15]

12. See Putnam, "E Pluribus Unum."

13. The Pew Landscape Survey of 2007 found that nearly 40 percent of all marriages cross religious affiliations. In 2010, Putnam and Campbell in *American Grace* reported that 50 percent of Americans are married to somebody that came from a different religious tradition, and that 33 percent of all marriages retain that religious diversity. America remains an unusually religious country for an industrial nation, but its religious commitments are very flexible. Whatever else may be said, "brand loyalty" appears to be diminishing by the day. For a summary of the survey results, see *The Economist*, "Brand Disloyalty: America Is a Nation of Spiritual Shoppers," February 28, 2008, https://www.economist.com/united-states/2008/02/28/brand-disloyalty.

14. See Putnam, "E Pluribus Unum." Only time will tell whether the social stratification associated with the ethno-racial categories will also dissipate in a manner similar to the decrease in social stratification along religious lines.

15. One of the ironies of the increased religious mobility brought on by an increased social mobility is the lack of physical mobility. David Brooks, in "The Neighborhood Is the Unit of Change," *New York Times*, October 18, 2018, https://www.nytimes.com/2018/10/18/opinion/neighborhood-social-infrastructure-community.html, notes that the typical American adult lives eighteen miles from home, the typical college student enrolls in a college thirteen miles from

Evangelicals Are More
Pluralistic Than They Realize

Evangelicals are an interesting test case when it comes to the pluralization and privatization of religion in late secular modernity. The movement may be the most studied and least understood of the major modern religious movements in the West.[16] It has been well studied in the last forty years because of its size and apparent influence over American religious sensibilities. In the last decade especially, its political sensibilities have come to define its essence in the minds of the media. What has often been lost in the contemporary imagination is that the movement is and has always been deeply pluralistic.

Who speaks for evangelicals? This is a question without a clear answer precisely because of the nature of the movement. It is a democratized coalition of diverse religious traditions built around a fragile consensus on the authority of Scripture, the personal nature of salvation, the unique work of Jesus Christ, and the manifest importance of the Christian life.[17] There is no confessional document of the various evangelical church bodies that contains any political statements. There

---

home, and 63 percent of our Facebook friends live within a hundred miles of us. He writes in summary, "Americans move less these days, not more."

16. The secondary literature on the history and nature of evangelicalism is enormous. A brief listing of major works on evangelicalism would include George M. Marsden, *Fundamentalism and American Culture* (New York: Oxford University Press, 1980); Donald W. Dayton and Robert K. Johnston, eds., *The Variety of American Evangelicalism* (Downers Grove, IL: InterVarsity Press, 1991); Randall Balmer, *Encyclopedia of Evangelicalism* (Waco, TX: Baylor University Press, 2004); Robert Wuthnow, *The Restructuring of American Religion: Society and Faith Since World War II* (Princeton: Princeton University Press, 1988); James Davison Hunter, *American Evangelicalism: Conservative Religion and the Quandary of Modernity* (New Brunswick, NJ: Rutgers University Press, 1982); Christian Smith, *American Evangelicalism: Embattled and Thriving* (Chicago: University of Chicago Press, 1998); and Mark A. Noll, *The Scandal of the Evangelical Mind* (Grand Rapids: Eerdmans, 1995). A helpful guide to primary sources of the movement is Barry Hankins, ed., *Evangelicalism and Fundamentalism: A Documentary Reader* (New York: New York University Press, 2008).

17. These mirror in some respect David W. Bebbington's frequently repeated fourfold description of evangelicalism: biblicism (the Bible as final authority), crucicentrism (a focus on the atoning work of Christ), conversionism (salvation occurs through a personal faith in Christ), and activism (the gospel is actively expressed in a transformed life). See Bebbington, *Evangelicalism in Modern Britain: A History from the 1730s to the 1980s* (Grand Rapids: Baker, 1989).

are undoubtedly politically charged individuals within evangelicalism, but to read all the various subgroups of evangelicals through political lenses is to misread the vast majority of evangelicals, even with regard to their actions in the public sphere.[18]

Evangelicalism is often referred to as a conservative religious movement, and in part this is accurate. Evangelicals of every stripe have been about the business of preserving the original meaning of the gospel of Jesus Christ. However, conserving the message of the gospel has often meant throwing tradition to the wind, and evangelicals have often been disdainful of the establishmentarian impulses of religious traditions.[19] Attempts to be "relevant" and "contemporary" have been hallmarks of evangelicals over the last century. The all-too-popular perception that evangelicals are culturally significant because they provide a link to safer, more secure days in the American past does not fit the fact of evangelicals' wary relationship to the religious traditions of the past. It has been a movement fascinated with youth culture and has steadfastly sustained a self-professed outsider status with relation to the religious establishment.[20]

The story of religion in the 1960s and following, with few exceptions, has been told in such a way as to suggest evangelicals were but a peripheral part of the social revolutions beginning in the postwar period. If given a role at all, evangelicalism was assigned the function of providing a safe haven against the inroads of secularism and pluralism in the era.[21] Evangelicals, or so the standard historiogra-

---

18. The *Evangelical Manifesto* (2008) (http://osguinness.com/publicstatement/the-evangelical-manifesto/), signed by a wide array of evangelical religious leaders, is evidence of the push-back from many within the movement of being stereotyped as an essentially political movement.

19. See Richard Lints, *Progressive and Conservative Religious Ideologies: The Tumultuous Decade of the 1960s* (London: Routledge, 2010).

20. See Darryl Hart, "Same as It Ever Was: The Future of Protestantism in the Global North," *American Theological Inquiry* 1, no. 1 (January 15, 2008): 38–53.

21. I am indebted to Christopher Lasch, *The True and Only Heaven: Progress and Its Critics* (New York: Norton, 1991), and Nathan O. Hatch, *The Democratization of American Christianity* (New Haven: Yale University Press, 1989), for the underlying framework that follows. Neither applies their insights directly to the 1960s, though the analogies with their respective concerns are not difficult to make, as the following will make clear.

phy suggests, were culturally significant in large measure because they revolted against the progressive agenda during the revolutionary decade of the 1960s.[22] If God was dead, as the front cover of *Time* magazine declared in April 1966, at least his memory was kept alive in evangelical circles.[23]

Lost in this standard historiography was the pluralist impulse embedded in many of the evangelical revivals in American history, and especially in the 1960s.[24] In many ways, the 1960s mirrored the Second Great Awakening (1820–1850), wherein institutional churches (local and denominational) were viewed as obstacles to genuine faith— but not because traditional faith itself was the problem. Evangelical conviction may have been thoroughly supernatural in its overall temper, but it was more than happy to embrace the modern progressive cultural protest against monolithic institutions—seen nowhere more clearly than in the countercultural youth revivals in the 1960s. Embedded in these revivals was a radical democratization of piety and an affirmation of the tools and economies of technology. Young people who embraced Jesus in this time were in part rebelling against the establishment patterns of their parents' religion. In the hands of young people, the freedom to choose Jesus replaced both the freedom to "do your own thing" and the inheritance of the shallow faith of their parents. "Choosing Jesus" was a form of cultural protest. In this regard, conservative religion was most definitely "radical"—visible in the period's new music, the clothes of the Jesus People, and the way

22. The evangelical Peter Marshall's bestselling text of American history is a self-conscious attempt to persuade his readers that the best traditions of the American past were evangelical in origin. See Marshall, *The Light and the Glory: Did God Have a Plan for America?* (New York: Fleming Revell, 1978). A fellow evangelical, Tim LaHaye, wrote the following recommendation on the dust jacket for Marshall's book: "*The Light and the Glory* reveals our true national heritage and inspires us to stay on God's course as a nation."

23. As early as (and as late as) 1978, the dean of American church historians, Sydney Ahlstrom, wrote, "Evangelical growth in this period can be explained essentially by the role it played in countering secularization." Ahlstrom, "National Trauma and Changing Religious Values," *Daedalus* (1978): 22.

24. I tell this story at much greater length in *Progressive and Conservative Religious Ideologies*, chapter 6.

evangelism moved toward people on the margins. It was little noticed at the time (nor has it been since) that religion was being realigned by virtue of the fragmentation of traditional religious institutions and denominations. On both the Left and the Right, but especially on the Right, future commentators would take it for granted that religious energy lay outside the older religious traditions. For those on both sides of the religious aisle, the traditional divisions between Baptists and Presbyterians, Lutherans and Episcopalians, Wesleyans and Pentecostals no longer mattered. Marriages across these historic denominational divides became almost routine. Revivals occurred outside of denominations. Religious figures of significance spoke not from within a theological tradition but apparently across those traditions. The emerging evangelical seminaries of the period were interdenominational and wary of representing any particular theological tradition.[25] The older religious divisions would virtually melt away in the last half of the twentieth century.

The realignment of culture along all-consuming Left-Right political lines brought with it a new "diversity discourse," including a new religious diversity discourse. When the discourse focused on the rift between progressive and conservative evangelicals, it inevitably pointed toward polarization. When evangelicals focused on the positive benefits of diversity within evangelicalism itself (e.g., transdenominational global evangelistic efforts), it was because diversity was seen as a good in itself, rather than as a means to an end. Evangelicals learned to celebrate the transcultural and global character of Christianity in an age when cultural diversity was everywhere present.

The impact of the pluralist impulse has been felt in the local church as well. In 2001, Robert Putnam argued that loneliness was virtually an epidemic, regardless of the class or social location of one's

---

25. The list of seminaries that gained prominence in this period all fit this profile: Fuller Theological Seminary, Trinity Evangelical Divinity School, Gordon-Conwell Theological Seminary, Dallas Theological Seminary, and Regent College.

community.[26] Small community organizations such as the bridge club, garden club, bowling leagues, and the local church decreasingly functioned as social glue. These were voluntary organizations in an era when the vast array of choices available undermined enduring commitments to any organization. The dominant civic organization in America had been and continues to be the local church. Nearly half of all voluntary association memberships in America were and are religious in nature. But as with so many other local organizations, the local church lost much of its traction in people's lives. Too many, other readily available options competed for their time. People attending a local church remained "religious" in their self-identity, but much of their religiosity was lived outside the regular rhythms of a local church. They attended churches less frequently and believed the differences between local churches had more to do with personalities than theological convictions.[27] As a result, many held commitment to any single church lightly, switching whenever another church had more to offer.

THE CONCEPTUAL STORY BEHIND THE PLURALIST IMPULSE

If modern technology and the mediums of communication pluralize both institutional structures and religious life, these changes also require an ideological framework to justify their enduring hold on modern consciousness. There must be a "story" of the "way life really is." The "story" may not be the primary motivation behind our intuitions, but without it the intuitions do not take hold collectively. The story provides the intellectual grid that maps the terrain on which the culture lives out its intuitions. Every enduring social imaginary is undergirded by an intellectual revolution. The two are not related in precise causal fashion. Great ideas may well "lead" the way, but often they serve as justifications for the notion of social and experiential

---

26. Robert Putnam, *Bowling Alone: The Collapse and Revival of American Communities* (New York: Simon & Schuster, 2001).

27. The exception here is the immigrant churches in the West that sustained an "outsider" status and whose distinctive religious traditions continued to be important.

change. As ordinary life changes in significant ways, we look for a new conceptual story (ideology?) that explains the changes. The stories provide a plausibility to the emergence of trends that otherwise might have been stopped. We then interpret our age in light of the intellectual stories that surround us. Even if we know very little about these stories, they unwittingly exert an inordinate power on our intuitions about the world we live in. The stories become taken for granted. They define the new normal. So what is the intellectual story behind the pluralist impulse?

Richard Rorty, who died in 2007, is a peculiarly clear public intellectual whose defense of pragmatism and pragmatic interpretations of cultural pluralism reflects well the spirit of the age. He taught at Princeton, the University of Virginia, and Stanford. He was persuaded science would not solve the fundamental problems of humanity, and that there was no way to claim an objective grasp of the world in light of the presence of human bias. In his flagship work signaling the dawning of a new intellectual era (then called postmodernism), Rorty displays his philosophical indebtedness to four philosophers, all of whom wrote their most influential works at the beginning of the cultural revolutions of the 1960s—W. V. O. Quine, Wilfred Sellars, Thomas Kuhn, and Ludwig Wittgenstein.[28] These figures provided an intellectual story whereby public intellectuals at the end of the twentieth century (clearly seen in Rorty) could take for granted that a singular intellectual account of reality was not viable in an age of such deep diversity. They (and Rorty) resisted the mythology that modern science had finally provided us with a definitive and objective grasp of the world. The sheer diversity of human opinions that persisted beyond the advent of modern science was an indication that humans were built for a constant and curious dialogue with the world—a dialogue with no

---

28. Richard Rorty, *Philosophy and the Mirror of Nature* (Princeton: Princeton University Press, 1979), is the first grand anti-realist reading of the history of philosophy by an American scholar.

conceivable end. Knowledge could no longer be conceived as a simple representation of the external world, what Rorty refers to as the "mirror of nature." This reflects his embrace of a pluralist social imaginary committed to modernity's endless conversation among diverse opinions.

Rorty's narrative of the rise and demise of the scientific account of knowledge proved compelling, replacing the prior standard secular account. According to Rorty, intellectual developments in the 1950s and 1960s trumpeted the dawning of a new era. The intellectual project of the Enlightenment was being abandoned, along with its optimism in scientific rationality.

The heart of the Enlightenment tradition—the so-called positivist paradigm—was its claim that the supernatural God, that is, the God of traditional Western Augustinian Christian theology, had died.[29] The rejection of the fundamental authority of God then brought the rejection of other institutional forms of authority, such as the church and the monarchy. In their place rose a veneration of human reason, and with it the scientific method. In this early modern tradition, the claims of science were revered as the primary means for an objective grasp of the world and the hope to solve the world's problems.

Over the last half of the nineteenth century, science was severed in a variety of ways from the discipline of philosophy. It occupied a separate space in the university curriculum. It developed its own professional associations and journals. But increasingly, philosophy's self-identity was wrapped up with its defense of the hard sciences—a defense little noticed by scientists but used ever so trenchantly by philosophers against an older religious supernaturalism.

The methodological empiricism of David Hume (1711–1776) provided a framework built on methods of the natural sciences—observation and description. By the early twentieth century, philosophers

---

29. This is the claim made famous at the end of the nineteenth century by Friedrich Nietzsche in his *Thus Spoke Zarathustra: A Book for Everyone and No One*, trans. R. J. Hollingdale (New York: Penguin, 1961 [orig. 1883]).

realized they could not make empirical discoveries in the same manner as scientists, but they could describe the language and fundamental commitments of science and thereby perform a great service on behalf of scientific naturalism.

The service consisted largely of analyzing the language of science and the competing vocabularies of religion, art, and ethics. As the Victorian age was coming to an end in the early twentieth century, these philosophers were confident that the antiquated claims of religious idealists and supernaturalists could be set aside once and for all. A new day dawned for philosophers as the optimism of the progressive era of the early twentieth century was reflected in their confidence in naturalism. This optimism was captured most significantly in the movement of logical positivism.[30] In the 1920s and 1930s, this cluster of influential philosophers manifested an obvious hostility toward all metaphysical and religious claims outside the bounds of science. Claims about God, the "good," or the "beautiful" had to be abandoned as nothing more than descriptions about someone's inner feelings. They believed the real subject matter of philosophy was language—the language of the natural sciences, in particular. In this sense, philosophy became a second-order discipline servicing the first-order claims about reality as understood by science. It is science, they believed, that gives us the only trustworthy knowledge of reality. There is not, and cannot be, a philosophical brand of knowledge that competes with science. What then is the task of the philosopher if not to speak about reality like a scientist? What philosophers can do "is to act as a sort of intellectual policeman, seeing that nobody trespasses into metaphysics."[31]

---

30. See especially the positivist manifesto titled "The Scientific Conception of the World" in *Empiricism and Sociology*, ed. Marie Meurath and Robert S. Cohen (Boston: Reidel, 1973), 299–318. Two sympathetic histories of logical positivism are Friedrich Stadler, *The Vienna Circle: Studies in the Origins, Development, and Influence of Logical Empiricism*, trans. Camilla Nielsen et al. (Vienna: Springer, 2001); and Michael Friedman, *Reconsidering Logical Positivism* (Cambridge: Cambridge University Press, 1999).

31. A. J. Ayer, "The Vienna Circle," in *The Revolution in Philosophy*, ed. A. J. Ayer (New York: Oxford University Press, 1956), 79.

In the late 1950s and early 1960s, this understanding of human knowledge was dealt an intellectual death blow in the work of Quine, Sellars, and Kuhn, and in the later work of Wittgenstein. This was an ironic development, because the very zenith of the Enlightenment intellectual project (at least in its English-speaking phase) had been reached in the 1930s with the work of logical positivists under the influence of Wittgenstein's early writings. In this philosophical revolution, the abandonment of philosophy's role as "intellectual policeman" was key. This prepared for the demise of confidence in a single, objective way of knowing. The beginning onslaught against this confidence came from Quine, the longtime chair of the philosophy department at Harvard. Writing in the 1950s, Quine argued that all claims to truth are relative to a conceptual scheme that is itself relative in time with respect to a society's interests. Our best beliefs are still posits, simply representing our best effort to say what the world is like. In a revealing quotation, Quine admits,

> For my part I do, qua lay physicist, believe in physical objects and not in Homer's gods; and I consider it a scientific error to believe otherwise. But in point of epistemological footing the physical objects and the gods differ only in degree and not in kind. Both sorts of entities enter our conception only as cultural posits. The myth of physical objects is epistemologically superior to most in that it has proved more efficacious than other myths as a device for working a manageable structure into the flux of experience.[32]

Physical objects (and the scientific theories that contain them) are a myth precisely because one can never get one's epistemological hands on the objects themselves with any certainty. The privileged and objective access to the world is a myth not far removed from the ancient mythologies of Greece and Rome.[33] There is an important dif-

---

32. W. V. O. Quine, "Two Dogmas of Experience," in *From a Logical Point of View: Nine Logico-Philosophical Essays* (Cambridge, MA: Harvard University Press, 1953), 44.

33. The other well-known attack on positivist epistemology from within its ranks came from Wilfred Sellars, *Science, Perception and Reality* (London: Routledge and Kegan Paul, 1963).

ference, though—the modern myths of the natural sciences seem to "work," and thereby help to better navigate the cascading revolutions of science and technology. But in terms of actual truth value, ancient myths and modern science stand on equal footing.

Other key questions emerged at midcentury that proved problematic for the positivist project: How can one reconcile an observational language of ordinary objects with the technical discourse of particle physics and quantum mechanics?[34] If science is objectively true, how can one account for the massive changes in scientific theories across the ages? Is naturalism itself simply another religious alternative to the ancient faiths?

According to Rorty, the work of Thomas Kuhn finally brought an end to the logical positivist tradition. A long-held conviction of natural scientists since the Enlightenment was the belief that "true science" only began with the early modern period. But Kuhn argues that, if all science prior to that point (e.g., Aristotelian dynamics, phlogistic chemistry) was not simply out of date but also genuinely "mythological," then myths can be produced by the same sorts of methods and held for the same sorts of reasons in modern science.

Central to Kuhn's alternative description of science is the notion of a "paradigm."[35] It was this notion that played a central role in undermining the apparent objectivity of science. Kuhn argues that all of science takes place within theoretical commitments that cannot simply be objective. Every scientific paradigm works with a set of problems and acceptable solutions, and those problems and solutions do not remain constant across paradigm shifts. They could be chosen for

---

Especially important is his attack on what he calls "the myth of the given."

34. On this point, see especially Gary Gutting, "Philosophy of Science," in *The Synoptic Vision: Essays on the Philosophy of Wilfrid Sellars*, ed. C. F. Delaney, Michael J. Loux, Gary Gutting, and W. David Solomon (Notre Dame: University of Notre Dame Press, 1977), 73–87.

35. See Margaret Masterman, "The Nature of a Paradigm," in *Criticism and the Growth of Knowledge*, ed. Imre Lakatos and Alan Musgrave (London: Cambridge University Press, 1970), for a wonderful, descriptive treatment of the myriad of ways in which "paradigm" was used in the philosophy of science literature in the early years of its usage, and even the widely divergent ways Kuhn put the term to use.

many different reasons—many of which are nonscientific in the older sense of that word. Politics and religion must be included in the rationale for shifts in scientific paradigms.

As Rorty reflected on this intellectual history across the twentieth century, he concluded that philosophy is better described as a kind of therapy. It cannot solve the perennial and perplexing problems of science or the enduring mysteries of the universe. It can merely help us discover ways in which the ordinary use of language may lead to conceptual mistakes, including the mistake that philosophy should have interesting theories about everything. The two sentences "you have a sore throat" and "you have a nice thought" appear to have the same "grammar" and can mistakenly lead one to conclude that throats are like thoughts and that the description of them ought to occur in philosophically similar ways. But thoughts are not after all like throats, said Rorty. The upshot is that we ought to be wary of any intellectual reflection that leads to grand theories and universal claims about the world. Experience is always filtered through an interpretive grid that helps us to get along in the world. One need not have a philosophical theory of truth in order to ascertain better (or worse) ways of navigating the contexts of one's life. Language, like philosophy, is simply a tool to help us navigate the ambiguities of life. Rorty argued that we need to stop seeing language as a mirror of reality, which leads inevitably to the mistaken notion that science gives us the only accurate description of the world and that philosophy explains what science is actually doing. Language is nothing more or less than a means to navigate the multiple options before us at any moment of our lives. It cannot provide us with certainty as to which path to take, but simply with a temporary rationale for the paths we do choose.[36]

---

36. For different ends, Jonathan Haidt reaches a similar conclusion about the nature of human reason. Reason is not the human ability to separate fact from fiction, but rather the intellectual mechanism by which our emotional choices are given credence after the fact. See Haidt, *The Righteous Mind: Why Good People Are Divided by Politics and Religion* (New York: Vintage, 2013).

In a world radically pluralized by modern technology, a Rortian framework supposes that language ought to be shaped to steer through the ambiguities of the newly acquired abundance of choices. Successful navigation will come only if we give up any "finally true" solution and instead learn to accept and celebrate the new diversity of options. There is no grand scheme of relativism here. There is just the reality of the particular cultural context in which we live. It is the only one we have access to, and it is a reality of a multiplicity of choices being imposed on us by the advanced technologies of our age.

There is no privileged place for philosophers in this brave new world. Rorty realized that the prophets of the new secular order were the folk musicians, the poets, and the novelists. We might now add filmmakers, television producers, and internet entrepreneurs to the list. Philosophers who thought of their work in coldly rational and objective fashion are now obsolete. They are no longer the police at the intersection of truth and falsehood. They have no special access to reality that is not readily available elsewhere. The newly reigning pragmatism that Rorty signaled also claims that no other specialist in the academy has privileged access to reality. All of us stand on an equal plane amid the ambiguities of language and reality.

Enlightenment intellectuals of previous centuries dreamed of a secular culture over which they might become philosopher-kings. Twentieth-century philosophers saw disenchantment with older religious views of the world take hold, only to realize that they were no longer needed in the secular revolution. In the virtual blink of an eye, singer-songwriters, filmmakers, and artists became the new influential voices shaping modern culture.

PRESENCE AMID PLURALISM

If the secular revolution were to prosper, what would keep it from descending into pure partisan relativism, in which everyone simply narrated reality according to their own desires—doing what was right in their own eyes? This was the question when the pluralist impulse became the dominant social imaginary at the end of the twentieth century. Is there, or could there be, any genuine "common good" when there is no objective vantage point from which to make an argument for it? If the pendulum had swung so far to the pluralist side, what sense could be made of the unity side? The national motto, *e pluribus unum*—out of the many, one—seems strangely out of place in late modernity. When diversity is interpreted in light of the pluralist impulse, any attempt to speak of a community (large or small, national or regional) as a unity appears hopeless. Unity looks more like small tribal communities at war with other tribal communities. And yet there remains a deep yearning for communities that reach across our differences, a yearning that cannot be explained within the pragmatic intellectual story accompanying the cultural movement from fate to choice.

Once upon a time, history may have been written by the victors, but in today's pragmatic environment there is no single history, only histories in the plural—each a story from a particular vantage point, the most privileged coming from those whose stories were previously disregarded. The challenge ahead for Christians is not to recover a long-lost Christian civilization where they ruled the roost and commanded the cultural armies. Falling into this trap will only enhance the cultural rifts that prevent genuine conversation across tribal divides. Christians must learn to stand in the grand tradition of Augustine by resolutely resisting the criticism that religious conviction is the source of our present cultural problems, while also affirming the possibility that religion can contribute to those problems when it is used as a political hammer to keep unbelievers outside the corridors of cultural power. Christians must learn anew the difference between the earthly city and the heavenly city. The earthly cities of politics and culture do not operate by the same rules as the heavenly city. However, on this side of paradise it is also true that those who have a sense of belonging to the heavenly city must live out their faith in the earthly city with grace and compassion. Whether Augustine contributed to the rise of Christendom in the West is debatable. What is not debatable is that Augustine understood the complicated relationship of Christianity to the Roman Empire of his day. His theological goal was not to replace one earthly empire with another, as if Christianizing an empire would bring heaven down to earth.[37] Utopian pretensions may seem admirable in the abstract, but given the flawed and fragile character of human nature, those pretensions will always lead to disaster. We turn in the next several chapters to the resources available in the Christian faith to underwrite a "faithful presence" in a diverse secular culture whose animating behaviors reflect a deep set of pluralist impulses.[38]

---

37. The literature on Augustine and his defense of Christianity in the face of Roman criticism is vast. A helpful place to start is Jean Bethke Elshtain, *Augustine.*

38. I am here intentionally borrowing James Davison Hunter's notable phrase, which serves as his guiding principle for a Christian's interaction with late modernity. See Hunter, *To Change the World: The Irony, Tragedy, and Possibility of Christianity in the Late Modern World* (New York: Oxford University Press, 2010).

The greatest religious challenge is: can I see God's image in someone who is not in my image? Whose colour, culture, or class is not mine.

—JONATHAN SACKS, "ON THE DIGNITY OF DIFFERENCE"

5

PERSONAL IDENTITY
AND THE DIFFERENCES
THAT MAKE A DIFFERENCE

FIXED AND FLEXIBLE IDENTITIES

For most of us, high school was a time of searching anxiously for a group identity. Star athletes belonged to the jocks. Slightly lower down the pecking order were the socially savvy kids who knew how to use their relational sensibilities. Significantly lower but still possessing some credibility were the really bright students who excelled at any subject they encountered. The nerds were those whose interests veered toward technological gadgets and other unusual hobbies. Our yearning to belong to some group meant that our own identity was often a function of the stereotypes associated with that group. But at ten- and twenty-year high school reunions, we realize the old stereotypes did not persevere beyond those adolescent years. Predicting "success" (whatever that might have meant in high school) based on stereotyped group identity had little in common with the actual outcomes of a person's life. As contexts changed, so did the groups to which people belonged. However, taking identity clues from the groups to which we belong is inevitable, for God has made us relational creatures who find our significance and purpose outside of ourselves.

Our individual identities are tied to the groups to which we belong, but the sheer volume of groups, the conflicting groups to which we

belong, and the transitory nature of those groups has meant that identity is increasingly fragile and fluid for most of us. The influence of these
diverse contexts and groups are the clues that shape our self-identity.
Given the large number and diversity of identity clues, it should not
be surprising that ours is an age of great identity confusion. When we
get competing identity clues, there arises an ambiguity in our sense
of significance and purpose in the world.[1] Our nuclear family may
communicate one set of clues, our immediate vocational peer group
another; still other clues come from our ethnic or racial identity group,
which may or may not overlap with those received from our social
relationships. The pervasiveness of global brands shaping personal
habits, combined with the attendant explosion of consumer choices,
has also given the illusion that our identities are endlessly flexible.[2] It
is no wonder that anxiousness over our self-identity is very much a
function of the age in which we live.

The power of external influences on personal identity is not new
to our age, but the amount, strength, and diversity of those influences
in our time has overwhelmed previous cultural patterns. A striking
example is the pattern of parent-children relationships. In an age of
individualism, teenagers often interpret their parents' instruction as
intrusive rather than constructive. The loss of extended family traditions has made parenting much more of an individual than a team
sport.[3] The rise of social media and mass marketing has made parenting a far more complex project than anything with which our ancestors

---

1. See Richard Lints, *Identity and Idolatry: The Image of God and Its Inversion*, New Studies
in Biblical Theology (Downers Grove, IL: InterVarsity Press, 2015). I tease out many of the
different identity clues inside a larger biblical theology of identity.

2. See George Ritzer, *The McDonaldization of Society: Into the Digital Age*, 9th ed. (New
York: Sage, 2019 [original 1992]).

3. The Pew Research Center gives evidence of a consistently rising percentage of children
in America in the last fifty years who have been raised in single-parent homes. The United
States now has the largest percentage of children (24 percent) being raised in single-parent
households in the world. See Stephanie Kramer, "U.S. Has World's Highest Rate of Children
Living in Single-Parent Households," Pew Research Center, December 12, 2019, https://www.
pewresearch.org/fact-tank/2019/12/12/u-s-children-more-likely-than-children-in-other-coun-
tries-to-live-with-just-one-parent/.

had to wrestle.[4] The grand epic mythologies of the ancient world surely exerted identity-shaping influence on their cultural elites, but the pervasiveness of modern mythologies as told through film and television effectively makes a parent's voice almost extraneous as an identity clue for children today.

Common wisdom affirms that social context influences who we think we are and shapes the diverse ways in which we understand the differences that surround us.[5] While difficult to quantify, there is no doubt that human behavior is shaped by these surrounding realities. Our social contexts mold us as we are daily bombarded through seeing, hearing, and perceiving. Those perceptions in turn influence how we listen to those who are different from us as well.

While these fluid culture-shaping influences are inescapable, it would be naive to dismiss the aspects of human nature that remain constant across cultures. Classic Christian convictions seek to make sense of these fixed points that tie us together. God has made us in his image, an imprint that has persisted across the ages and across the globe. Despite the significance of cultural narratives, the enduring core of human identity cannot be completely dissolved by any particular context. Though the cultural conditions of late modernity are unique, they are not powerful enough to eradicate our persistent identity as images of God.[6] We speak because God is a speaking God. We are drawn to beauty because God has made us to seek beauty. Our moral sense is grounded in the reality that God distinguishes between right and wrong and has created us as responsible moral agents. The living God has created us to yearn for safety and significance outside

---

4. See Mitchell Stevens, *The Rise of the Image, the Fall of the Word* (New York: Oxford University Press, 2017), for an extended portrait of the power of visual images in contemporary culture (as opposed to words) to shape an individual's meaning and purpose of life.

5. By many accounts, one of the earliest and most influential reckonings of this was Peter Berger and Thomas Luckmann, *The Social Construction of Reality: A Treatise in the Sociology of Knowledge* (Garden City, NY: Anchor, 1967).

6. Richard Lints, "The Vinyl Narratives: The Metanarratives of Postmodernity and the Recovery of a Churchly Theology," in *A Confessing Theology for Postmodern Times*, ed. Michael S. Horton (Wheaton: Crossway, 2000), 91–110.

ourselves. In these and a host of other ways, human identity remains firmly tied in its central core to the God who made humans in his image.

These contrasting convictions—that identity is both fixed and flexible—must be held together in tension. We must affirm humans as morally responsible agents while also recognizing that many of our choices are profoundly influenced by forces outside of our control. At the intersection of these two convictions lies an indissoluble mystery. Leaning too strongly in one direction or the other inevitably produces an inaccurate picture of who we are. Our choices are not simply determined by the complex of social clues fed into our brains, nor are they simply made free of any outside influences. We are morally responsible agents in the choices we make, and our choices are profoundly influenced by the social contexts of our lives.[7]

The fixed and flexible parts of human identity can be difficult to clarify due to the relational character of persons. This is part of being created in God's image.[8] The social dimension of our identities and perceptions points at the fact that our relationships (visual, virtual, personal, communal) profoundly influence our sense of who we are and how we act.[9] We are creatures inside a social dynamic. That dynamic consists of a set of perceptions of our world, individual perceptions that are also part of a communal and cultural context. Not only do our perceptions influence how we evaluate the appropriateness of our actions, but we are also influenced by the perceptions others have toward us and their judgments of our actions. Our identity is bound up with this ongoing conversation between our perceptions of ourselves and the perceptions others have of us. Self-consciousness

---

7. It is important to hold both sides of the nurture-nature distinction in tension.

8. Lints, *Identity and Idolatry*.

9. Karl Barth's discussion is often cited as the locus for this renaissance of relational-trinitarian discussions of personhood. See his *Church Dogmatics*, vol. I/1, *The Doctrine of the Word of God*, 2nd ed., G. W. Bromiley and T. F. Torrance, eds. (Edinburgh: T&T Clark, 1975). Stanley Grenz, *The Social God and the Relational Self: A Trinitarian Theology of the Imago Dei* (Louisville: Westminster John Knox, 2001), offers a summary of the renaissance and its impact on theological questions of personhood. From a popular-cultural vantage point with roughly corresponding consequences, see David Brooks, *The Social Animal* (New York: Random House, 2012).

is the sense that we are both subjects with perceptions as well as objects being perceived. The great mystery is experiencing ourselves simultaneously as objects and as subjects—as if two persons in one[10]—viewing others and one viewing how others view us. We take cues from others and give cues to ourselves.

Our identities are shaped by those around us even as we also influence the identities of those around us. We view them through our filters even as we are viewed through theirs. Every conversation takes place with expectations from both sides. We tell stories through our own narratives while also being part of the narratives of others. We are a character in our own novel, so to speak, but we also are characters in the novels being written by others. We may be unaware of the stories within which we are placing persons around us and likewise unaware of the stories in which our own past has played a central role. We are at best coauthors of our own story.[11]

In our attempts to interpret others, we forget they are not simply characters of our own creation. We are often lulled into thinking our own act of "shaping" is innocent and trivial, although sometimes it is neither. We feel violated when others distort their perceptions of us but do not recognize when we have done the same. Motives and actions can be distorted in either direction—unfairly assigning blame or credit toward others or even toward ourselves.

In the next section, the relationship of marriage serves as a poignant illustration of the unique (and often hidden) pressures that individuals must navigate within the social imaginary of our times. Marriage brings to the surface the peculiarly modern ways in which individuals both interpret their differences and also how they deal with their differences. The influence of the modern social imaginary is often experienced irrespective of the marriage partners' own personal religious convictions, most especially when those religious

---

10. The old dictum "Talk to yourself, don't just listen to yourself" captures this dynamic of self-identity.

11. Stanley Hauerwas, "The Virtues of Alasdair MacIntyre," *First Things* (October 2007), https://www.firstthings.com/article/2007/10/the-virtues-of-alasdair-macintyre.

convictions sit lightly on the individuals. This analysis of modern marriages leads then in the following section to a comparison between the social imaginary of our times and the theological imaginary of Scripture as it pertains to the matters of interpreting and dealing with difference more broadly.

LATE MODERN SECULAR MARRIAGE: WHAT IT LOOKS LIKE FOR INDIVIDUALS

Marriage is a primary institution in which difference is negotiated—constructively or not. It is an "image" within which husbands and wives carry on a distinctive kind of relationship. That image has a variety of influences in every culture. In the late modern secular world, those influences come from diverse quarters, often in conflicting ways. The modern secular marriage, an invention of the nineteenth century, presupposes a radical separation of domestic life from the world of work. As Christopher Lasch has argued,

> The decline of household production and the rise of wage labor made it possible to conceive of the family as a private retreat from a public world increasingly dominated by impersonal mechanisms of the market. The image of the family as a haven in a heartless world helped Americans to manage the ambivalent emotions evoked by the new industrialization. On the one hand they wanted the comforts and conveniences furnished by industrial progress; on the other hand the agency of progress—the capitalist market—appeared to foster a type of acquisitive individualism that left no room for the finer things in life: loving-kindness, spontaneous affection, what John Stuart Mill called the "culture of feelings."[12]

The social context of late modernity inevitably influences the expectations married couples have toward each other. The

---

12. See Christopher Lasch, *Women and the Common Life: Love, Marriage and Feminism* (New York: Norton, 1997), 102.

understanding of marriage as an institutional framework for a life-long commitment of husband and wife is all but lost, undermining the tendency to subordinate one's own impulses and intuitions for the maintenance of the family system and the flourishing of children. Marriage has increasingly become a nonbinding relationship in which the primary aim is the emotional and sexual satisfaction of each individual. It is more a temporary contract than a binding covenant.

Statistics bear out that the understanding of marriage as covenant has largely vanished in late modernity. Divorce rates have continued to increase twofold in every generation over the last century. Cohabitation was virtually absent as the twentieth century dawned; now nearly 60 percent of everyone under the age of forty will cohabit at some point.[13] Gone is the notion of marriage as a primary vehicle for the restraint of selfish desires and intentions, replaced by the requirement that one feel fulfilled by one's partner.

In the preindustrial period, children were viewed as an economic benefit; their labor helped support the agrarian enterprise of the family. Over time, industrialization reversed that economic equation. During the twentieth century, children became "expensive"—a drag on the economic well-being of the family—and marriages were reshaped with new cultural expectations of child-rearing. With self-fulfillment as the goal of the marriage relationship, child-rearing became the arena in which experts advised parents on how best to produce self-fulfilled children. When the experts included mass marketers, a new "youth culture" was created, inculcating children as consumers and placing demands on parents to meet all their children's needs. Seeds of this change could be seen as early as the "flapper culture" of the 1920s, but it really exploded onto the national consciousness in the 1960s with radical generational changes in music, fashion, and entertainment. John F. Kennedy's youthful image, the Beatles's appearance on the Ed Sullivan Show, and the rise of the Jesus People all sounded the death knell for the privileging

---

13. See Pew Research Study on Marriage and Cohabitation in the U.S. accessed at https://www.pewresearch.org/fact-tank/2019/11/06/key-findings-on-marriage-and-cohabitation-in-the-u-s/.

of age over youth. Television, advertising, and concerts all announced the late twentieth century as the age of youthfulness.

At the same time, there was a revolution in morals. During the twentieth century, notions of "duty" or "service" as the prime motivation for actions in the family increasingly seemed outdated. In the eighteenth century, the Enlightenment tried to find a rational basis for traditional moral maxims without reference to a sacred story.[14] As a result, ethicists in the twentieth century incoherently attempted to ground normative claims in the arbitrary whims of individual decision, replacing the older virtues with far more "flexible" norms—most often shaped by the social contexts of consumer culture. This attachment of moral norms to the satisfaction of temporal human pleasures resulted in the celebration of sexual freedom, the legality of no-fault divorce, and the abandonment of marriage as a lifelong project. Husbands and wives became consumers-in-chief who viewed their attraction to each other through the primary lens of intense romantic passion and sexual excitement.[15]

These cultural shifts cause both persons in the marriage, shaped by the cultural nexus of relationships into which they have been catechized, to act as autonomous individuals. These expectations influence the way they understand marital fidelity, and relational fidelity more generally. In a predictable twist, this understanding of marriage as an institution whose primary goal is self-actualization has reshaped expectations of divine fidelity. Rather than God's enduring commitment to his people serving as the corrective to human experiences of infidelity, the human expectations that a spouse fulfill one's needs and goals leads us to expect the

---

14. Alasdair MacIntyre's critique of the Enlightenment project and the resulting incoherence of twentieth-century moral emotivism has renewed interest in virtue ethics and the project of situating moral norms within a larger story about the ends for which humans have been created. See especially MacIntyre, *After Virtue* (Notre Dame: University of Notre Dame Press, 1981).

15. To illustrate this declension in marriage norms, MacIntyre cites Bertrand Russell riding a bicycle one day in 1902, realizing he was no longer in love with his first wife, and shortly thereafter divorcing her. MacIntyre comments, "Any attitude whose discovery while riding a bicycle in a sudden flash, is only an aesthetic reaction, and has to be considered irrelevant to the commitment which a genuine marriage involves, and to the genuinely ethical/moral character which underwrites marriage itself." MacIntyre, *After Virtue*, 40.

same of God.[16] If divine fidelity was once the moral ground of a marital covenant, in late secular modernity the reverse has taken place: the reenvisioned marriage contract has altered the way we see God's faithfulness.

THEOLOGICAL IMAGINARY: CREATOR AND CREATURE

All of us reflect the world we live in while retaining the imprint of the Creator who brought us into being, even if we do not recognize it. That imprint is what I call the *theological imaginary*. It is the deep structures of the Creator/creature relationship in which all of our lives are embedded. As with the social imaginary, the theological imaginary functions in the background of our consciousness, evidenced by the patterns and habits of our interactions with the world around us. It is the framework by which we yearn for meaning and purpose, as well as safety and security. It echoes in our moral instinct that all of human life is sacred and in our intuitive repulsion that comes when human life is treated with disdain. It is manifest when we blame God for events even if we do not believe in God, or when we thank God for what otherwise may appear to be ordinary events. Making sense of these imprints on our mental landscape requires a reference outside of the social imaginary. It is *theological* precisely because of the Creator-creature relationship that forms the skeleton of the structure. It is an *imaginary* in the sense that it gives rise to instincts and intuitions that shape many other dimensions of the mental landscape and influence what we think is possible and important.

The biblical account of the *imago Dei* (image of God) is the ground of the theological imaginary of Scripture. It points to the created reflection of God in human creatures from the beginning—profoundly affirming that humans are created as images of God. There is nothing peculiarly complex about this phrase, but there is an enormous theological claim

---

16. Trevor Hart, "Imagination and Responsible Reading," in *Renewing Biblical Interpretation*, ed. Craig Bartholomew, Colin Greene, and Karl Möller (Carlisle, UK: Paternoster, 2000), 334–37.

at stake. That claim is simply that humans find themselves by looking outside of themselves, and most particularly as they sense a delight in that which God delights in, and thereby reflect the God who made them in his image. Their theological imaginary is not formed by their unique physical or psychological characteristics, but rather by the imprint left on their souls by the God who made them in his image.

This imprint is reflective of the character of God in whom love, beauty, justice, and goodness fully reside. Our yearning for love, for beauty, for justice, and for goodness emerges from the imprint of the divine nature in humankind. None of these virtues or values could emerge simply by the will of a person or group. Affirming that an action is good cannot simply mean, "I like that action." It may be true that good actions are in fact liked, but liking an action is fundamentally different from the goodness of its character. The goodness of an action (or its justice or its beauty) lies in the nature of the action itself, not in our approbation of it. In other words, each of these virtues possesses an objective (and transcendent) character. Justice ceases to be justice if it only applies within the confines of one's desires. Beauty cannot finally be reducible to taste, and love cannot be the same as self-interest. Each of these "delights of God" requires an objective basis outside of and yet made concrete within human experience. Each serves as a bridge from the immanent to the transcendent. Pondering them also provides a powerful reminder that humans did not invent or create the virtues, and places everyone on equal footing before the God who created us all. As the virtues are embedded in the character of God, they resist being captured by our own stereotypes—despite our persistent efforts.

Humankind is like God, but unlike God we have limits. We are derived copies, not the original. We possess an exalted status as reflections of the very Creator of the universe but also a humble status as merely derived copies of the original.[17] We are "like" God, bearing

---

17. See Henri Blocher, *In the Beginning: The Opening Chapters of Genesis* (Downers Grove, IL: InterVarsity Press, 1984).

some resemblance to God, but we are "merely" like God insofar as we are not God. Herein lies the tension within the human heart of experiencing what we are and what we are not.

In contrast to ancient Canaanite mythologies and their anthropomorphic deities, Genesis clearly asserts the transcendence of God but strangely also his dwelling within the created order. It is God who speaks creation into being, and it is God who speaks to and with our human parents. God speaks as a person-in-relationship. God does not speak to humankind as an equal but does grant them a relationship by virtue of his words. The God who speaks creates beings who speak, though they do not speak identically to their Creator. With words they create worlds of meaning, but the creature's words do not sovereignly call reality into being as does the divine Word. With words humans make promises, utter commands, and express compassion—as God does. But the promises, commands, and compassion of God bear none of the frailty of human speech and intentions. There is an absolute uniqueness to the divine speech by virtue of the reality that God alone is God.

God's words in the first chapter of Genesis constitute speech acts of a performative nature.[18] The words accomplish what is connoted in the words themselves. When God says, "Let there be light," light is thereby enacted or performed. The act of creating is identical with the speaking of the words. What God says frames the created order and possesses a logical priority to creation. God's speech acts tell us both that God is a communicative being and that his communication is logically prior to our existence as communicative beings. We speak because God speaks. Words matter to us precisely because they matter to God.

In the liturgy of creation in Genesis 1, the reflection of God in humankind is unmistakably connected to our relational character. We

---

18. Nicholas Wolterstorff, *Divine Discourse: Philosophical Reflections on the Claim that God Speaks* (Cambridge: Cambridge University Press, 1995), defends the claim that God speaks not by virtue of having vocal cords but rather by authorizing discourse as his own.

are constituted as social beings, as persons whose identity is bound up in a dialogical relationship to others. The reflection of God shines against the backdrop of an integral human relationship—male and female. That relationship, in turn, is a sign pointing to God's personal and relational identity. In the immediate context of Genesis 1:27, the language of male and female underwrites the affirmation that God created more than one: God created "them." In this, God created a plurality.[19] Male and female point to a relationship of significant difference and similarity.[20] While the language of male/female is not grounded in any sort of sexual or gendered resemblance to God, it does call attention to a covenantal relationship of significant difference and similarity.[21]

There is an important clue in Genesis 1 that the God who created humankind in the plural contains some kind of plurality in his own being. The divine plural of Genesis 1:26 ("let us make") has been the subject of a multitude of interpretive explanations.[22] The verb

---

19. It is not appreciated often enough how the singular and plural are interwoven in Genesis 1:26–27. God acts in the singular, and God acts in the plural. God creates a human in the singular, and God creates humans in the plural. In an account replete with numerical nuances, this must be intentional. See Lints, *Identity and Idolatry*, for a greater elaboration of this interweaving of the singular and plural in the book of Genesis.

20. Stanley Grenz's discussion of Karl Barth's contention that the *imago Dei* is constituted by the male-female relationship is most helpful. See Grenz, *The Social God and the Relational Self*. He both affirms the importance of the male-female relationship and places it in the larger construct of "community" themes present in the canon. We must keep "difference" at the heart of the exposition of the *imago Dei*, and this is secured in the language of male and female.

21. See Gordon Hugenberger, *Marriage as a Covenant: A Study of Biblical Law and Ethics Governing Marriage, Developed from the Perspective of Malachi* (Leiden: Brill, 1994), for a biblical-theological argument grounding marriage in its covenantal framework.

22. The range of alternatives include an address to creation, an address to the heavenly court, a plural of deliberation, a plural of majesty, an unfiltered remnant of pagan polytheism (most doubtful), or a plural of divine persons. Gunnlaugur Jónsson, *The Image of God: Genesis 1:26–28 in a Century of Old Testament Research* (London: Coronet, 1988), offers a helpful summary of the historic alternatives. It is difficult to discern which options are plausible given the paucity of contextual clues. Early Jewish midrash seemed to favor the angels, but overall early Jewish tradition is eclectic on the question. See Umberto Cassuto, *A Commentary on the Book of Genesis*, vol. 1 (Jerusalem: Magnes Press, 1961); Jon Levenson, *Creation and the Persistence of Evil: The Jewish Drama of Divine Omnipotence* (San Francisco: Harper & Row 1988); and Norbert Samuelson, *The First Seven Days: A Philosophical Commentary on the Creation in Genesis* (Atlanta: Scholars Press, 1992). Early Christian commentary overwhelmingly favored a foreshadowing of

"to make" (Hebrew 'āśâ) used in Genesis 1:26 was used previously in Genesis 1:7, 16, and 25, but in each of these the verb had been in the first-person singular of God. In 1:26, when the plural is used, the reader expects a partner to be named, but no partner appears. Is the partner missing or merely implicit?[23] An obvious possibility is the Spirit of God, who is already mentioned in verse 2 and also appears later in Genesis (6:3; 41:8).[24] Of further note, 1:27 introduces the result of the plural verb of 1:26, concluding with a reference to a plurality of persons—male and female.[25] The interplay of singular and plural appears again in Genesis 3:22, at the end of the account of the fall, and again the mention of a plurality of human persons (Adam and Eve) is close at hand.[26] All of this points to the possible plurality of persons within God, which the early church overwhelmingly interpreted as a foreshadowing of the Trinity.

The plurality of persons forms the basis of the biblical intuition that persons are always intended to be "persons-in-relationship."

---

the Trinity in the plural of 1:26. See Andrew Louth, *Genesis 1–11*, Ancient Christian Commentary on Scripture, Old Testament 1 (Downers Grove, IL: InterVarsity Press, 2001). Mainstream exegetes in the first half of the twentieth century seemed assured that the Trinity could not be a part of v. 26 since the author/editor could not have had any knowledge of the Trinity. The strongest argument against taking the plural of 1:26 as a plurality of divine persons is the polemic against pagan polytheism in the primeval history of Genesis 1–11. See Gerhard F. Hasel, *Old Testament Theology: Basic Issues in the Current Debate*, 4th ed. (Grand Rapids: Eerdmans, 1991); and Victor Hamilton, *The Book of Genesis: Chapters 1–17*, New International Commentary on the Old Testament (Grand Rapids: Eerdmans, 1990).

23. Though some commentators have suggested the plural of v. 26 need not suppose a partner, the overwhelming majority of commentators (both Jewish and Christian) have argued that an implicit partner is required by the context. The two most favored by interpreters are the angelic court and some partner within God himself.

24. This is defended by D. J. A. Clines, "Humanity as the Image of God," in *On the Way to the Postmodern: Old Testament Essays, 1967–1998* (Sheffield: Sheffield Academic Press, 1998), 2:447–97.

25. Karl Barth infers an actual personal duality in God by reference to the creatures God has made "male and female" in v. 27. The problem for Barth is that the duality in God cannot be a sexual duality as implied by "male and female." Barth partially responds to the problem by noting that human persons (male and female) are reflections of divine persons who relate to each other as "I" and "Thou," as do human persons. See Karl Barth, *Church Dogmatics* III/4, ed. G. W. Bromiley and T. F. Torrance (Edinburgh: T & T Clark, 1961).

26. The other contextual clues in Genesis that imply a plurality of persons are the theophanies of divine plurality in Gen 11:7; 18:1–2; 32:28.

And the peculiar relationship of humankind to God is framed by the uniqueness of the Creator-creature dynamic—namely, that creatures are created to find delight in that which their Creator delights in and to desire that which their Creator desires. In this regard, image bearers find their telos, or purpose, in the honoring relationship to the original. We are made to yearn for something beyond ourselves in which our deepest longings are fulfilled.

The language of the *imago Dei* also illuminates how we are to understand differences. The primary difference is surely with reference to God.[27] Desiring to be "as God" has been the great temptation from Genesis 3 onward. It is the tendency to reimagine a god in our image, effectively reducing God to a more manageable size, and failing to grasp the importance of our difference from God. Reckoning and respecting the essential differences with our Creator stabilizes our sense of significance and safety. By analogy, respecting and appreciating the differences with other human persons enables the very kind of relationships to emerge that bring out the creaturely virtues. Being patient with others means that we do not require others to behave just like us. Being gentle with others requires that we respect differences. Being faithful to another is most manifest when our differences with the other do not undermine our commitment to them. Being merciful to another means that we forgive even differences by which we are wronged. In all these ways, relationships are intended to reflect the character of God, which is only possible when we are constituted as "beings-involved-in-relationships-of-similarity-and-diversity."[28]

All of this supports the reality that meaning and significance are found in social contexts, which in turn provide interpretive clues

---

27. The *imago Dei* does not refer to a list of human attributes that more technically belong to ontological accounts of human identity rather than theological accounts. David Kelsey makes this claim by arguing that that the *imago Dei* is substantially insignificant in providing details of a Christian account of human nature. See Kelsey, "Personal Bodies: A Theological Anthropological Proposal," in *Personal Identity in Theological Perspective*, ed. Richard Lints, Michael S. Horton, and Mark R. Talbot (Grand Rapids: Eerdmans, 2006), 139–58.

28. See Miroslav Volf, *Exclusion and Embrace*.

about the many social spaces we associate with difference in our late modern secular democracy—race, ethnicity, gender, and class, to name but a few. These also surely include the differences manifest in families, in places of work or worship, in politics, and across generational lines. All these diversities occur in socially defined spaces and require both a recognition of those socially defined expectations and a theological imaginary that sees those relationships from a different perspective. These social and theological expectations overlap as well as stand in tension. The mystery of the "sometimes-overlapping" and "sometimes-in-tension" of these two perspectives lies behind the complexity of being reflective beings—reflecting both the social realities of our context and the theological character of the God who made us. Our reflective identity means that we are both fragile and fixed.

THEOLOGICAL IMAGINARY:
IMAGE BEARER AND IDOL MAKER

In the biblical theological imaginary, the gravest threat to the *imago Dei* is graven images (that is, idols). Idolatry is what most centrally distorts the security and significance of the creature. The idol maker is the theological opposite of the image bearer, although they may be one and the same person. Bearing the image of God and the crafting of idols are two sides of the same conceptual coin. The Creator has made human creatures who can seamlessly move from delighting in what God delights in to finding their greatest delight elsewhere. The human heart can define beauty or justice or goodness for itself and all too easily manipulate others (or be manipulated by others) on the basis of a self-centered conception of identity.

As "images," we gain our ontological weight from what we honor, how we find our significance, and where our security lies. In Scripture, people are a thin or thick reality depending on the object of their deepest desires. If their object of desire is the living God, they are filled with life, securing a thick identity. If the objects of their ultimate desires are focused on the created order rather than the Creator, their identity will inevitably be as thin and transient as the objects of their desire. Locating our significance and security in a place or person without ontological ultimacy launches us on a fleeting search for stability precisely where it cannot be found.

Another way to frame this issue is to distinguish the projects of finding meaning and creating meaning. Finding meaning is recognizing the larger narrative into which our life fits and realizing that meaning comes as we embrace our place in that narrative. Creating meaning is the attempt to write a different narrative on our own terms to make our place in our own narrative more important than what it otherwise might be. The fundamental difference is whether the larger narrative of life is of our own making. The ancients as well as the church across the ages have resolutely affirmed the fixed nature of reality and our responsibility to make peace with our place in that reality. The mythology of late secular modernity centers on the intuition that reality is what we make it to be. In this Facebook model of personal identity, the self is created as a homepage, we link to others to illustrate our significance, but we also "like" and "unlike" those associations with others at will.[29] Each of us creates the story that tells the meaning of our lives, often with and through a set of images that make life appear different than it actually is.

Tragic or difficult experiences often challenge the notion that we can create our own meaning and the story into which it fits. The loss of a loved one, a debilitating and persistent disease, or deep intractable conflict have a way of reminding us that the story of our lives is not written with our happiness always in view, nor can we simply rewrite the story.

The hope of creating our own ultimate meaning is doomed from the start. Since our created meaning lacks attachment to something or someone with ontological solidity, it always remains transient and

---

29. Mark Lilla, *The Once and Future Liberal*, 85. He writes further, "If the young student accepts the all-American idea that her own unique identity is something she gets to construct and change as fancy strikes her, she can hardly be expected to have an enduring political attachment to others, and certainly cannot be expected to hear the call of duty toward them."

fragile. Surely we have personal responsibility for "living into" the larger narrative of reality, but the effort to create meaning from the created order is doubly "thin"—we suppose that what we create can return the favor by giving significance to that which created it, but the transiency of the creature is not overcome by the creation of our own hands (or lives). However, what the logic of this myth does illuminate is the desire to find significance and meaning outside of ourselves, which seems intuitively obvious upon reflection.

The metaphor of Facebook identities offers another important reminder of the danger of supposing that meaning and purpose can be created by the one in need of meaning and purpose in the first place. As with Facebook, the act of creating an image for ourselves in turn refashions us after its own likeness. The image we create becomes the standard we now must live up to. Images of an exciting and storied life create internal stress for the one who desperately yearns for that but knows full well that life is not always exciting nor storied.

These self-made images are as dangerous as outside love interests are dangerous to a marriage. Dangerous liaisons may appear exciting and stimulating until reality sets in—relationships are costly, especially those entered without regard for the emotional dimensions. The self-made image of adultery reflects disordered desires (such as the desire for gratification on terms more convenient and comfortable).[30] Like idolatry, self-made images involve errors in belief—namely, that some part of the created order can satisfy our deepest longings.[31] If there is only one God, there is only one object worthy of ultimate worship and adoration.[32] This means that our ultimate pleasure cannot be self-de-

---

30. Even "good" desires may become idolatrous when they become ends in themselves rather than means to a greater end. Timothy Keller writes, "Making an idol out of love may mean allowing the lover to exploit and abuse you." Keller, *Counterfeit Gods: The Empty Promise of Money, Sex, and Power, and the Only Promise That Matters* (New York: Penguin, 2009), 24.

31. See Paul Helm, "Review of Halbertal and Margalit on Idolatry," *Mind* 414 (1995): 419–27.

32. Kenneth Seeskin, *No Other Gods: The Modern Struggle against Idolatry* (West Orange, NJ: Behrman House, 1995), writes, "If there is only one God, there is only one thing in the universe worthy of worship; everything else is part of the created order and subject to the will of God. In fact, the division between God and creation is so decisive that not only are

fined. Ordering our lives in accord with that reality brings to the fore
the contrary-to-late-secular-modern expectation that temporal pleasures are not worthy competitors for the delights that God defines.

THE END OF THE STORY: THE SOCIAL
AND THEOLOGICAL IMAGINARIES

It is becoming increasingly obvious that human persons are essentially social. The pendulum is swinging in our public consciousness
away from rugged individualism toward notions of personhood
rooted in communities.[33] Christians ought to celebrate this in part
because it opens the door to recognizing more clearly the nature of
our unity and diversity as created beings framed by the Scriptures. If
the cultural pendulum were to swing too far toward the submerging
of identity into a singular community, individuals would too easily
lose moral responsibility for their own actions. That is not likely to
happen anytime soon in the West, although there are communities
outside the West where this has cultural strength. In most cultures
where late secular modernity holds sway, individualism ("what's in
it for me?") shows no signs of losing its traction, even as we become
more self-conscious of the influence of communities on our identity.[34]

The biblical account runs against the grain of the contemporary
intuition that personal identity is equivalent to the traits of ethnicity,
race, sexual orientation, or gender. The web of relationships described
in the Scriptures is far richer and more complex than any one of
these could encompass. Reducing personal identity to a singular social
identity cannot do justice to the complexity of communities to which
individuals actually belong, nor to their own individual moral responsibility. These social contexts do provide identity clues, but we should

heavenly bodies, mortal creatures and sea monsters not divine, they cannot even serve as
images of the divine" (15).

33. Robert Putnam, *Bowling Alone: The Collapse and Revival of American Community* (New
York: Simon & Schuster, 2001), charts this pendulum swing.

34. Putnam, *Bowling Alone*, amply testifies to the enduring strength of individualism in
our contemporary consumer culture.

not suppose they exhaust the fullness of our identity. Even more significant, none of these characteristics adequately encompass the fullness of the divine-human relationship at the heart of an accurate description of personal identity.

The sociality of the human person is never a sociality *simpliciter*— never merely a set of human relationships abstracted from a concrete historical context. We belong to an actual past as well as to a genuine present. Try as we might to escape historical influences, they remain an ever-present reality. A stubborn voice continually reminds us of the past in our own memory, but it does so in selective ways. We do not remember everything that ever happened to us. We tend to remember events or episodes that shaped us, and even with these memories we exercise a selective control, placing ourselves in the story of our past in self-serving ways.

We also do this as groups or communities. We too often tell ourselves half-truths about the past. For example, as the last of the "greatest generation" passes away, our collective memory calls to mind the unbelievable sacrifices they made in two world wars and the Great Depression, but we often forget that freedom from external tyranny on American soil did not always translate into civic freedoms for many immigrants and African Americans. We can also reverse the historical narrative to denigrate those same heroic sacrifices because they were accompanied by contradictory actions in other areas. In both directions, the complexity of human identities is missed.

As argued in chapter 2, the history of American democracy can be told as an inclusion narrative or an exclusion narrative. Our collective memory tends to lean in one direction or the other, but a sufficiently complex conceptual framework is needed to explain both narratives existing side by side.[35] The clear conviction of the founders that all

---

35. In what follows, I am indebted to Mark A. Noll, *God and Race in American Politics: A Short History* (Princeton: Princeton University Press, 2008). In his final chapter, he captures as succinctly and as simply as possible the theological convictions that lie behind the real and apparent contradictions of these realities. I know of no better short theological treatment of this history.

persons are created equal was rooted in the long Christian tradition associated with the *imago Dei*, and yet many in the early founding of the republic also failed to see the incongruity of this Christian claim with the practices of slavery. The history of American Christianity shows many instances of remarkable generosity toward those on the margins of society, while also showing too many instances of hostility to strangers. The history of race and religion in America requires a framework that is sensitive to the contradictions both in the church and within the human heart, if also still retaining deep mysteries.

To account for the display of manifest good and overwhelming depravity in the history of race and religion and politics, we must resist a naive optimism toward human nature as well as an all-encompassing cynicism toward human hypocrisy. There are other variables such as economics, technology, media, and geography that must be brought to bear on any sensitive interpretations of these conflicting realities. By themselves, they cannot adequately account for the contradictions whereby oppression and liberation reside side by side, or where love and hatred can be expressed by the same group or person. The paradoxical presence of justice alongside injustice, of generosity with greed, of compassion with spite, of inclusion and exclusion together are layered throughout history, much to our present chagrin. These contradictions cry out for an affirmation both of the goodness of the created order and the persistence of evil in the depths of every human heart and community. We must reckon both with common grace and the myriad ways that grace is resisted. We must seek the mystery of human nature, in which even the best motives are mixed with self-interest and acts of goodness come from unexpected places of human depravity.

We need a transcendent account of the fragility and fixed nature of human identity, which is inevitably more complex than we would like. This account affirms the goodness of the Creator and of his creation and also of the great mystery of human fallenness and the persistence of individual and corporate sin. Whatever else salvation means on this side of the grave, it does not mean perfection. The history of redemption moves from creation to fall to forgiveness in Christ. Christians have long recognized (often inconsistently) that divine forgiveness rather than human merit is the sole basis for a reconciled relationship to God. This recognition implies that the transformation of human character is always and only partial, and never forms the grounds on which humans can boast before God.[36] If this is so, then in reckoning with the deep contradictions in the behavior of Christians as they have dealt with deep difference, we must neither suppose that Christians have nothing to be ashamed about nor that Christians have always been on the wrong side of history. The gospel requires a different framework for understanding ourselves, leading both to a greater sense of humility and conviction and a greater yearning for God's forgiveness.

Trite as it may seem, the attitude we need in the face of the contradictions of human nature is not hopelessness but resolve—a resolve to work through differences in concrete ways. The brokenness of our past calls us to put our relationships back together precisely because God has put our relationship to him back together. Our resolve must be a reflection of his resolve. That resolve should be shown in marriages, in neighborhoods, in spaces of work, in our circle of friendships—in short, in all of life. In the following chapter, I consider three models from Scripture that may guide and motivate renewed ways to live into the unity-in-diversity for which we have been created.

---

36. I have spelled this out at greater length in "Living by Faith—Alone? Reformed Responses to Antinomianism," in *Sanctification: Explorations in Theology and Practice*, ed. Kelly M. Kapic (Downers Grove, IL: IVP Academic, 2014), 35–56.

Our finite ears cannot receive the whole hymn of this divine life, but we are given not one part only of the tremendous symphony, but a divine fourfold melody. In this Divine song each evangelist [of the four Gospels] has his part to sing, and each part is complete in itself; while the Holy Spirit is the composer of all, the author at once of their diversity, suiting the part to the voice that is to sing it, and of their concordant harmony by which we may get a foretaste of that grander music which it shall be ours to hear "when we shall see Him as He is."

—BENJAMIN B. WARFIELD, "WHY FOUR GOSPELS?"

6

DIVERSE MODELS OF DIVERSITY

The world of Jesus and the early church was vastly different from ours, but nonetheless contains parallels. It was defined by deep religious pluralism, where diverse cultures and worldviews regularly bumped into each other. But it was also a world of empires with only a sprinkling of early city-state democracies. The ancient world did not know a sharp distinction between the natural and supernatural or between religion and politics. It was a world where the language of the self was largely hidden from view, and when present it was woven into the fabric of tribe, city, or empire.

This was a world whose social imaginary was surely quite different from ours. The differences that made a difference in the historic contexts of Scripture are not the same as those of today. We need wisdom to perceive those contexts and apply the most appropriate principles to today. Wisdom grapples not only with moral principles and laws but also with the circumstances in which those principles may apply. Wisdom recognizes that laws cannot be applied the same way in every context. Speed limits are generally applicable to all drivers, but exceptions exist, such as when an ambulance is en route to the hospital or a state trooper is in pursuit of a criminal. Such exceptions are not violations of the law, nor do they undermine the trustworthiness of the law. Wisdom teaches us how to navigate these exceptions

by virtue of taking into account the circumstances. Wisdom is critical in moving us from the historical contexts of Scripture to our own
peculiar circumstances, pointing out where analogies between the
two make sense and where they may not.

Wisdom also takes seriously the ways in which Scripture uses metaphors to interpret different circumstances across redemptive history.
For example, the church is described as the "bride of Christ," using
a metaphor partially borrowed from the Old Testament description
of Israel as Yahweh's bride. This is a way to interpret the church's
relationship to Jesus without providing an exhaustive list of what to
do in every situation. It is not to be translated out of the theological
imaginary, but rather evokes within church members the character
of their new relationship to Jesus. So it is with the image of the body
of Christ used in the New Testament depiction of the church. This
image shapes the church's wisdom in thinking through how different
members in the church are to relate to each other.

Also, Scriptures rarely speak of the diversity of Israel or the
church without first referencing their unity. Their ultimate security
lay in their single-minded devotion to the one God of the universe.
This unity of purpose granted Israel and then the church their fundamental identity. Differences were permitted and encouraged within
Israel and the church, but it was their ultimate unity in their fidelity
to the one God that was paramount. This unity is the proper conceptual ground for theologically and morally appropriate notions
of diversity.

In what follows, I will bring three conceptual models from
Scripture to bear on our contemporary experience inside and outside
the church to illuminate the complex relationship of unity and diversity. These models—redemptive history, marriage, and the Trinity—
provide wisdom and guidelines for "bumping into" the all-pervasive
diversity of our times. Each of these models is illuminated in Scripture
in concrete historical circumstances, as well as "applied" across
diverse historical situations. In this way, they provide clues for how
we might approach diversity in our own times.

REDEMPTIVE HISTORY: THE STORY
OF THE ONE AND THE MANY

Reading the Scriptures as they are intended to be read provides a window into the complicated conceptual puzzle we have been considering. The Scriptures themselves ought to be conceived of as an extended work of unity-in-diversity. We cannot say that *all* of Scripture is a divine rule book or *all* of Scripture is a set of morality tales. No fair reading of Scripture can reduce the whole to one simple function. Likewise, a fair reading should not so intensely historicize or pluralize the Scriptures that the unifying central story is lost. On the contrary, a fair reading reveals a single story told in and through countless diverse episodes, genres, and settings.

Christians across the ages have read the Bible as one book and as sixty-six books, primarily because of the claim that the Bible is a book authored by God as well as by many human authors. The intention of the human author is disclosed most nearly in the entire context of his own writing. The same applies to the divine Author's intention. God's intentions are most clearly displayed from the context of the Bible as a whole. Christians have read the Scriptures from both perspectives—namely, as one story, the divine drama so to speak, and as historical narratives recorded for us by multiple human authors.[1]

Understanding certain parts of reality is often "art rather than science," and this surely applies to reading complex pieces of literature such as the Bible, which confesses to be the word of God as well as the words of multiple human authors. Scripture should be read with attention to its unfolding plotline from Genesis to Revelation, whose climax is found in Jesus as the fulfillment of all the hopes of God's people.[2] In this regard, it provides a significant conceptual resource for contemplating unity and diversity in the present age.

---

1. See Kevin Vanhoozer, *The Drama of Doctrine: A Canonical-Linguistic Approach to Christian Theology* (Louisville: Westminster John Knox, 2005), and Michael S. Horton, *Covenant and Eschatology: The Divine Drama* (Louisville: Westminster John Knox, 2002).

2. See Graeme Goldsworthy, *According to Plan: The Unfolding Revelation of God in the Bible* (Downers Grove, IL: InterVarsity Press, 2002).

There is an inherent unity to the Scriptures because the divine Author intends it, but it is not a uniformity of a single truth revealed all at once in one form. The organic unfolding of the message of the Bible across its many ages reveals a perfect seed eventually growing into a perfect tree, though not every dimension of the tree is manifest as it grows across the years. This "organic unity" of the Bible frees us to read each passage or book in the context of its respective context, locally and as part of the whole canon. The structural unity-in-diversity of the theological framework does not originate with the reader or any system imposed on the text but with the unity-in-diversity of the divine and human authors of the text. It has unity because of its one divine Author, while it has diversity because the divine plan (story) unfolds in and through history.

Understanding the Bible in this way is a powerful reminder that God communicates as a master storyteller, often using grand historical narratives and epic poetry and complex proverbs as well as didactic lessons and apocalyptic dreams. The thread holding all of these together is the reality of God's overarching authorship, as well as God's bringing about the redemption of a people climactically in and through the life, death, and resurrection of Jesus. Put simply, it is God's gospel that unfolds across the whole of the Bible.

The complex act of divine wisdom revealed across the Scriptures by the organic ordering and executing of redemptive history illustrates the difficulty of any simplistic rendering of unity and difference. From the perspective of human history, we encounter countless unique characters along the way as well as diverse genres through which the story is told—from epic poetry to enigmatic parables to apocalyptic dreams to autobiographical prayers. From one angle, this is a collection of many stories. From another angle, it is a single story. How do we make sense of this, and what is the significance to the task of understanding unity and diversity?

The "Jesus story" makes sense only in light of all that has come before it. The abiding promise of God's presence to Abraham in Genesis 12 makes apparent that God's presence comes in diverse ways and times. God came to Moses in the burning bush. God came to Israel in the wilderness in the cloud by day and the fire by night. God's presence settled on the holy of holies in Solomon's temple—and entrance into the holy of holies came only once a year and only then by the high priest. Climactically, God's presence was manifest in the flesh with the coming of Jesus. This theme of God's presence will be consummated at the end of time in the new heavens and the new earth. Divine presence connects all the "stories" describing God showing up—and thereby connecting the Jesus story with all prior stories.[3]

Consider another example. The entire complex of meaning surrounding Israel's temple is required to understand what happened on the cross. The original context of the temple helps explain the meaning of terms like "sacrifice," "substitute," "atonement," and so on, which then are woven together into an interpretive framework for understanding the death of Jesus. Additionally, the great event of Israel's exodus from Egypt echoes across the Scriptures as the framework for understanding God's saving work in history. God delivered Israel out of bondage by an act of sovereign mercy in order that Israel's departure out of Egypt would secure their worship of Yahweh. This pattern of sovereign deliverance followed by worship forms the backbone of the New Testament proclamation of the gospel. When the people of Israel pleaded with God for a human king in order to successfully survive in the ancient world of competing empires, God granted their request (1 Sam 8). Saul was anointed Israel's first king, followed by David and then Solomon. During this period, not only were there clear signs that these earthly kings were morally flawed and unable to fulfill Israel's desire for protection against the competing empires, but also the yearning for an earthly king undermined Israel's loyalty to the sovereign king of the universe, Yahweh. This conflicted relationship between earthly institutions and divine realities remains a

3. For a detailed treatment of the presence of God across the entire canon, see G. K. Beale, *The Temple and the Church's Mission: A Biblical Theology of the Dwelling Place of God*, New Studies in Biblical Theology (Downers Grove, IL: IVP Academic, 2004).

consistent theme—most poignantly picked up with the inauguration of the ministry of Jesus. The divine king of the universe announces salvation not by virtue of earthly power or position but by virtue of weakness and humility. The narrative thread of the "kingdom" runs consistently from Saul to the end of the book of Revelation, finding its ironic climax in the life and death of an itinerant prophet who is also the king of the universe.

Notably, it is not simply Old Testament events that serve as the interpretive ground for New Testament events—all that follows the cross and resurrection of Jesus are interpreted through the lens of these archetypal events. Followers of Jesus must die to themselves even as Jesus died (Rom 6:5). Baptism comes to be viewed as a theological echo of Jesus's death on the cross (Rom 6:4). Likewise, the resurrection of Jesus forms a pattern for the life of the Christian even prior to their own resurrection (Rom 6:5).

A wise interpreter of Scripture seeks to capture this historical unfolding of themes that faithfully represent God's authorship of the grand narrative of redemption—beginning with creation and climaxing in the death and resurrection of Jesus.[4] The links between passages should not be arbitrary, nor should they wrench any passage from its original meaning. When God asks Abraham to offer his son Isaac as a sacrifice in Genesis 22, surely it is not arbitrary to see the way in which this prepares for God himself offering up his son Jesus as a sacrifice. The former episode (Abraham/Isaac) prepares us to see more clearly the latter (God/Jesus). In the life, death, and resurrection of Jesus, God has done a brand-new work—but it is a work he prepared beforehand in actions and described by terms (redemption, adoption, sacrifice, and so on) that are directly applied to the work of Jesus.

As the Old Testament prophets wrote, "for those with eyes to see" God revealed the gospel progressively over many successive eras,

---

4. On this point see the forthcoming work edited by D. A. Carson, Gregory K. Beale, Benjamin Gladd, and Andrew Naselli, *Dictionary of the New Testament Use of the Old Testament* (Grand Rapids: Baker Academic, 2023).

and embedded it as the story of many diverse individuals and institutions. God's revelation was not delivered in a static fashion, as if he were offering a theology lecture, then simply recounting the lecture in linear form. God's revelation of the gospel unfolds over time. When the apostle Paul cited Genesis 15:6 in Romans 4:3 ("Abraham believed God, and it was counted to him as righteousness") it was because the beginning of the gospel of God's gracious dealings with his people goes all the way back to Genesis.

Ultimately, God is the "glue" that holds the Scripture together. God is a being whose trinitarian character belies easy oversimplifications. God's voice is not a monotone. God's mercy is a surprising dimension of God's justice. He faithfully acts as he has promised, often contrary to expectations, forgiving when we expected judgment and bringing life from death. God's promise to Abraham's particular descendants is a promise to all nations. He gives unbreakable laws and yet surprisingly suffers punishment himself on behalf of guilty parties. God inspires poetry and apocalyptic literature, which are to be read very differently than law, attesting to the richness and depth and thickness of human life. God presents an overarching purpose to history found by paying attention to the overarching story of redemption, but the overarching story does not minimize or undermine the reality of day-to-day experiences.

There are different kinds of differences. Some are genre related. Some are owing to the diversity of human authors through whom God has chosen to work. Each human author wrote with goals and purposes without loss of his own distinctive personality and context. Some of the New Testament letters were written with specific churches and situations in mind. Others were written with more general audiences and purposes in view. Some of the biblical authors used terms in unique ways, recognizable only in the fuller context of their entire corpus of writings. Some differences may be accounted for by diversity of pastoral concerns, others by differing theological motives, and still others by distinct literary styles of the human author in different redemptive historical epochs.[5] God works through these human vessels, with the emphasis on working *through them*.

An adequate theological vision should seek to capture the complexity and richness of the unity and diversity of Scripture. Such a theological vision is deeply instilled with wisdom—able to understand and embrace the varieties of God's speech.[6] Wisdom knows that God communicates truth; truth, however, is often dressed not as a tenseless proposition but as poetry, providence, or proverb. Wisdom breathes deeply as God narrates the story of redemption across many historically diverse circumstances and fills in many subplots to shape our own view of the past. On the surface, life may seem ordinary, without much apparent purpose, and with the odds stacked against it. But somehow, in the mystery of God's providence, the very foundations of history will bring all things to their proper consummation. It is this ability to "see" history differently and our lives as part of that redemptive story that comes by seeing the patterns revealed across the Scriptures.

In Genesis, Joseph's imprisonment at the hands of Pharaoh seemed like a divine defeat. But this was no mere accident of history—just one chapter in the unfolding of the divine plan. This execution of the divine plan did not remove culpability from Joseph's brothers. They were fully responsible for their actions. Yet in a strange manner, these same actions furthered the divine plan. Joseph finally tells his brothers, "You intended to harm me, but God intended it for good to accomplish what is now being done, the saving of many lives" (Gen 50:20 NIV). The unfolding of God's redemptive purposes in the events surrounding the life of Joseph did not remove the story from the plane

---

5. See D. A. Carson, "Unity and Diversity in the New Testament: The Possibility of Systematic Theology" in *Scripture and Truth*, ed. D. A. Carson and John Woodbridge (Grand Rapids: Zondervan, 1983), 65–95.

6. Richard B. Gaffin Jr. writes, "Revelation is not so much divinely given gnosis to provide us with knowledge concerning the nature of God, man, and the world as it is divinely inspired interpretation of God's activity of redeeming men so that they might worship and serve him in the world." Gaffin, "Introductory Essay," in *Redemptive History and Biblical Interpretation: The Shorter Writings of Geerhardus Vos*, ed. Richard B. Gaffin Jr. (Phillipsburg, NJ: P&R, 1980), xvii.

of human history. The Egyptian political and penal systems were not separated out from the divine story, neither were Pharaoh's seemingly arbitrary whims disconnected from God's providential involvement and oversight. God works in and through human history without making it any less human. Biblical history is at once both factual (Joseph's brothers are culpable) and purposeful (God remains faithful to the promises originally delivered to Abraham). Our theological vision ought to reflect this blending of the divine and the human in the unfolding of Scripture—a lens to understand our own lives.

The very rich diversity of forms in the canon strongly argues that our model of unity must be sufficiently complex to account for the surprising diversity in the divine communication of redemption. Wisdom, rather than mere observation, recognizes this complexity and is not daunted by it.[7] Thinking of redemptive history as a "model" of unity and diversity pushes us to suppose that unity should not swallow up diversity, but neither should diversity block all attempts at finding meaningful unity. On this side of the grave, wisdom encourages us to see how valuable and unexpected their relationship is.

Marriage: A Relationship of the One and the Many

Marriage may be the most pervasive metaphor in the canon, highlighting the manner in which the overriding concern for unity actually protects the significant differences represented in the relationship. The description of marriage begins in the early chapters of Genesis and runs through the wedding supper of the Lamb in Revelation 19. The words instituting marriage in Genesis 2 do not merely function to cement a social contract between consenting

---

7. Oliver O'Donovan comments on how Christians relate to the overwhelming diversity of political situations: "No context is the same as any other, no one theological undertaking will exactly mirror another; and yet as each enterprise takes seriously its own authorization in the gospel of Jesus Christ, it will find that it is in a symbiotic relation to every other enterprise that does so. The gospel is one gospel which has manifold implications for us as we believe and obey it." O'Donovan, *The Desire of the Nations*, 21.

parties but are a deep and enduring theological claim on the man and woman's reflected identity as a unity-in-diversity. The final words in Revelation remind us of the telos of all creation—namely, the creature's consummation in the eternal relational bond to Jesus. Marriage is both a concrete institution created by God and a metaphor that points to the relationship of God's people to God. Throughout the New Testament, the apostles also use the analogy of marriage to describe the unity-in-diversity of the church in its relationship to Jesus. The marriage analogy is further extended with the organic analogy of vines and branches (John 15) as well as a human body with many different but interconnected parts (1 Cor 12 and Rom 12). The overriding unity does not minimize or undermine the significant diversities within these analogies—the hand cannot say to the foot, "I do not need you."

The institution of marriage illustrates the concreteness of the unity-in-diversity pattern and points at the underlying reality of persons as fully persons when they are in relationship. Illustrated by marriage, "diverse-persons-in-a-united-relationship" expresses an essential dimension of being created to flourish in the context of being bound to others. We flourish when we belong to each other in a natural manner. Marriage is intended as a relationship that manifests this in peculiar ways, fundamentally owing to the key differences that wife and husband bring to the marriage. In marriage, two human beings with considerable differences are bound together. This is true of all human relationships, but what marks marriage as peculiar is the concrete physical differences between wife and husband. This difference is the vehicle by which they are to express their commitment. Difference matters in marriage.

Genesis 1:27 is the introduction of the male-female construct that prepares for the description of marriage in Genesis 2:20–25. The "male and female" language of Genesis 1–2 points to a relationship of difference. While maleness and femaleness are not grounded in sexual or gendered resemblance to God, they do call attention to a covenantal relationship of difference and similarity.[8] This is how both Mark's and Matthew's Gospels interpret the use of "male and female" in Genesis 1:27. In Mark 10:3–9 and Matthew 19:1–7, Jesus connects the creation of "male and female" in Genesis 1 with the covenant of marriage established in Genesis 2. He moves without comment from Genesis 1:27 to Genesis 2:21 as if no explanation were needed, assuming a natural and necessary connection between male and female.

God has created us as social creatures who bear individual responsibility for our actions, as well as being "incomplete" outside a social network of relationships. In an important sense, persons find their meaning and significance only in relation to another person different from themselves.[9] The primary social relationship to which marriage points, but is not a substitute for, is between human persons and God.[10] The bridegroom-bride imagery is one of the earthly metaphors created to point at the divine-human relationship, with the clear proviso that all human relationships are but a faint reflection of the divine-human relationship simply by virtue of the radical difference between God and his human creatures. The mystery at the heart of marriage, of two becoming one, is an important analogy of the relationship between Christ and his church. The relational bond is mysterious precisely because of the significant differences between the partners. They are not the same—resulting in a richer, deeper, and more profound union.

Broken marriage is highlighted in Scripture as a strong analogy to the disordering of the divine-human relationship. The language of adultery is used as a powerful analogy of the ways in which God's

---

8. See Gordon Hugenberger, *Marriage as a Covenant: A Study of Biblical Law and Ethics Governing Marriage Developed from the Perspective of Malachi* (Leiden: Brill, 1994), for a biblical-theological argument grounding marriage in a covenantal framework. Though Hugenberger draws his argument specifically from Malachi, it is much wider in scope and draws attention to the echoes across the Old Testament canon.

9. See Miroslav Volf, *Exclusion and Embrace.*

10. This is most clearly elaborated in Ephesians 5, where marriage is directly compared to the relationship between Christ and the church. Significantly, there abounds a "mystery" at the heart of both relationships—of how the two could become one while remaining two.

people stray from the covenant relationship with God.[11] The overlapping of the concepts of adultery and idolatry illuminate the disordered desires of the human heart when it strays from God.[12] There
is no more powerful parable of this reality than the book of Hosea.
The prophet Hosea was given instructions to marry a prostitute, not
because she had turned away from her prostitution, but because
Hosea was to express a love for her not grounded in what he received
in return. This served as a powerful reminder of God's love given
freely, not based on what God received in return. Human dysfunction, by which the original covenant relationship to God is broken
in the end, is not an obstacle too great for God's sovereign love.[13] In
Romans 8:31–38 Paul summarizes this remarkable reality that nothing, not even human dysfunction, can separate us from divine love.

Humans have been created for meaningful relationships. We are
not intended to be lonely automatons. Even the most introverted
need relationships to discover the fullness of who they are. The primary relationship that gives meaning is the relationship of the creature to the Creator of the universe, who is wise, just, and loving. In
a committed relationship to the Creator, those very same characteristics are reflected in the human character. This reflective relationship ultimately satisfies the human longing for significance. The
principle in ordinary terms is simple—those who you hang out with
influence who you are and who you become. The adage "like father
like son" rehearses this simple social reality. Children are profoundly
influenced by their parents both in view of nature and nurture. This
likeness is not deterministic or wholly exhaustive. Children are
never *exact* copies of their parents. But there is a dynamic at work
between individuals and the communities in which they are formed.

---

11. The best biblical-theological treatment of the relationship between adultery and idolatry
is Raymond Ortlund Jr., *Whoredom: God's Unfaithful Wife in Biblical Theology*, New Studies in
Biblical Theology (Grand Rapids: Eerdmans, 1996).

12. See the book of Hosea for an extended exposition of the overlapping character of the
concepts of adultery and idolatry.

13. See Hugenberger's rich theological work *Marriage as a Covenant* for an extended argument to this effect.

Individuals are both personal agents in their own right and "individuals-in-community" whose identity is bound up with their communities, both for good and for ill.

Sociologists use the term "social capital" to refer to the economic benefits accruing to people by virtue of the social networks they inhabit.[14] Social capital is a difficult thing to precisely quantify, but it is clear that the relationships one is embedded in have much to do with economic flourishing or floundering.[15] There is economic value in having a strong family support network, a circle of friends that includes contacts with key leaders, neighbors who provide help in time of trouble, and so on. Strong social networks also have value in terms of job placement and promotion opportunities. Students with a strong family support system have a much better chance at academic success. Coaches put into place strong support networks to encourage their athletes to progress toward strong physical and mental conditioning. Cities and towns thrive by virtue of the strength of their community organizations linking their citizens together in meaningful ways. Conversely, those towns and cities that fail often lack strong mediating structures, such as churches, synagogues, and other voluntary organizations.[16] Social-survey data strongly suggests that individuals with a high degree of commitment to a local church are much less likely to engage in spousal abuse, less likely to abandon their children, and more likely to lead socially fulfilling lives.[17] This is never a perfect equation; churches can be dysfunctional. But broadly speaking, being committed to a strong community makes a positive

---

14. For one of the clearest expositions of "social capital," see Robert Putnam, "E Pluribus Unum," 137–74.

15. J. D. Vance, in *Hillbilly Elegy: A Memoir of a Family and Culture in Crisis* (New York: Harper, 2016), powerfully illustrates the lack of social capital in much of deep rural America, what he refers to as "hillbilly culture."

16. See Timothy Carney, *Alienated America: Why Some Places Thrive While Other Places Collapse* (New York: Harper, 2019).

17. Brad Wilcox, "The Latest Social Science Is Wrong: Religion Is Good for Families and Kids," *Washington Post*, December 15, 2015, https://www.washingtonpost.com/posteverything/wp/2015/12/15/the-latest-social-science-is-wrong-religion-is-good-for-families-and-kids/.

contribution to a person's character. Human relationships matter because of the strength of the commitments that bind us together as the means to effectively deal with our differences. The bonds that tie people together are stronger when their differences are part and parcel of their commitment to each other.

People in long-lasting marriages are often much more realistic about each partner's flaws. Marriage is hard work and ordinarily is not lived on the mountaintop of passionate sexual delight and pure emotional happiness. The tediousness and ordinariness of marriage is actually its greatest benefit over time, as lifelong commitment cuts against the grain of self-interest. The divine love for which marriage is a metaphor reveals an inner logic to the relational character of persons, found most deeply in the gospel. The logic is this: God's life-giving love toward us is not earned by virtue of what we offer to him, but rather is expressed in the divine grace toward us in the sacrifice of his Son for our forgiveness and well-being. It is not what God gets from us that matters, but what God gives by his grace. Marriage reminds us that it is not what we get from the other that matters, but what we give. The diversity at the heart of marriage reflects this strange logic of the gospel, by which we get life by giving life away—the very means by which our union to Christ is rich and deep and satisfying.

THE TRINITY: THE MYSTERY
OF THE ONE AND THE MANY

If marriage is the most consistent scriptural analogy for our cove-nantal relationship with God, theologians across the ages have con-sidered the Trinity as the most significant model for understanding the unity-in-diversity of the created order. Without betraying the deep mystery at the heart of Scripture's confession of the Trinity, we can still recognize that the perennial question of unity and diver-sity is reflected in Scripture's testimony to God's tripersonal nature. God's triunity and the consistent concern with the relationship of unity and diversity across the New Testament appear to argue for a strong analogy between the relationships in the Trinity and creaturely relationships of unity-in-diversity.[18] The nature of the analogy may seem straightforward, but as historians of theology know, the precise nature of the analogy is quite difficult to pin down.

Theologians have long spoken into two particular questions: How close does the creation reflect the Creator? and, How is it possible to describe the relationship of "reflection" (that is, the creation reflecting the Creator) without standing on both sides of the relationship? At one end of the spectrum are those who have argued that if God created the world, then the world must reflect the God who made it.[19] At the other end lie those who are wary of too closely equating the Creator with the creation.[20] While our theological intuitions might lean one direction or the other, it is important that we affirm that God is the ground of how we are to think about the created order.

Many theologians who have affirmed a strongly reflective relationship between God and the world have emphasized the three persons in the Trinity as a social community with integral relationships between them. Part of the rationale for this emphasis is that it provides theological grounds for the relational character of human persons—as reflective of the God who made them. This framework is intended to combat the dangers of hyper-individualism in Western culture by providing a basis for a thicker social polity rooted in communities

18. Miroslav Volf comments, "The question is not whether the Trinity should serve as a model for human community; the question is rather in which respects and to what extent it should do so." Volf, "The Trinity Is Our Social Program: The Doctrine of the Trinity and the Shape of Social Engagement," Modern Theology 14, no. 3 (1998): 405.

19. A lucid and compelling exposition of this argument can be found in Peter Leithart, Traces of the Trinity: Signs of God in Creation and Human Experience (Grand Rapids: Brazos, 2015). Leithart sketches out the vast number of perichoretic (interrelated) relationships in the created order, almost all of which are barely noticeable to late modern, democratic, individualistic eyes. All things are what they are because of the indwelling presence of other things in them. This is mostly clearly seen for Leithart in human relationships, which require an affirmation of "individuals-in-community" to account for their genuine identity.

20. Calvin and post-Reformation orthodoxy more generally stood on this side of the spectrum. Calvin argued that Scripture does not speculate about the relationship of human personhood to the divine persons, but Scripture does affirm that the language of "persons" as applied to the Godhead is indeed scriptural and the church should not shy away from using this language. See John Calvin, Institutes of the Christian Religion (1559), ed. John T. McNeill, trans. Ford Lewis Battles, Library of Christian Classics (Philadelphia: Westminster, 1960), 1.13.

of persons-in-relationships.[21] It privileges divine relationality (three persons in relationship) and deemphasizes the unity and simplicity of God. Other theologians have argued that this perspective comes close to denying classical monotheism, and it is not necessary to conceive the persons of the Trinity as individuals-in-relationship in order to combat the ills of Western individualism. Rather, God's gracious and just moral character is an adequate basis for defining a virtuous society and criticizing hyper-individualism.[22]

Both sides agree that the problem with modernity is its commitment to individualism corresponding to a disengaged "objectivity" that sees the human person as one object in the universe independent of other individuals. This is possible only when human persons are considered as static entities similar in kind to any other physical object. On this rendering, modern Western culture has pushed aside the older social order and privileged the static physical order.[23] The describable universe resides in tangible material objects and cannot account for persons as integrally relational.[24] This perspective became particularly potent

---

21. One of the most significant voices in this regard is Colin Gunton, seen mostly clearly in his work *The One, the Three and the Many* (Cambridge: Cambridge University Press, 1993). Gunton seeks to rehabilitate notions of social cohesion through a greater emphasis on the divine trinitarian community. He supposes the theological root cause of hyper-individualism lies in its static understanding of human persons, which in turn is grounded in a prior commitment to a static notion of God. Gunton (incorrectly, in my mind) lays most of the blame for static understandings of human nature at the feet of Augustine and his alleged Platonizing tendencies. A most thoughtful and trenchant critique of Gunton's treatment of Augustine is Lewis Ayres, "(Mis)adventures in Trinitarian Ontology," in *The Trinity and an Entangled World: Relationality in Physical Science and Theology*, ed. John Polkinghorne (Grand Rapids: Eerdmans, 2010), 135–40. See also Lewis Ayres, *Augustine and the Trinity* (Cambridge: Cambridge University Press, 2010).

22. Two contemporary theologians worth mentioning in this regard are Katherine Sonderegger, *Systematic Theology*, vol. 1, *The Doctrine of God* (Minneapolis: Fortress, 2015); and Stephen Holmes, *The Quest for the Trinity: The Doctrine of God in Scripture, History and Modernity* (Downers Grove, IL: IVP Academic, 2012).

23. One might think of the relationship between these two orders as analogous to the way in which particle physics understands the relation between quantum objects and objects of ordinary perception. The core datum of the universe is in subatomic particles, though it "appears" as if ordinary objects exist in an otherwise-predictable Newtonian ordered universe.

24. This was coterminous with the rise of Descartes's description of a human as a lonely "thinking thing." See René Descartes, *Meditations on First Philosophy* (1641), in *Discourse on Method and Meditations on First Philosophy*, trans. Donald A. Cress, 3rd ed. (Indianapolis: Hackett, 1993), 46–105.

with the advent of the modern democratic nation-state, in which each individual person is politically empowered by his or her right to vote. On this view, individuals are no longer simply subjects of the reigning king but are independent and autonomous political agents.[25]

With the enormous economic benefits of early modern democratization came a dark shadow. Charles Dickens and others in the latter part of the nineteenth century wrote in gloomy detail of the dehumanizing consequences of the Industrial Revolution, as well as the potential for political chaos without a wise sovereign overseeing the direction of the empire and constraining the dysfunctions of industrialization. In the twentieth century, the mass destruction wrought by the world wars served as the warning against the utopian pretensions of the modern world. The root suspicion lay in the claim that modernity freed individuals from moral constraints, leaving them with nothing but the arbitrariness of their own natural desires. Individuals, viewed this way, inevitably became mere objects to be exploited—by robber barons, by mass marketers, by political tyrants, or by their own self-destructive inner tendencies.

Theologians across the spectrum suppose that the Trinity in some fashion can provide important conceptual resources to solve the "problem of modernity," though they lean in different directions for a solution.[26] There may be no consensus among Christian theologians on the proper use of the analogy between the Trinity and the human social order, but there remains agreement that the Trinity is an important model of unity-in-diversity across Scripture.[27] Drawing attention to

---

25. Nathan O. Hatch skillfully sketches out the religious consequences of this transformation of the political sphere in his magisterial work *The Democratization of American Christianity*. Also note that the cultural transformations of the Industrial Revolution democratized work and vocation. No longer was vocation tied to the skill passed on from father to son, but work itself exploded outside of the traditional craft and guild society and was reducible in many instances to its physical components.

26. On this see the collection of essays: Kevin J. Vanhoozer, ed., *The Trinity in a Pluralistic Age: Theological Essays on Culture and Religion* (Grand Rapids: Eerdmans, 1993).

27. Miroslav Volf follows this same general line: "To think in Trinitarian ways means to escape this dichotomy between universalization and pluralization. If unity and multiplicity are equiprimal in God, then He is the ground of both unity and multiplicity. Since God is the

the Trinity as model leads to two key texts in the New Testament—
Ephesians 4:1–6 and 1 Corinthians 12:4–11. There are a host of other
trinitarian texts in the New Testament, but these two describe the
analogy between the divine persons and the human social order.[28] The
trinitarian references in the two texts read as follows:

> There is one body and one Spirit—just as you were called to
> the one hope that belongs to your call—one Lord, one faith,
> one baptism, one God and Father of all, who is over all and
> through all and in all. (Eph 4:4–6)

> Now there are varieties of gifts, but the same Spirit; and there
> are varieties of service, but the same Lord; and there are vari-
> eties of activities, but it is the same God who empowers them
> all in everyone. (1 Cor 12:4–6)

Despite the differences in context and tone, the arguments in 1
Corinthians 12 and Ephesians 4 are strikingly similar. The reference
to Father, Son, and Spirit as the ground for correctly understanding
the social fabric of the church is preceded by discussion of diverse
gifts (the gifts of the Spirit in 1 Cor 12, and the gifts of ecclesial officers in Eph 4) and a reference to the body metaphor—one body with
many members.

On the surface, both texts appear to address the delicate balance
of the unity and diversity of the body—the metaphor suggests to
some that Paul is primarily concerned with protecting an appropriate
diversity in the church rather than arguing for its unity. The history of
interpretation of both texts makes scant mention of their trinitarian

---

one God, reality does not, as Aristotle's metaphor suggests, degenerate into individual scenes
like a bad play; yet since the one God is a communion of the divine persons, the world drama
does not degenerate into a boring monologue. Trinitarian thinking suggests that in a successful
world drama, unity and multiplicity must enjoy a complementary relationship." Volf, *After
Our Likeness: The Church as the Image of the Trinity*, Sacra Doctrina: Christian Theology for a
Postmodern Age (Grand Rapids: Eerdmans, 1997), 191.

28. On the wider matter of Paul's understanding of the Trinity across his corpus, see
Wesley Hill, *Paul and the Trinity: Persons, Relations, and the Pauline Letters* (Grand Rapids:
Eerdmans, 2015).

shape, but rather interprets the trinitarian reference by means of the body metaphor. Like the body with many members, so the Trinity is one with many members. But in fact, neither of these texts appeal to the Trinity in terms of diverse divine persons in relation to each other. The appeal to the Trinity is oriented to the oneness of the church, not principally its diversity. The repetition of "one" in the Ephesians text must drive the interpretative task, rather than being subsumed under a preexisting assumption about the "persons-in-community" of the Trinity. Likewise, the language of "same" in 1 Corinthians 12 hammers home the point not of unity-in-diversity, but of oneness.

Setting the context well, Ben Witherington summarizes the background to the Ephesians 4 passage:

> Probably citing an early confessional formula, Paul offers up some of the practical and theological bases of that unity in v. 4, with a sevenfold use of the word "one." Father, Son, and Spirit turn out to be the basis for the existence of and the exhortation to unity. A Trinitarian structure anchors this statement, with the one Spirit anchoring v. 4, the one Lord anchoring v. 5, and the one God and the Father of all anchoring v. 6. The repetition of the terms "one" and "all" and the asyndeton here have rhetorical force, adding weight to the exhortation.[29]

On the surface of both passages is a straightforward concern for the unity of the church. The trinitarian framework appeals to the overriding concern for the way in which the church is rooted in the reality of the Father, Son, and Spirit. The Trinity is not being used as a model of the church in its diversity but in its unity. What then is the nature of the argument?

Commentary on these verses in the early church emphasized the fragmented nature of the church as the apostle Paul's fundamental concern. Representatively, John Chrysostom comments, "The

---

29. Ben Witherington III, *The Letters to Philemon, the Colossians, and the Ephesians: A Socio-rhetorical Commentary on the Captivity Epistles* (Grand Rapids: Eerdmans, 2007), 286.

purpose for which the Spirit was given was to bring into unity all who remain separated by ethnic and cultural divisions: young and old, rich and poor, women and men."[30] The work of the Spirit is to unify the diverse elements of the body of Christ, transcending ethnic, gender, and social boundaries. Even as the Father created everything in harmony, so the Spirit works to draw everything back into harmony. Thus in accordance with the work of the Spirit, the members of the (ecclesial) body, diverse as they may be, are to strive for unity.

But what exactly is "unity"? Is it closer to a "union" or to a "community"? Is it more like the "two-becoming-one" of a chemical compound consisting of two separate elements that, when conjoined, have a single chemical makeup, or a community of diverse people agreeing on common beliefs, lived out with common traditions, and expressing common habits?

There were voices in the early church that said unity meant union, not merely community. The hope of the church, according to Jerome, is the consummation of the kingdom of God, when the collective members of the body of Christ will finally be restored as the "perfect man."[31] Commenting on Ephesians 4:5–6, he writes, "There is one Lord and one God, because the dominion of the Father and Son is a single Godhead. The faith is said to be one because we believe similarly in Father, Son and Holy Spirit as one God."[32] Unity is not simply diverse elements working together, but the actual union of diverse elements into one. The "many" take on a different reality in their being constituted "one."

Augustine viewed Ephesians 4:6 as trinitarian not only by virtue of its appeal to the Spirit, Son, and Father but also because of its emphasis on the unity of the being of God: "Those who read very closely

---

30. John Chrysostom, *Homily on Ephesians* 9.4.1–3, quoted in *Galatians, Ephesians, Philippians*, ed. Mark J. Edwards, Ancient Christian Commentary on Scripture, New Testament 8 (Downers Grove, IL: InterVarsity Press, 1999), 159.

31. Jerome, *Epistle to the Ephesians* 2.4.3–4, quoted in Edwards, *Galatians, Ephesians, Philippians*, 160.

32. Jerome, *Epistle to the Ephesians* 2.4.5–6, quoted in Edwards, *Galatians, Ephesians, Philippians*, 160.

recognize the Trinity in this passage. ... All things are *from God,* who owes his existence to no one. All things are *through him,* as though to say through the Mediator. All things are *in him,* as though to say in the One who contains them, that is reconciles them into one."[33] The persons of the Godhead have not become distinguishable realities but in their respective persons accomplish the divine mission in unison.

Roy Ciampa and Brian Rosner argue that Paul's primary concern in 1 Corinthians 12 is worship that is fitting for the one true and living God, as the body of Christ stands over against the idolatrous and pluralistic background of the Corinthian Christians, from which the church has been redeemed.

> The main emphasis of the chapter, then, turns out to be the oneness of the Christian community based on the oneness of the God/Lord/Spirit who establishes and serves as the patron of the community (in implied contradistinctions to divisions, or at least a lack of unity, that might be expected to exist among pagans pursuing diverse blessings from different patron gods/idols, each presumed to offer different benefits/gifts to its followers).[34]

They emphasize the irony of a reference to monotheism (and its accompanying command of monolatry) as grounded by appeal to the Trinity. In a pluralistic context, Paul was well aware that difference quickly turned into division, rooted in the belief in many gods. By contrast, the oneness of God was in fact the framework within which monolatry became compelling.

The upshot of this brief exegetical interlude is that the trinitarian shape of these passages is in fact a surprising reference to the oneness of God. The repeated emphasis on "one" in the Ephesians 4 text makes this clear. There are not three gods, but one God who works

---

33. Augustine, *On Faith and the Creed* 19, quoted in Edwards, *Galatians, Ephesians, Philippians,* 161 (emphasis original).

34. Roy E. Ciampa and Brian Rosner, *The First Letter to the Corinthians,* Pillar New Testament Commentary (Grand Rapids: Eerdmans, 2010), 561.

all things.[35] There are not many members in the Godhead, each of whom is separable from the others, as there are not many faiths, nor many baptisms, nor many bodies, nor many hopes. There is but one faith, one baptism, one body, one hope, one God.

These passages also show the significance of the unity of the Godhead as the ground for constraining the church's intrinsic tendencies toward fragmentation. They do not draw any direct analogy between the divine persons and human persons, though they do point at the way in which human persons are to "work together" as a reflection of the singular mission of Father, Son, and Spirit. The diversity of the church is derived from the providential ordering of God to illuminate its rich and complex unity. While diversity always poses a threat to unity, it should not be construed as always and only a threat. The source of differing gifts lies in the one God, and therefore they may never rightly be grounds for divisions in the church but rather opportunities for a richer and more nuanced unity.[36] The diverse officers of Ephesians 4 should not be construed as a democracy wherein all simply vote according to their own desires; rather, they work toward a consensus reflecting the unity-in-diversity of the mission of the church.[37]

A brief comment on John 17 is also in order, as this text is often referred to as the key New Testament passage addressing the unity of the church.[38] The relationship between Father and Son at the heart of

---

35. The three persons of the Trinity are not collapsible into an undifferentiated unity, but neither does the threeness of God cancel out the one being of God. In this regard, the threeness and the oneness of God are equally fundamental. See Volf, "The Trinity Is Our Social Program," 403–23.

36. In a preceding passage, 1 Cor 11:2–16, Paul leverages the distinction between the Father and the Son to provide a model for at least one micro-community—husband and wife. Whatever else may be said about the echoes of unity-in-diversity in this passage, the overriding claim in v. 12, "All things are from God," regulates any appropriation of the diversity-in-unity paradigm. The mysterious union of the husband-wife relationship that Paul so eloquently addresses in Ephesians 5 is rooted in the common source from which both husband and wife have come—namely, the one God.

37. I address this issue at greater length in chapter 8.

38. A more extensive treatment of the Trinity in the Gospel of John can be found in Royce Gruenler, The Trinity in the Gospel of John: A Thematic Commentary on the Fourth Gospel (Grand Rapids: Baker, 1986).

this passage serves as a template for the relationships among Jesus's followers. However, we should not equate the divine relationship of Father and Son to the human relationships in the church. Verse 3 affirms there is only one "true God," which frames the argument on the unity of the church. And there is no mention of diversity in the Godhead but simply an appeal to the unity of the Father and Son in verse 21. Throughout the passage, unity is grounded in the dynamic of love, which is so prevalent in the previous chapters (John 15–16). The relational dimension between Father and Son is simply and mysteriously affirmed alongside of monotheism. So the reality of the church's unity (by virtue of the love manifest among its members—17:11) is mysteriously affirmed alongside the fundamental commitment to the church's important diversities.

We must preserve the otherness of God, so central to the biblical witness, while protecting genuine experiences of God among his creatures. There is deep mystery in the encounter with God side by side with an accurate comprehension of the God encountered. Ephesians 4 and 1 Corinthians 12 affirm the absolute oneness of God as the ground for the unity of the church, while refusing to ground the differences among members of the church to any differences in the divine persons of the Trinity. Both texts affirm the oneness of God as the ground of the "individuals-in-community" character of the church while not allowing us to peek behind the curtain of the divine community. The mystery of the Creator-creature relationship remains mysterious. The Creator and the creature are absolutely different and importantly similar at the same time.

This leads to the conclusion that the oneness of God is absolutely foundational to the biblical witness, but also mysterious. When God "shows up," his identity is never in doubt, but God's identity is never fully captured by the human encounter. In the aftermath of their many direct experiences of God, Israel was left speechless, wanting both to flee from God and to have more of God. Words are used to describe the experience, but the words never do justice to the full identity of

God who was genuinely present in the experience.[39] God is know-
able and unknowable at the same time. There thus remains a mystery
behind the experience of unity-in-difference in the church even while
the church should be crystal clear in its aspiration to experience this
unity-in-difference.

In the next chapter, I turn to the ways in which the church has
understood its unity-in-diversity across the ages, before then turning
to consider the ways the biblical models of Scripture, marriage, and
the Trinity, as well as the lessons from the history of the church, help
us understand how the church may better work toward an effective
unity-in-diversity in our own time.

---

39. Katherine Sonderegger writes of the "hidden presence" of God, "There is no end to
the Mystery of the One. The superabundant mystery of this predicate is not a sign of our *failure*
in knowledge, but rather our *success*. It is because we know truly and properly—because we
obey in faith the first commandment—that God is mystery. There is no veil that is lifted, such
that we see something or Someone beyond the One, even when we, by grace are past death."
Sonderegger, *Doctrine of God*, 24–25.

It has been granted to the Americans less than any other nation of the earth to realize on earth the visible unity of the Church of God.

—DIETRICH BONHOEFFER, *NO RUSTY SWORDS*

7

THE DIVERSE STORIES OF
THE CHURCH'S DIVERSITY

The Uniting and Dividing of Protestants

Ecclesiastical divisions in America in the twentieth century have most often happened along a Left-to-Right spectrum defined by the political language of conservative and liberal. Prior to the twentieth century, church divisions would have been defined in theological language—disputes over predestination or clerical authority or the sacraments. The Protestant solution to these differences was the embrace of diverse denominations. Methodists and Lutherans and Baptists and Presbyterians and Anglicans all belonged to a common Protestant tradition, but each held to their own peculiar theological distinctives. In this age of polarization, these standing differences among Protestant church bodies has come to be viewed as a tragic disaster. To many, denominationalism itself is the besetting sin of the American church, the legacy of its connection to the diverse ecclesiologies of the Protestant Reformation.[1] It is also one of the sharpest criticisms leveled at Protestants by Roman Catholics.[2]

---

1. See John Frame, *Evangelical Reunion: Denominations and the One Body of Christ* (Grand Rapids: Baker, 1991); Peter Leithart, *The End of Protestantism: Pursuing Unity in a Fragmented Church* (Grand Rapids: Brazos, 2016).

2. This is nicely summarized by Stephen Beale, "Just How Many Protestant Denominations Are There?," *National Catholic Register*, October 31, 2017, https://www.ncregister.com/blog/sbeale/just-how-many-protestant-denominations-are-there.

There has always been a diversity of churches in Christianity, but there is something about denominations, so the argument goes, that displays an unhealthy diversity or fragmentation. But exactly which kinds of diversity are healthy, and which are unhealthy? Is organizational and hierarchical unity an adequate historical and theological understanding of diversity and unity? Or, to the contrary, might organizational unity be neither a sufficient nor a necessary condition of the fulfilment of Jesus's words?

Before we consider these questions, note that there is little historical correlation between the organizational unity of the church and its vitality, its fidelity to the Great Tradition, or to its missionary calling. The house-church movement in China and the African Independent Churches are two notable modern examples that manifest little organizational unity but great missional energy and a desire to be faithful to the Great Tradition in their own cultural settings.[3] In both, the churches are more Protestant in character, but they formally do not belong to any Protestant or Roman Catholic body. These "new" ecclesiological shapes took form when the church spread into lands that were not party to the great schisms in the history of the church—the East-West schism in 1054 and the Protestant–Roman Catholic schism in 1517. The churches in China gained a foothold not because of organizational connections to other churches but because of their intense missionary zeal and fidelity to the Great Tradition. The state has not been protective or even neutral with respect to the church, but often has persecuted the church.[4] Without state sanction

---

3. Rodney Stark goes so far as to argue that the "free religious marketplace" is the reason why churches have thrived in the American setting in contrast to the European settings. The sheer diversity of churches in America has meant, according to Stark, that they have to expend greater energy to build a congregation in order to sustain their own vocation. This "competition" forces churches to be clearer about their mission and their audience. See Stark, *The Triumph of Christianity* (San Francisco: HarperOne, 2011), especially chapter 20, "Pluralism and American Piety."

4. The most striking example of the church's vitality in a hostile missionary setting is surely China over the last fifty years. This reality is poignantly portrayed in David Aikman, *Jesus in Beijing* (New York: Regnery, 2003). For detailed demographic data on Christianity in China see Daniel H. Bays, *A New History of Christianity in China* (Malden, MA: Wiley-Blackwell,

or support, these house churches often took shape in sharp contrast to the cultural and political structures that surrounded them, while also not mirroring the structures of churches in the West. The political pressures on the house churches remains intense in many parts of China, and as a result they have retained a "movement" structure that looks very different from ecclesial structures in the West. Time will tell how long this structure will persist.

History also shows far too many instances whereby organizational structures have permitted and encouraged churches to seek public recognition and access to the corridors of power, both of which are frequently dangerous. These temptations may fall on large organizational bodies of churches or small independent bodies of churches. The church fulfills its mission neither because it is large or small, organizationally united or not, but by other measures altogether. The history of the church itself bears out this claim, as does the apostolic testimony.

In what follows, I look at the historical contexts both of the diversity of the church and the church's sense of dealing with diversity that have influenced the church's present identity. I will also examine the ways the church has conceived of the unity toward which it is to strive. Thinking historically about unity and diversity as it relates to the church might aid the church in navigating its mission in the present.[5]

Before beginning, we do well to remember that experiences of diversity are not always problematic. Diverse readings of biblical texts often illuminate depths of meaning not illuminated by the private readings of an individual. Listening to diverse voices in a congregation may prevent the abuse of power when all authority would otherwise be consolidated into the hands of a few. And as noted earlier, the early church confidently affirmed the integrity of four different

---

2011), and Todd Johnson and Gina Zurlo, eds., *World Christian Encyclopedia: A Comparative Survey of Churches and Religions in the Modern World,* 3rd ed. (Edinburgh: Edinburgh University Press, 2020).

5. The evidence suggests that churches in America that over-adapt to the pluralist impulse inevitably decline, but ironically churches that under-adapt by sequestering themselves into homogeneous communities lose their vitality and decline. See Stark, *Triumph of Christianity,* especially chapter 20.

Gospels (Matthew, Mark, Luke, and John) and saw no need to harmonize them. Jesus's reality and that of the kingdom he ushered in were too deep and too rich and too complex to be captured by a single account. In each of these ways, diversity actually contributed to a fuller and more thorough understanding of the complex world God has created and redeemed.

The other side of that reminder, however, is that Jesus commanded his disciples that the church be united (John 17). Across the ages, church divisions have often undermined this mandate, and yet no enduring consensus has ever been reached as to how to bring to pass the unity at which Jesus was pointing.[6] "Ecumenism" is the word often given to the project of unifying the church across its many divisions. But there is a deep divide over the very concept of ecumenism in our day—between those who suppose that church unity is *the* primary goal of our time, and those who suppose ecumenism distracts from the core mission of the church. The all too easy dichotomy between the liberal push for inclusion and unity versus the evangelical commitment to mission and evangelism masks the underlying complexity of the theological identity of the church. If the church is called to mission and to unity, how can these be reconciled? The beginnings of an answer can be found by not confusing these two constructs. The mission of the church is not its unity, but neither is its unity identical to its mission. How could this be so? We begin to answer this question by exploring the church's reckoning with these realities in historical context.

EMPIRE AND ECCLESIOLOGY: THE CHURCH'S HISTORICAL DIVERSITY

All sorts of diversity emerged early in the life of the church: theology, culture, polity, personality, language, and so on. Prior to Constantine in the early fourth century, church leadership fell most directly on

---

6. This may be due in part to disagreements about the nature of unity itself. See Geoffrey Bromiley, *The Unity and Disunity of The Church* (Grand Rapids: Eerdmans, 1958), for the most incisive modern treatment of this exegetical and theological issue.

the shoulders of bishops acting on behalf of their local network of churches. The organizational unity of the increasingly large number of local churches was only loosely configured. The geographically and culturally diverse churches were connected by the bishops in larger urban centers whose relationships with each other were informal and tied to the apostolic witness to Jesus and to the bishops' direct or indirect contact with the apostles or with those who had been in contact with the apostles. As a result, the significant controversies of the first three hundred years of the church's life were largely grounded in disputes about the proper way to interpret the writings and testimony of the apostles. There was no "supreme court" of bishops to definitively resolve the disagreements, but there was an original "constitution" to which appeals were made—the apostolic tradition as it had been passed down orally and in writing.

The primary concern of the bishops was maintaining the unity of the meaning of the confession that Jesus was Lord as it had been passed down to them from the apostles. The unity of the church derived from that confession of Jesus as Lord, or so it was hoped. A secondary concern was how Christians should get along with each other locally—manifesting a unity of spirit in their communities. As cultural outsiders during the first three centuries in most parts of the Roman Empire, churches retained a missionary ethos, thinking less about their own ecclesiastical unity than their witness to their still largely pagan neighbors.[7]

Significant differences emerged as the gospel spread into diverse cultural locations in the first three centuries of the church's life. There would be no "center" that held the bishops together organizationally or culturally until well into the fourth century. Emperor Constantine (272–337) engineered a state-sponsored unity of the church that became more permanent in the West under the emperor Theodosius

---

7. This distinction between the missionary task and the ecumenical task should not be so sharply divided as to suppose that one precluded the other. Both emerged from the apostolic testimony. See Alan Kreider, *The Patient Ferment of the Early Church: The Improbable Rise of Christianity in the Roman Empire* (Grand Rapids: Baker Academic, 2016).

in 380, and this effectively lasted for nearly a millennium.[8] From Constantine forward, ecumenical councils were called by various emperors (only some of which came at the request of the bishops) as the means to resolve disputes. The unity of the church was framed around the settled findings of the councils, and their declarations of the fourth and fifth centuries moved the church into a different mode of dealing with differences. The final court of appeal was still the apostolic tradition (the "faith delivered once and for all to the saints"), but now there was an executive branch of the church that enforced the tradition throughout the churches, or at least attempted to do so with imperial aid. This enforcement of authority was inextricably tied to the imperial authority by which the councils had been called and that granted to them legitimacy throughout the empire.

As a result, the framework whereby state authority undergirds and thereby privileges the place of Christianity in a culture is often called the Constantinian Option. This is not to say, however, that the church across the thousand years of near consensus on the relation of church and empire did not have divergent understandings of the church's role in the culture. Complex negotiations occurred as to the appropriate authority of the state relative to the mission and identity of the church.[9] Dominant personalities played outsized roles, as did the enduring conflicts between people groups and wars between various parts of the empire and interactions with surrounding empires. With the fall of the Western Roman Empire in the fifth century and the rise of what we now call the Byzantine Empire, the relationship of the various cities and bishops shifted cultural authority to the east, though Latin Christianity remained a significant if persecuted

---

8. Theodosius issued the Edict of Thessalonica in 380, which marked Christianity as the official religion of the Roman Empire. In 381 he called together bishops to the Council of Constantinople to affirm the tradition of Nicene Christianity and thereafter increasingly restricted the civil rights of any other religious tradition in the empire.

9. The differences between the church in the Eastern Roman Empire (Greek speaking) and the church in the Western Roman Empire (Latin speaking) remained significant during most of this thousand-year period, eventually culminating in the Great Schism in 1054.

presence centered on Rome.[10] Overlaid onto all these issues, from the seventh century onward, was the emergence of, expansion of, and confrontation with Islam.

The unity of the church was always fragile during late antiquity, though it may seem sturdy if one's focus is only on the succession of popes during this era. From almost every other angle, the church displayed a remarkable amount of diversity and division between Theodosius and the end of the Byzantine Empire in 1453.[11] Internal dissent was significant throughout much of the history of the Byzantine Empire. Emperors vacillated in their support for or opposition to one group or another. The unity of the church was often a function of changing whims from emperor to emperor.[12] There was continual tension between political and ecclesial authority.

It is this mixing of political and ecclesial authority that has led many Christians in the present age to cast significant doubt on the model of church unity built around or tied in any way to political authority.[13] Rodney Stark has argued again and again that the cultural and political establishment of the church historically led to its

10. The Byzantine Empire was largely the continuation of the Eastern side of the Roman Empire and was known throughout its history as the Roman Empire. However, Rome played a secondary imperial role to Constantinople, and disputes between various factions within the church were messy because of the ambiguous relationship between emperors and the multitude of diverse bishops throughout the empire. See Judith Herrin, *Margins and Metropolis: Authority Across the Byzantine Empire* (Princeton: Princeton University Press, 2013).

11. The balance of power between Eastern Christianity and Western Christianity largely depended on the sentiments of the emperors as well as the collection of bishops in the major urban centers of the empire. The divide was fully rent asunder in the Great Schism of 1054, when the bishop of Rome fully excommunicated the bishops associated with Constantinople over the matter of the relations within the Trinity. See Henry Chadwick, *East and West: The Making of a Rift of the Church; From Apostolic Times Until the Council of Florence* (Oxford: Oxford University Press, 2005).

12. From the earliest period of Constantianism, this was evident in the number of times Athanasius, the champion of the Nicene Council (325), was banished by succeeding emperors and brought back to prominence by other emperors during the years after Nicaea. This pattern would be repeated many times over in the centuries ahead as diverse emperors granted wide privileges to diverse parties within Christendom while casting others out.

13. See Stanley Hauerwas, *After Christendom: How the Church Is to Behave if Freedom, Justice, and A Christian Nation Are Bad Ideas* (Nashville: Abingdon, 1991), for an especially pointed criticism of the Constantinian Option.

decline, even if it also manifested organizational unity on the surface. The environment in which the church thrives is always the missionary context where the claims of Christianity engage the claims of diverse religions or diverse cultural settings unprotected by political authority.[14] Whenever the church was given a noncompete clause, so to speak, it lost its vitality.

However, it would not be accurate to suggest that the church had no missionary encounter with diverse cultural contexts over the thousand years of "Christendom." The confrontation with Islam from the seventh through eleventh centuries, as well as its evangelistic efforts in northern Europe during much of the later Middle Ages, testifies to the wide and broad cultural competition in which churches were engaged during significant periods of time. The expansion (and sometimes decline) of the church into formerly pagan lands over this period testifies to the missionary zeal it was able to retain in spite of and/or because of its political underpinnings.

NATION AND CHURCH: THE TRANSITIONAL DIVERSITY OF THE CHURCH

The relation of ecclesial and political authority shifted significantly with the Protestant Reformation in the sixteenth century, and with that shift came different conceptions of church unity. The protection of the Reformers by the magistrates of the diverse nation-states of northern Europe was essential to sustaining any outward evidence of the unity of the church—analogous in some measure to the way in which the alliance between emperor and pope appeared to secure

---

14. Evidence shows the church thrives best in missionary contexts, and those missionary contexts exercise a significant influence on the church. But the church's understanding of its mission may result in very different church identities. If the primary concern is to reach middle-class consumers with many entertainment options, the church may well take the form of being another entertainment option. In an impoverished area, the church may take on activities associated with social-service agencies. According to Stark's thesis, the church thrives in a "free market" of religious institutions. This may be true, but as David F. Wells and many others have argued, the temptation of the church in a free market is succumbing to the very consumer orientation of those markets, and thereby a transformation of its very mission. See Wells, *Losing Our Virtue: Why the Church Must Recover Its Moral Vision* (Grand Rapids: Eerdmans, 1998).

the unity of the church through much of the Middle Ages. Churches across northern Europe during the post-Reformation period wrestled with the dynamic between state-sponsored unity and confessionally defined unity. Clergy stood with a foot often on both sides of that divide—their income derived from taxes and wealthy benefactors, but their credentials coming from their church superiors in accord with an ecclesial confession.

The migration from an imperial church with a strong, monarch-like pope to a cluster of nationally established churches did not happen smoothly, nor was it the result of any strategic plan of an ecclesial body. The churches across northern Europe slowly adapted to the changing political environments even as those same environments were influenced by quasi-religious convictions about the danger of condensed power.[15]

The division of Protestants and Roman Catholics in the Reformation era gave rise to two different ecclesiologies. Rome believed in the Constantinian Option, whereby the church's power was effectively coequal and analogous with that of the emperor. The unity of the church was bounded by the authority of the bishop of Rome. Protestants across northern Europe were captured in diverse ways by the sentiment that ecclesial authority that was too centralized and too closely tied to imperial authority was too easily abused, though they still believed that church and state must be connected somehow.[16] The convulsive separation of the Reformation churches

---

15. Neither Luther nor Calvin had well-developed convictions about religious liberty. In different ways, both thought faith was a matter of private conscience that could not be imposed by political power, but they also believed that dissent from the established church must be limited. A helpful comparison between Luther and Calvin can be found in Robert Kolb and Carl R. Trueman, *Between Wittenberg and Geneva: Lutheran and Reformed Theology in Conversation* (Grand Rapids: Baker Academic, 2017).

16. The national churches of the post-Reformation period (the Church of England, the Lutheran churches of the Scandinavian countries, the Reformed church in the cantons of Switzerland, etc.) served as a bridge between the ecclesiology of one single established church (Rome) and multiple nonestablished churches (the United States with its disestablishment clause of the First Amendment). The exception here is the early Anabaptists of the Reformation era, who strongly believed that there should be no ties that bind political and ecclesiastical authority together. This loose association of groups has often been referred to as the Radical

from Rome could not have taken place without those cultural sentiments being relatively well established in northern Europe. In other
words, as with all cultural movements, the Reformation came to
pass because of a complex of historical, cultural, economic, and
political factors.[17]

For example, the widespread reform movements within the
Roman Catholic Church undoubtedly influenced the shape of the
Protestant Reformation. The invention of the modern printing press
in Germany influenced the dissemination of Protestant ideas and as a
result effected change across northern Europe that would have been
impossible a hundred years earlier.[18]

The political environment also influenced popular support for
Luther and the other Reformers. The city-states in the south of
Europe contained fewer republican sentiments than those in the north.
Increasingly, the political centers in northern Europe were secular—
that is, disconnected from the authority of the Vatican. As a result, the
city-states in southern Europe may have been less convinced of the
need to revolt against the political and ecclesiastical power of Rome.
The fact that the Reformation succeeded in Germany, failed in France,
and never took root in Spain was at least in part a function of the
diverse political orientations of these three regions.[19]

Reformation, since adherents challenged even the greatly modified relationship of church and
state found among the magisterial Reformers.

17. Attempts to downplay the significance of actual theological conflicts between Rome
and the Reformers fails to do justice to the way the conflicts themselves were interpreted at
that time. The divorce between Rome and the Reformers was spelled out in straightforward
theological terms, at least after 1522. Protestants separated from Rome on matters of papal
authority and the doctrine of justification by faith alone, a split confirmed at the Roman Catholic
Council of Trent (1540–1544). It should not be forgotten, however, that on issues such as the
two natures of Christ, the reality of the Trinity, etc., there continued to be wide agreement
between Protestants and Roman Catholics.

18. This factor may partially explain the failure of the reform movements associated with
John Wycliffe and Jan Hus in the century prior to Luther and Calvin.

19. There was a brief time of peaceable coexistence between Rome and the Reformers
(Huguenots) in France between the Edict of Nantes (1598) and its revocation in 1685. The
peace did not last because of public sentiment that the Reformation was undermining the
unity of the French republic.

Protestants did not have the theological option of constructing the unity of the church along imperial lines. The unity of the Roman Catholic Church depended on the centralization of its power in the Vatican, and this was in part a primary criticism of Rome by the Protestants. The unity of Protestants, though they were protected by the magistrates in the countries of northern Europe, centered instead on a set of confessional convictions—namely, that God who had created, sustained, and brought redemption into the world would one day bring the consummation of his kingdom to pass.[20] This was a theological unity, but one that would be realized only eschatologically at the consummation.[21] Ecclesial unity was only secondarily expressed organizationally. The primary form of unity was a commitment to the marks of true Christian churches. For Protestants, those marks were the faithful preaching of the work of God in salvation, the genuine discipline of the church, and the practice of the sacraments, which were the manifest signs or marks of the work of God in salvation. So Calvin wrote, "The pure ministry of the Word and pure mode of celebrating the sacraments, are, as we say, sufficient pledge and guarantee that we may safely embrace as church any society in which both these marks exist. The principle extends to the point that we must not reject it so long as it retains them, even if it otherwise swarms with many faults."[22]

Church authority was necessary to keep unity, but it was not the ground of that unity. There was theological diversity among

---

20. See Michael S. Horton, *People and Place: A Covenant Ecclesiology* (Louisville: Westminster John Knox, 2008), for an extended argument of this post-Reformation framing of the issues.

21. Drawing out the consequences of framing church unity eschatologically, Darryl Hart writes, "This ideal of unity has the advantage of uniting all believers, the living and the dead, from Abraham and Paul to J. Gresham Machen, my parents, and me. That seems like a fairly profound understanding of unity since it encompasses that great cloud of witnesses that has gone before us. Yes, it is abstract. That is the way of mysteries. But it is also amazing to ponder that we are united in Christ with believers who have finished the race and have passed into glory." Hart, "Is This Really the End? A Review Article," *Ordained Servant*, February 2017, https://www.opc.org/os.html?article_id=605&issue_id=122.

22. John Calvin, *Institutes of the Christian Religion* (1559), ed. John T. McNeill, trans. Ford Lewis Battles, Library of Christian Classics (Philadelphia: Westminster, 1960), 4.1.12.

Protestants about matters such as the sacraments and church polity, and at times that diversity did undermine their sense of being united by the work of God in salvation.[23] By virtue of not having a centralized ecclesial authority, Protestant disputes often were messy. The actions by some Protestant bodies did not always reflect an affirmation of other Protestant bodies, and because of this, it was not clear how the unity of the Protestant church would survive. This tension between visible unity and eschatological unity is an enduring legacy of the Reformation—one day the church will be united, and yet the visible unity of the church cannot take precedence over the core convictions of Christians as they work out their understanding of the gospel. When theological unity around the work of God in salvation was realized, even if only partially, it came to be more nearly connected to the unity of churches in the individual nation-states—Lutheranism in Germany and the Scandinavian countries, Anglicanism in England, and the Reformed churches in Switzerland.[24]

In the post-Reformation period, different Protestant traditions developed different systems of church government reflective in some measure of the nation in which they developed and the historical circumstances that brought them into being. Henry VIII's divorce from Catherine of Aragon initiated not only the English Reformation but also the transformation of the governance of the churches of England away from the papacy and the Holy Roman Empire toward an uneasy alliance with the political authority of the British monarchy. Anglicanism retained a hierarchical polity, but without papal authority. The national churches in Germany, the Netherlands, Switzerland, and the Scandinavian countries each reflected their own peculiar political

---

23. The fact of diverse traditions is no less true of Catholicism in the sixteenth century. There were a number of influential communities of interpretation that differed markedly from each other. However, they all remained under the one institutional umbrella of the Catholic Church. Unity in the Catholic Church revolved around its single unifying head. Its (considerable) diversity was subservient to its fundamental unity.

24. This unified connection between church and state in northern Europe is often referred to as the magisterial Reformation, since it was the magistrates of the diverse countries that provided the means by which particular churches were established in their lands.

contexts while also consistently defining the boundaries of the church as identical with the boundaries of the nation.

The emergence of formal political toleration of diverse ecclesial traditions on the continent of Europe after the Thirty Years' War (1618–1648) and the Peace of Westphalia (1648) brought with it the beginnings of serious theological reflection on the separation of the church and the civil authorities. The sheer number of church traditions permitted to coexist in the same geographical space required some theological justification, though it was difficult to discern how to sustain a united country without a united church.[25] The full-blown disestablishment of the church did not effectively take place until after the American Revolution and then primarily in the United States, and it is fair to say that this disestablishment was driven more by the changing political realities than by the force of theological argument.[26]

DEMOCRACY AND DENOMINATIONS:
DIVERSE HISTORIES OF CHURCHES

In the transition from the Old World order of Europe to the New World frontier of America, denominations served as dissenting voices against religious hegemony, even as members of the non-conforming denominations were treated as second-class citizens in their own countries. These church bodies were the means to protect dissent while also (mostly) remaining loyal to the larger social project of the nation-states of Europe. The Dissenting churches of

---

25. Dissenting churches slowly gained toleration, but it would take more than two centuries to be fully realized—well into the eighteenth century. Most of the American colonies had an "established church" prior to the American Revolution. Establishment meant the colonies provided direct aid to the church. Some colonies even required officeholders to affirm the theological tenets of the established church. See Mark A. Noll and Luke E. Harlow, eds., *Religion and American Politics: From the Colonial Period to the 1980s* (New York: Oxford University Press, 2007).

26. Brian J. Grim and Roger Finke have argued that there is still a high degree of state favoritism shown to "established churches" in most of the countries of Europe to this day. See Grim and Finke, "International Religion Indexes: Government Regulation, Government Favoritism and Social Regulation of Religion," *Interdisciplinary Journal of Research on Religion* 2 (2006): 1–40.

England in the early eighteenth century (Presbyterian, Baptist, and Congregationalist) sought civil protections from the established Church of England while remaining loyal to the British crown.[27] The Nonconformist churches saw themselves as prophetic corrections to the state church while not supporting any large-scale insurrections against the Crown—that is, not until these denominations found life in the American colonies.

In the context of burgeoning democratic sentiments gaining currency in the monarchies of Europe, denominations came to function as carriers of concrete theological traditions freeing themselves from the political contexts out of which they were originally birthed.[28] Democracy appeared not as a carrier of tradition but somewhat opposed to tradition, at least as those traditions were represented by the European monarchies. The revolt against the centralization of political power came to be viewed also as a revolt against the millennia-old tradition of imperial rule by monarchs. Early democracies in the West were held together by a commitment to the separation of powers and by a constitutional declaration of individual civil rights, both of which provided a significant hedge against the power of a centralized government and the monarchy.[29] For a season, democracies appeared as a consensus framework of politics with diverse religious traditions, but over time, those same religious traditions diverged as to

---

27. A brief history of English denominationalism can be found in William H. Swatos Jr., "Denomination/Denominationalism," in *Encyclopedia of Religion and Society*, ed. William H. Swatos Jr. (Walnut Creek, CA: AltaMira, 1998), 134–36.

28. Seeds of later movements toward religious disestablishment could be found in 1568 with the Edict of Torda in Hungary. While not establishing full religious freedom, the edict did grant each local congregation to choose its own preacher across the full spectrum of Catholic, Orthodox, Reformed, and even antitrinitarian groups. It is likely that the Hungarian territory had always to negotiate compromise between Roman Catholicism and Orthodoxy since it sat on the frontier between the two. See Diarmaid MacCulloch, *The Reformation: A History* (New York: Viking, 2003), 254–55.

29. Historians of the American Revolution continually remind the modern reader that notions of a "united" nation made up of tightly connected states was a highly contested issue during and after the Revolution. The colonists were clear they did not want a centralized monarchy, and most feared an empowered federal government would run counter to the very ideals of the Revolution. See Joseph Ellis, *The Quartet*.

how democracy should function. The freedom of religion enshrined in modern democracies encouraged a plurality of religious traditions, which thereby undermined the claim that a unified religious tradition was necessary for a unified nation-state.[30]

The diverse denominational structures became the assumed framework of Protestant churches in the American Revolution. It would be fair to say that the diversity of denominations gained cultural traction by virtue of being situated in the vibrant but fragile democracy of colonial America. The religious traditions of Europe were transformed into distinctive denominational structures once they were established on American soil.[31] Denominational identity depended on a theological rationale for internal coherence and a socially sanctioned means of dealing with differences with other church bodies, most especially after the freedom-of-religion clause was signed into law in the Bill of Rights in 1791. In the United States, formal ecclesiastical coherence tended to be developed along three (broad) lines—the hierarchical episcopate, the republican federation, and the autonomous congregation—each of which had to compete with the others in the context of the disestablishment of churches. These models of church polity focused on the structural coherences normally associated with the powers of church office and mirrored in some sense diverse models of political authority.

Denominations learned how to survive and eventually thrive within American democracy by means of their constitutionally guaranteed rights and freedoms. They eventually were accorded civil space across all the colonies in protection from the oppressing powers of

---

30. This is the claim with which Jeffrey Stout opens his magisterial work *Democracy and Tradition* (Princeton: Princeton University Press, 2004).

31. In the century prior to the American Revolution the Congregationalists largely established their territory north of New York and the Anglicans were dominant in the southern colonies. The Congregationalists framed their existence in America against the backdrop of freedom from British rule while at the same time limiting the freedom of congregations that veered too far from congregational orthodoxy. What makes this period of Congregational history even more of an enigma is the reality that church membership and attendance in New England during this time was well under 20 percent of the population. In essence the Congregationalists restrained religious freedom in a region that was largely irreligious.

any state or establishment church. In turn, early American democracy respected religiously sanctioned communities as a prime mediating structure through which the virtues of the common good were extolled and sustained.[32] American democracy needed the social glue of a commonly articulated set of ideals held up by the churches apart from the ascendence of any one of denomination. The vast array of diverse churches nonetheless served as a moral ballast for a developing national polity that otherwise would not have had any grounds for its moral authority.[33]

The American churches played distinctive roles in this development once they were freed from the political shackles of the European landscape. This proved especially important to the state churches that had come from northern Europe as they became less defined by their countries of origin. Lutherans were still German but slightly less so in the upper Midwest. Presbyterians were less Scottish in the mid-Atlantic colonies. Anglicans became Episcopalians as the English state church crossed the Atlantic. Baptists and Methodists, which had never been defined by ethnicity, easily became acclimated throughout the American South. Roman Catholics tended to be Irish or Italian for much longer durations, though their ethnic identities eventually diminished as well. The Congregationalist churches of New England and the Methodist and Baptist churches of the South were original to the American landscape. These "free churches" also provided strong theological precedents for the many independent and autonomous local congregations that would eventually litter the early American frontier.

---

32. This may have been (mostly) true at the official level of established law. Unfortunately, discrimination against certain religious bodies remained a part of popular culture throughout the nineteenth and twentieth centuries. The glaring example is the Black church both before and after the Civil War. See Michael Battle, *The Black Church in America: African American Spirituality* (Malden, MA: Wiley-Blackwell, 2006).

33. One finds echoes of this claim in Alasdair MacIntyre, *After Virtue* (Notre Dame: University of Notre Press, 1981), where he argues that the loss of a common moral vision rooted in an enduring religious tradition in the second half of the twentieth century in America has meant that democracy has been left with irreconcilable moral conflicts.

At first these diverse denominational ecclesiologies tended to be regionally specific—Congregationalists in New England; Presbyterians in the Mid-Atlantic; Anglicans, Baptists, and Methodists in the South; Lutherans in the upper Midwest; Roman Catholics in large urban centers. Migration patterns increasingly confused these regional boundaries, and by the twentieth century one could find different polities in every region of the country.

However, much of the religious energy in colonial America was not found in the formal structures of the ecclesial polities but rather in the missionary endeavors of the churches. Prior to 1789, most of the American colonies still had established churches with significant privileges granted to one religious body. Contrary to common wisdom, by all outward measures the churches were significantly more vital in those colonies without an established church than in those colonies with an established church.[34] The freedom-of-religion clause also brought (at least implicitly) a significant shift in the shape of ecclesial organization and concepts of church unity. Diverse churches sprang up without any single governing authority to define how they were to be united to other churches. The unity of churches, when any thought about it, was largely informal and ad hoc. To use Timothy Smith's metaphor, the Protestant churches were a mosaic.[35] Christianity in America had some common patterns when looked at from far enough away, but its parts did not always seem to fit when looked at too closely. It was a loose federation, bound together not by organization but by a common Protestant zeal for the spread of the gospel, and those churches on the frontier far removed from state protection or privileges (the Baptists and Methodists, in particular) seemed especially adept at growing and expanding. Alexis de Tocqueville famously

---

34. Stark also makes the claim in *The Triumph of Christianity* that the church grew significantly across all the colonies in the half century after the Bill of Rights. Stark's numbers of church growth in this period are much more optimistic than standard histories of religion in colonial America, but the overall trend of growth would still support his thesis.

35. See Timothy Smith, *Revivalism and Social Reform: American Protestantism on the Eve of the Civil War* (Baltimore: Johns Hopkins University Press, 1980).

reported in the 1830s that religion thrived in the midst of the chaos
of American democracy, in contrast to its very constrained presence
in Europe.[36] The churches in America were surely not unified in any
outward fashion, but the ability to adapt to the democratic temper
of the nation granted them (virtually) unconstrained opportunities
to evangelize and expand.[37]

Churches were still largely organized along denominational lines
throughout the nineteenth century, but with rare exceptions, none of
the denominations viewed themselves as the "one true church." This
permitted and at times encouraged a wider confessional conversation
among the various branches of the Protestant churches. Unlike Roman
Catholicism and Eastern Orthodoxy, Protestants had a built-in structural context for dissent—both political dissent and dissent from each
other. Protestants in America had to learn how to compete in the open
religious marketplace since they were shorn of establishment privileges.
Under increasing social pluralization and democratization, denominations often became fiercely independent, and under the conditions
of a consumer culture in the twentieth century, they became fiercely
protective of their "market share." One of the results was the increasing
inability of people in the pews to see any remnant of the visible unity
of the gospel beyond local congregational life. However, as Stark has
argued, the competition for market share also made churches more
liable to communicate with urgency and vitality. When churches lost

---

36. Alexis de Tocqueville, *Democracy in America*, trans. and ed. Harvey Mansfield and
Delba Winthrop (Chicago: University of Chicago Press, 2000 [original 1835–1840]). "There is
no country in the world where the Christian religion retains greater influence over the souls
of men than in America. ... In the United States, Christian sects are infinitely diversified and
perpetually modified; but Christianity itself is an established and irresistible fact" (280).

37. This is a central theme of Nathan O. Hatch's *The Democratization of American Christianity*
(New Haven: Yale University Press, 1989). Adapting to democracy meant an increasing embrace
of populism and pluralism. Reflecting on the Second Great Awakening (1800–1830), he writes,
"This awakening developed inversely to that commonly depicted, however, instead of fostering
a unified, cohesive movement, it splintered American Christianity and magnified the diversity
of institutions claiming to be the church. It sprang from a populist upsurge rather than from
changing mores of established parishes. The movement captured the aspirations of society's
outsiders. The heart of the movement was a revolution in communications, preaching, print,
and song; and these measures were instrumental in building mass popular movements" (226).

their sense of mission, they lost market share.[38] Any formal notion of the unity of the church seemed less of a priority than its vital evangelistic mission in the open marketplace of American culture.

As the new nation found its cultural authority in the voice of the people, so churches also found their visible authority in the voices of ordinary people and preachers. The Protestant principle of the priesthood of all believers was transformed on American soil into an affirmation of the diversity of Protestants, all of whom had some claim on belonging to the one true church. Modern religious historians remind us that the church's adaptation to the democratic temper ran in fits and starts throughout much of the nineteenth and twentieth centuries.[39] Religious intolerance reared its ugly head all too often, and America's original sin of slavery remained a tragic legacy in and among churches. The "inclusion" narrative of American democracy did not always accurately describe the expansion of diverse churches in American history, but surely the long arc of history suggests that the American churches wrestled with inclusion and diversity more persistently than any other nation on earth, even if it did this with many ugly episodes along the way.[40]

From Civil Religion to the Culture Wars

One of the strange ironies of Christianity in America by the time the twentieth century rolled around was the rising conviction in some circles that America was and should be a Christian nation—effectively

---

38. As the twentieth century came to a close, gaining market share also brought enormous consumer pressures on the church, with many within the evangelical wing of the church also seeking political alliances to maintain their voice in the public square. On both counts the results were disastrous. See David F. Wells, *The Courage to Be Protestant: Reformation Faith in Today's World*, 2nd ed. (Grand Rapids: Eerdmans, 2017). Also D. G. Hart, *From Billy Graham to Sarah Palin: Evangelicals and the Betrayal of American Conservatism* (Grand Rapid: Eerdmans, 2011).

39. See George M. Marsden's now classic work, *Fundamentalism and American Culture*, 2nd ed. (New York: Oxford University Press, 2006).

40. See Mark A. Noll, *A History of Christianity in The United States and Canada*, 2nd ed. (Grand Rapids: Eerdmans, 2019). Not only is Noll especially sensitive to portray the enduring influence of the church in North America, but he is also painfully honest about its dark underside.

affirming that there is an established and privileged religion in America. However, the toleration of many different kinds of Christian churches across America made it difficult to know what kind of Christianity was to be established and privileged. One answer during the first half of the twentieth century was an ambiguous Christianity.[41] In the frequently repeated words of Dwight Eisenhower from 1954, "Our Government makes no sense unless it is founded on a deeply held religious faith, and I don't care what it is." By "religious faith" he surely meant Christianity, just not any concrete instantiation of it. This was an affirmation of the establishment of religion so ambiguous and pluralized it would not offend anyone—or so the guardians of this civil religion believed. This homogenization of Christianity actually roiled many genuinely religious people of the era.[42] The political establishment at midcentury was hopelessly enamored of a religion so nebulous as to prohibit any concrete religious tradition from speaking with conviction into the public square. It was, however, one (unfortunate) way to think about the unity of the church across all its many diversities.

A related but very different tactic to recover church unity that emerged at midcentury was the founding of the World Council of Churches in 1948 and the National Council of Churches in 1950. The ecumenical movement wrestled with the question of whether and how it was possible to work toward full organic unity of all the member churches. Its work continued to bump up against the reality

---

41. In the popular mind, the "Christian America" movement is most often associated with a cluster of conservative evangelicals in the 1980s (Francis Schaeffer, Jerry Falwell, James Dobson, etc.). Though the civil religion movements at midcentury and the evangelical movement in the 1980s appear different, they share an underlying intuition of the Christian founding of America. The classic criticism of these temptations in the analogous British context can be found in the work of Lesslie Newbigin, the Scottish bishop who returned from India after a lifetime of mission work to discover that Britain was far more of a mission field than anything he had encountered in India, though most of the British still conceived of Britain as a Christian nation. See Newbigin, *Foolishness to the Greeks: The Gospel and Western Culture* (Grand Rapids: Eerdmans, 1988). A more contemporary, practical, and popular distillation of these themes can be found in Timothy Keller, *How to Reach the West Again: Six Essential Elements of a Missionary Encounter* (New York: Redeemer City to City Press, 2020).

42. See George M. Marsden, *The Twilight of the American Enlightenment: The 1950s and the Crisis of Liberal Belief* (New York: Basic Books, 2014).

of enduring church division among its constituents and never saw significant union among any of its member churches. This movement was largely the brainchild of liberal Protestantism and undoubtedly fostered greater collaboration among member churches on a host of socially progressive projects. And from an outsider's perspective, it surely appeared that the differences between the churches became smaller over time—though their histories and distinctives continued to serve as the primary hindrance to full organic union. The lasting legacy of the World Council of Churches may well be that it oversaw the massive decline in the influence and membership of its mainline constituent churches during the last half of the twentieth century.[43]

As the twentieth century wore on, the major denominations on American soil divided along sociopolitical lines.[44] Religious identity became more and more identified with one's sociopolitical convictions, and religious conservatives and religious liberals became the two great parties of American religious life.[45] These culture-war definitions had the unintended consequence of flattening out the differences among denominations. Evangelical Presbyterians and evangelical Methodists were likely to see themselves as allies and their liberal counterparts as foes. The increasing importance of politics during this period was reflected in the assumption that the political spectrum was the primary way in which church life was defined. Even new denominations tended to emerge either as conservative or liberal in the cultural space they occupied. Parachurch and nondenominational ministries did not escape the liberal-conservative divisions either.

---

43. David A. Hollinger makes the ironic claim that the demise of the mainline denominations was actually a positive result of their ecumenical strategy. This implied that their embrace of a liberal religion would be best manifest in a religiously tinged secularity rather than a distinctive set of ecclesiastical structures. See Hollinger, *After Cloven Tongues of Fire: Protestant Liberalism in Modern American History* (Princeton: Princeton University Press, 2013).

44. Robert Wuthnow, *The Restructuring of American Religion: Society and Faith Since World War II* (Princeton: Princeton University Press, 1987), is generally credited for formulating the map of this reorganization of denominations along party lines.

45. See D. G. Hart, *The Lost Soul of American Protestantism* (Lanham, MD: Rowman & Littlefield, 2002).

These definitions reinforced the notion that religious people were more centrally identified by political tradition than creed or confession.[46] Roman Catholics found it difficult to assimilate to the democratic culture through much of the twentieth century in part because of their sense of belonging to a different political order that was not easily categorized as conservative or liberal. Many distinctively confessional Protestants also seemed out of place on the liberal-conservative spectrum.[47] On the politically conservative side, Jerry Falwell's Moral Majority tended not to have very many Missouri Synod Lutherans, Orthodox Presbyterians, or Christian Reformed folk, which by other accounts appeared quite conservative theologically, because these church bodies had intentionally separated themselves from political loyalties. In addition, Black churches tend to remain theologically conservative while being politically aligned to the Left, and thus do not fit easily into the either/or categories of the culture wars.[48] In a cultural context allegedly freed from political oversight and control, the unity and diversity of the church took on a very political cast. The irony is too rich to miss.

Another model of unity emerged at midcentury with the rise of the National Association of Evangelicals (1942). Its intention was to open up communication lines among many of the loosely connected evangelical churches and organizations. The Billy Graham crusades and the Lausanne movement walked closely beside the National Association of Evangelicals in its concern for mission. This gave rise to a different conception of unity than that found among the mainline

46. See D. G. Hart, "Live by the Polls, Die by the Polls," in *Evangelicals: Who They Have Been, Are Now, and Could Be*, ed. Mark A. Noll, David W. Bebbington, and George M. Marsden (Grand Rapids: Eerdmans, 2019), 228–33.

47. Hart, in *The Lost Soul of American Protestantism*, argues for a "third way" to configure Protestants who do not fit on the liberal-conservative spectrum. He suggests that pietism is the common heritage of churches defined by the liberal-conservative framework, since pietism privileges religious experience and thus abandons the public spheres of life to a secular rationality.

48. See Jemar Tisby, "Are Black Christians Evangelicals?," in Noll, Bebbington, and Marsden, *Evangelicals*, 262–72.

churches or within Catholicism.[49] It had little interest in organizational unity and was more concerned with letting a thousand flowers bloom in mission.[50]

THE ESCHATOLOGICAL STRANGENESS
OF ECCLESIAL UNITY

History ought to teach us to be wary of any final solution to the issue of church unity, though it also teaches us that we should never stop reflecting on unity and working toward it. As Geoffrey Bromiley puts it, "Throughout its history, the church has always and everywhere maintained an awareness of its unity. It has extended to many different lands and races and cultures. It has taken many different forms. It has been split by innumerable dissensions and disagreements. It has passed through many crises and vicissitudes. It has known ages of the most violent individualism as well as the most submissive collectivism. But for all the legitimate or illegitimate variety it has never lost the sense of its ultimate and indestructible unity."[51]

But then, in what does the unity of the church consist? And what of Bonhoeffer's criticism lodged at the outset of this chapter? At the heart of the answer is that there is a transcendent reality neither entirely absent nor present in the earthly realm. In contrast to the intuitions of secularism, Christian hope lies in the reality that God has come in the flesh, that eternity has entered into time, even if it is also true that temporal structures are but indicators of a greater reality to

---

49. Donald Bloesch rightly chides the "beguiling romanticism" among disenchanted Protestants who suppose that the return to Rome will solve the unity question. He criticizes the claim of Carl E. Braaten and Robert W. Jenson et al., in *In One Body through the Cross: The Princeton Proposal for Christian Unity* (Grand Rapids: Eerdmans, 2003), that there can be no discipline of pastors and parishes without the Catholic ecclesial structure headed by the pope. Bloesch notes the "Roman church is not theologically healthy nor missiologically vital. It has not held fast to the gospel of free justification through faith in the living Christ." Donald Bloesch, *The Church: Sacraments, Worship, Ministry, Mission*, Christian Foundations 6 (Downers Grove, IL: InterVarsity Press, 2002), 255.

50. The next chapter describes and dissects this "mission" model of unity in the context of the history of the fragmentation of evangelicals.

51. Geoffrey W. Bromiley, *The Unity and Disunity of the Church* (Grand Rapids: Eerdmans, 1958), 9.

come in eternity. The unity of the church is centered on Christ, who is manifest in the flesh but whose work has not been fully consummated. This unity is real and genuine and not simply invisible. But neither is it captured by any earthly historical condition—until such time as history is consummated and God puts everything right.

The church's unity has already been accomplished in Christ's life, death, and resurrection, yet is still waiting to be fully accomplished. The mistake in identifying it with any particular organizational unity of the church is in attempting to find the center in an entirely historical factor, as if the church were only or primarily a human entity like so many others. The church exists on earth, but it also and primarily exists on the plane of eternity. It exists in the tension of the already and the not yet. It is the mission of the church that most fully expresses this tension. It is to that model of missional unity that we turn in the next chapter.

We are forced to do something that the Western church has never had to do since the days of their own birth—to discover the form and substance of a missionary church in terms that are valid in a world that has rejected the power and the influence of the Western nations.

—LESSLIE NEWBIGIN, *THE OPEN SECRET*

8

THE DIVERSITY OF A
UNIFIED MISSION

Lesslie Newbigin's prescient insight into the post-Christian West led to much soul searching about the mission of the church. He exploded the myth that mission was primarily about churches in the West sending missionaries to countries outside of the West. He forcefully pressed the issue that the church in the West must learn to think of its own context as a missionary context. As the twenty-first century dawned, it became clear that the West was increasingly secular and the church in the West must recover a sense of being missionaries in this post-Christian context. The church had failed to realize that mission was not only about sending people to far-off parts of the globe, but also (and primarily) about being a missionary presence in its own context. Newbigin's clarion call to think of mission as the sum and substance of the church's identity poured like a cold shower over much of the church in the West. Whether Christendom was ever an actual reality or simply a theoretical framework, it was now clear that the West was no longer Christian in any identifiable sense. Modern liberal democracies in the last half of the twentieth century were secular in their orientation, and Christianity, where it existed, had become a marginal voice.

This diagnosis makes good theological sense. There is no time or place in which the gracious work of God will have completely

penetrated the lives of those in that context (inside the church or
outside), and this explains why mission should always have an eschatological focus: Its task is never finished.[1] The church reflects the
gospel in its life and in its mission in the way it lives "life together" in
the midst of those who do not share in its common life.[2] This holds
in tension the dual realities that the gracious work of God is present
along with the brokenness of the human condition.

Newbigin believed church unity was grounded in God's grace
and disunity was grounded in human brokenness.[3] However, disunity is not to be equated with difference at all times. There are different kinds of difference, and disunity is simply one species of it.
If the church saw its calling in missionary terms, it might be able to
see ecclesial diversity emerge naturally from the diversity of contexts into which it was planted. These contextual differences are
not intrinsically a form of disunity, though often they have been
interpreted as such. Making mission central to its identity helps
the church think more directly about its context, which will ultimately shape the way the church's mission is lived out. The church
should look different in midtown Manhattan than it does in the
lower Bronx. The church should look different in Puerto Rico than
it does in Portland, Oregon. Different contexts will determine its
complexion and reflection in various geographical locations. But
how should context shape the way the mission is lived out? And
how do we know when the church is under-adapting or over-adapt-
ing to its cultural context?

---

1. Newbigin helpfully refers to the church's mission as "hope in action." See Lesslie
Newbigin, *The Open Secret: An Introduction to the Theology of Mission* (Grand Rapids: Eerdmans,
1978), chapter 6.

2. This is Dietrich Bonhoeffer's term for the practices of Christians gathered together by
the gospel. See Bonhoeffer, *Life Together*, trans. John W. Doberstein (New York: Harper &
Row, 1954).

3. Lesslie Newbigin, *The Reunion of the Church: A Defense of the South India Scheme* (London:
SCM, 1948). He speaks of the unity of the church in familial language as the "reunion" of
churches, assuming that union is the natural state of the church, from which disunity arose.

Missional Unity and the Task
of Contextualization

This mission of the church is not defined by its organizational unity. Rather, its unity arises from its mission. That mission defines the identity of the church, while the context of the church influences its concrete organizational shape. Inevitably, the mission must be grounded in and founded on the gracious work of God in the gospel. The mission of God is the precursor to the mission of the church, which in turn is the precursor to how the church adapts to its cultural context.[4] The visible structures of the church enable the mission to be carried out and are not themselves equated to the mission. The unity toward which the church's mission points is the unity created by the gospel, not its organizational shape. The irony is that this kind of missional unity ought to enable churches to envision their calling as different from other churches in other times and places.[5]

The mission of the church may be compared to a pair of glasses through which the church views its central vocation in the world and how that might be accomplished.[6] They are theological glasses insofar as we understand mission as arising from the work of God. Naturally, churches in diverse settings will "see" their vocation lived out in different ways, though no church wears perfectly formed glasses on this side of eternity. These glasses are intended to clarify but may instead

---

4. This is often referred to as the *missio Dei* (the mission of God), rightly locating the origin of the mission of the church in the mission of God. See Newbigin, *Reunion of the Church*, especially the introduction.

5. To take but one example, the recent growth in church planting in small towns has given rise to a literature that thinks very differently about the visible church structures in those settings than that envisioned by the literature that has grown out of the great global-cities church-planting projects of the last thirty years. See the similarity and difference between Timothy Keller's manual for planting churches in large global cities, *Center Church* (Grand Rapids: Zondervan, 2011) and Stephen Witmer's work on church planting in small towns, *A Big Gospel in Small Places: Why Ministry in Forgotten Communities Matters* (Downers Grove, IL: InterVarsity Press, 2019).

6. I used the analogy of a "theological vision" in an earlier work, *The Fabric of Theology: A Prolegomenon to Evangelical Theology* (Grand Rapids: Eerdmans, 1993), to illuminate the means by which we move from interpreting Scripture to interpreting life.

distort the cultural context of a church's mission, thereby altering the mission of the church—what has been called "mission drift."[7]

At the most generic level, every church faces the daunting task of interpreting and translating its mission for its peculiar setting. Contextualization is simply the application of mission to a specific time and place. In this sense, mission comes prior to contextualization and ought to be the prime driver of contextualization. The task of building organizational structures in a specific time and place emerges from a church's sense of mission; therefore, even though different churches may have many elements of a mission in common, the task may give rise to different contextualizations.

This project of contextualization is both commendable and dangerous. It is commendable when the church realizes that its essential identity is not its organizational shape or its particular cultural form. Then it is freed to live the reality that God's gracious work can be carried on in many diverse cultural contexts. In this regard, the church is unlike any other earthly organization. In the words of Edmund Clowney, "The church is to be understood not sociologically as an organization of a certain kind, fitting into the pattern of a given society. Rather, the church is defined in relation to God: The Father, the Son and the Spirit. The assembly that defines the church is not the gathering of the saints in either a house or a civic auditorium. It is the gathering of the saints with the angels in the presence of the Living God (Heb 12:22–24)."[8] The church is present in the world by virtue of the presence of the Triune God through the reconciling work of the gospel. The church's tangible organizational structure and cultural form is not the source of its identity, though it must have a concrete form by which Christians show forth the reality of the Triune God in their midst.

---

7. See Peter Greer, *Mission Drift: The Unspoken Crisis Facing Leaders, Charities and Church* (Minneapolis: Bethany House, 2015).

8. Edmund P. Clowney, *Living in Christ's Church* (Philadelphia: Great Commission Publications, 1986), 109.

But churches over-adapt to their cultural context when they lose their distinctiveness from the cultural setting, and their words and practices are indistinguishable from the ordinary habits of the world around it. Churches under-adapt when their rhetoric and practices become so isolating from the world around them they lose all ability to communicate a compelling gospel vision to their cultural neighbors.

The impulse to over-adapt can be seen in the ecumenical movement of the twentieth century in the World Council of Churches.[9] Under emerging leadership, missionary interest shifted toward an accommodation with the world's religions, and as early as 1928, the International Missionary Council (precursor to the World Council of Churches) was debating whether Christian mission to non-Christians was appropriate and began instead to prioritize the merits of synthesizing Christianity with the other great religions of the world in order to form a united world faith.[10] The offense of the gospel was lost in the desire to adapt to the emerging global context of modern communications and trade.

This impulse may also be seen at the other end of the theological spectrum. In the American context, the Christian Right emerged from the neo-evangelical movement, which had itself emerged out of the shadows of Christian fundamentalism at midcentury. The initial impulse of the neo-evangelicals was to engage American culture more confidently with the claims of the gospel, and thereby abandon the separatist (under-adapting) impulse of their fundamentalist forebears.[11] The mission to engage encouraged some to press for greater cultural privileges and increased access to the corridors of political

---

9. The World Missionary Conference of 1910, held in Edinburgh, is often seen as the originating conference for the rise of the ecumenical movement.

10. See Edmund P. Clowney, *The Church*, Contours of Christian Theology (Downers Grove, IL: InterVarsity Press, 1995), 145.

11. Carl F. H. Henry was representative of this separation from the fundamentalist tradition. His book *The Uneasy Conscience of Modern Fundamentalism* (1947; repr., Grand Rapids: Eerdmans, 2003) signaled a new era for conservative Christians in engaging the great cultural questions of the day.

power. The strategy was to recover elements of a time when America was "more Christian"—namely, when it was the unofficial established religion of the land. In reality, the attempt to use the political levers of power to encourage the mission of the church backfired, and the Christian Right came to be viewed as simply another political movement rather than a gospel-centered community.[12]

The under-adapting impulse can be seen on both ends of the theological spectrum as well. The big, steepled mainline churches whose pews were filled in the 1950s failed to reckon with the cultural shifts taking place toward the end of the twentieth century and frequently supposed the boomer generation wanted to worship in precisely the same way their parents had. As a result, their membership declined in staggering numbers. They had become irrelevant. On the other end of the spectrum were conservative churches in that same era who continued to preach as if everyone still believed in heaven and hell, still believed in sin, and still believed in moral absolutes. They believed in an unchanging gospel but failed to recognize the radical shifts taking place in the culture surrounding them.

Contextualization after Christendom and Outside Christendom

The remarkable expansion of Christianity in the global South and East in the second half of the twentieth century has reminded us there is an integral relationship between the unity of the church's mission and the cultural flexibility of the church. Even as the forces of liberal democracy have (re)shaped the church in the post-Christian West, the resurgence of Christianity in the South and East has given rise to a diverse set of organizational structures for post-Western Christianity.[13] Churches in the South and East largely sprang up outside any

---

12. See the trenchant critique of this cultural strategy in James Davison Hunter, *To Change the World: The Irony, Tragedy, and Possibility of Christianity in the Late Modern World* (New York: Oxford University Press, 2010).

13. Lamin Sanneh, *Whose Religion Is Christianity? The Gospel beyond the West* (Grand Rapids: Eerdmans, 2003).

connection to Christendom.[14] As a result, church structures, organizations, and networks have varied as greatly as the cultural spaces
in which the diverse churches have appeared.[15] The expansion of
Christianity in Korea and in China in the last decades of the twentieth century took two very different structural forms—namely, the
megachurch in Korea and the house church in China.[16]

There has been no comparable expansion of churches in the
West—even though these churches still enjoy cultural privileges as the
shadow of Christendom grows increasingly faint. These churches have
too often succumbed to the temptation of structuring their communal
life to protect those privileges. Churches that live on the margins of a
culture, outside of the corridors of power, are forced to think about
why they exist rather than merely maintain their existence. Churches
in America have lived with the tension of not being established by
the authority of the state, but nonetheless enjoying a privileged place
in culture. As theologian George Lindbeck has noted, the American
church is in an "awkward intermediate stage of having once been
established but not yet clearly disestablished."[17] The tension between
cultural protections and the lack of cultural influence has grown in

---

14. Sanneh, *Whose Religion Is Christianity*: "What is at issue now is the surprising scale
and depth of the worldwide Christian resurgence, a resurgence that seems to proceed without
Western organizational structures, including academic recognition, and is occurring amidst
widespread political instability and the collapse of public institutions, part of what it means to
speak of a post-Western Christianity" (3).

15. Many religious revivals outside of the West have been led by pastors with large personalities who, adept at adapting church structures to the context, operated like bishops in
the early church. Inevitably, the complex relationship of ecclesial power and worldly behavior
led to morally shady behavior on the part of some. To take but one example, see the financial
difficulties associated with David Yonggi Cho, longtime pastor of the world's largest church
in Korea, Yoido Full Gospel Church, reported by Ruth Moon, "Founder of World's Largest
Megachurch Convicted of Embezzling $12 Million," *Christianity Today*, February 24, 2014,
https://www.christianitytoday.com/news/2014/february/founder-of-worlds-largest-mega-
church-convicted-cho-yoido.html.

16. See Ed Stetzer and Daniel Im, *Planting Missional Churches: Your Guide to Starting
Churches That Multiply* (Nashville: B&H Academic, 2016), 346.

17. George Lindbeck, *The Nature of Doctrine: Religion and Theology in a Postliberal Age*
(Louisville: Westminster John Knox, 1984), 8. Disestablishment in Lindbeck's sense refers to
being not merely formally free of ties to political powers but also genuinely outside the sphere
of any cultural advantages.

recent decades as the secularity of cultural elites has increased. A spectrum of divergent responses has emerged in this unusual time in the United States.[18] There are loud voices in the evangelical coalition that have urged for renewed pressure on politicians to preserve the privileges of earlier generations of Christians in America—ranging from the protection of tax-exempt status for churches to freedom from antidiscrimination laws mandating certain hiring practices.[19] These patterns of church-state relations in America were originally part of the bargain in the early republic in which churches were disestablished but all Christian churches (and eventually all officially recognized religious bodies) were given certain limited privileges. At the other end of the strategic spectrum, some have argued that the project of late modern democracy is itself fatally flawed and churches need to abandon attempts to preserve their former privileges.[20] This response works on the assumption that liberal democracy is the product of the Enlightenment and is a tool for domesticating religion by giving it limited space to operate, requiring it to abandon its exclusive claims as entry ticket to the public square. On this rendering, churches must abandon any desire to be culturally relevant and learn instead to be strangers in a strange land.[21]

The irony between the situation of the church in the West and the expanding church in the global South is captured well by Stanley Hauerwas:

---

18. Stanley Hauerwas captures the spectrum of responses in *After Christendom: How the Church Is to Behave if Freedom, Justice, and a Christian Nation Are Bad Ideas* (Nashville: Abingdon, 1991).

19. Both the National Association of Evangelicals and the Council of Christian Colleges and Universities maintain extensive lobbying efforts in Washington, DC, to preserve these privileges.

20. Several conservative Roman Catholic scholars have argued in this fashion. See, e.g., Patrick Deneen, *Why Liberalism Failed* (New Haven: Yale University Press, 2019). On the Protestant side, see Hauerwas, *After Christendom*, and for a deeper theoretical dive, see several of the essays in John Milbank, *The Future of Love: A Political Theology* (Eugene OR: Cascade, 2009). An accessible version that has received wide notice is Rod Dreher, *The Benedict Option: A Strategy for Christians in a Post-Christian Nation* (New York: Sentinel, 2018), which argues for a monastic-like retreat from late modern consumer culture.

21. See Stanley Hauerwas and Will Willimon, *Resident Aliens: Life in the Christian Colony*, 25th anniv. ed. (Nashville: Abingdon Press, 2014 [original 1989]) and Dreher, *Benedict Option*.

We are puzzled by the fact that in countries where we have freedom of religion it is very difficult to make serious reference to God in the public arena. Of course we are not prohibited from confessing our belief in God as long as we make the appropriate social gestures that we understand such belief has no implications for our fellow citizens who do not have such beliefs. Yet suddenly in countries that have repressed the Christian faith for most of this century, Christians, exactly because they are Christians, have become the primary political actors. Indeed in those contexts it seems some even think it makes a difference, and it is a political difference, whether what Christians believe is true or false.[22]

EVANGELICALS: DIVERSE CONTEXTUALIZATIONS OF A SINGULAR MISSION?

Many American denominations have uneasily navigated the ecclesial pluralism outside their boundaries, but few have developed an effective theology of collaboration with other Protestant denominations. I would suggest that the lone American "tradition" that has developed a peculiarly modern and democratically informed construct of ecumenism (and, correspondingly, a diversity strategy) is evangelicalism—and more particularly the wide variety of networks of churches that refer to themselves as evangelical.[23] These networks are built on a

---

22. Hauerwas, *After Christendom*, 24. Hauerwas is using the language of "politics" in this context not to refer to formal political power, but rather to the influence of churches on the *polis*—that is to say, the national ethos itself.

23. Given the current political connotations of the term "evangelical," it is important to qualify the "tradition" to which I am referring. In reality, it is a subset of the evangelical tradition—and is distinguishable by virtue of a commitment to networks and to mission. There are many self-described evangelical churches that remain steadfastly denominational in their orientation or steadfastly independent. There are also many self-identifying evangelicals who do not have any connection to a church. It is largely this latter demographic that shows up in huge numbers as representative of the evangelical tradition on political surveys. On this latter point, see D. G. Hart, "Live by the Polls, Die by the Polls," in *Evangelicals: Who They Have Been, Are Now, and Could Be*, ed. Mark A. Noll, David W. Bebbington, and George M. Marsden (Grand Rapids: Eerdmans 2019), 228–33.

common mission with a much greater emphasis on voluntary partnership, reflecting a democratically infused construct of collaboration.[24] These networks tend to be both overlaid on denominational commitments as well as independent of them. The networks themselves are mostly built on a focused understanding of mission, whether it be church planting, urban mission, multiethnic ministry, or charismatic worship.[25] They have also tended not to be organizationally thick or concerned with questions of theological boundaries.[26]

These networks continue the long legacy of voluntary nonprofit associations in American history, while also representing a significant break from the way churches have historically related to established structures of authority. That break appeared first in denominational form with the rise of Baptist, Methodist, and independent churches on the American frontier in the nineteenth century. However, those church polities still had a denominational cast to them. This meant that mission was but one part of the church's portfolio, while other denominational activities, such as administration, education, credentialing, and so on, were very much part of the identity of the churches under these umbrellas. The vast increase of Baptist and Methodist churches on the American frontier through the nineteenth century surely was rooted in their belief in the congregation's independence from outside interference—a rallying cry that has been the hallmark

---

24. The emphasis is not on a single network of churches, but rather the vast number of networks of churches, most of which have been started within the last forty years. This would also include the large number of nondenominational churches that have started in the last forty years and also identify as evangelical. See Stetzer and Im, *Planting Missional Churches*. See also Ed Stetzer, "Defining Evangelicals in Research," National Association of Evangelicals, winter 2017/2018, https://www.nae.net/defining-evangelicals-research/.

25. There are literally hundreds of these networks, most of which focus on a single mission issue. So, e.g., the Willow Creek network of churches focuses on innovative church mission. The Acts 29 network of churches focuses on planting churches with a clear Reformed theological framework. The City to City network of churches focuses on church-planting movements in large global cities. The Mosaic network of churches focuses on planting multiethnic and multiracial churches.

26. Stetzer and Im, *Planting Missional Churches*. See especially chapter 28, "Networks and Denominations." There are exceptions to the "theologically thin" descriptions of networks, though the absence of the confessionalization process marks them as distinctive from denominations.

of American democracy. The rise of church networks in the second half of the twentieth century may be considered another chapter in this progression from establishment to disestablishment, but it also represents a different form of ecumenism, no longer bounded by denominational fences.[27]

Postwar evangelicalism intentionally had renewal movements at its core, while also relating to a wide variety of denominational identities.[28] The hope of neo-evangelical founders such as Carl F. H. Henry, Harold Ockenga, and Billy Graham was to create a movement large enough to stand as an alternative to mainline establishment Protestantism while not inventing an alternative denominational structure.[29] They therefore crafted structures of cooperation among renewal movements within formerly competing denominations and between significantly different kinds of parachurch organizations. The wider the movement became, the more nebulous its substantive identity.[30] We might say they attempted to represent "mere Christianity" or "generic Christianity." Their zeal for mission was unmistakable, even if their theological identities remained thin.[31]

---

27. As with movements more generally in democratic contexts, the question remains as to whether they will endure. Stetzer and Im pithily state, "If denominations want to become more effective they must become like networks (laser focused on mission and evangelism). If networks want to last, they need to become more like denominations (build structures and define beliefs)." Stetzer and Im, *Planting Missional Churches*, 345.

28. See Richard Lints, "Whose Evangelicalism? Which Renewal? The Task of Renewing a Renewal Movement," in *Renewing the Evangelical Mission*, ed. Richard Lints (Grand Rapids: Eerdmans, 2013).

29. A helpful historical narrative of the early neo-evangelical founders can be found in Garth Rosell, *The Surprising Work of God: Harold John Ockenga, Billy Graham, and the Rebirth of Evangelicalism* (Grand Rapids: Baker Academic, 2008).

30. D. G. Hart contends that there actually is no such substantive movement as evangelicalism. It is a construction without an actual identity: "Evangelicalism needs to be relinquished as a religious identity because it does not exist. ... The non-existence of an evangelical identity may prove to be, to borrow a phrase from Noll, the real scandal of modern evangelicalism, for despite the vast amounts of energy and resources expended on the topic, and notwithstanding the ever growing volume of literature on the movement, evangelicalism is little more than a construction." Hart, *Deconstructing Evangelicalism: Conservative Protestantism in the Age of Billy Graham* (Grand Rapids: Baker Academic, 2004), 17.

31. The criticism of the evangelical movement from within has come primarily (and rightly) at this point. Two books that came from the same Pew Foundation study of evangelicalism raise

Two of the more curious realities in these evangelical networks in a late modern democracy has been that evangelicalism has been a movement so large that it defies definition and also a movement willing to cross formerly impassable divides. It seems clear now that loosening denominational bonds has resulted in the loosening of bonds to theological traditions. As a result, the hard edges of the Christian faith have been flattened out in a culture wary of any universal truth claims.[32] The upside is that the postdenominational impulse has created conversations across bridges that a century ago would have seemed unimaginable; the evangelical movement(s) has quietly been the most ecumenical movement of the twentieth century. But this often has come with the loss of important theological claims.[33]

Mixed in with the mission of these networks is the complex set of intuitions about how best to interact with the elite culture that often sets the tone of public discourse in the United States. There has been a large segment of those inside the evangelical tent who embraced the mythology of a Christian America.[34] There have been many other networks under the evangelical tent that carried no political loyalties and thought of their mission in pragmatic terms related primarily

---

this point in strikingly different but complementary ways. David F. Wells, *No Place for Truth, or, Whatever Happened to Evangelical Theology* (Grand Rapids: Eerdmans, 1994), and Mark A. Noll, *The Scandal of the Evangelical Mind* (Grand Rapids: Eerdmans, 1994).

32. Mark Lilla, from outside the evangelical world altogether, comments, "Though this is still a churchgoing nation, the gospel now being preached, particularly in evangelical circles, has been infected with the same individualism, selfishness, and superficiality that have infected other sectors of American life." Lilla, *The Once and Future Liberal: After Identity Politics* (New York: Harper, 2017), 125.

33. It will also likely continue the long-standing tradition of being an antitraditional tradition rooted in being a renewal movement rather than a tradition—which, after all, is simply a unique tradition. This in part explains why the evangelical movement can be so "conservative" on some issues (family values, sex, the Bible) while throwing tradition to the wind on other issues (worship style, music, political loyalties). See my *Progressive and Conservative Religious Ideologies: The Tumultuous Decade of the 1960s* (London: Routledge, 2010), especially chapter 9, "Radical Retrieval: Evangelicals and the Story of the 1960s."

34. This impulse to return America to a primitive Christian state undoubtedly misinterprets the facts of history regarding the religious state of America in its early years. See Jon Butler, *New World Faiths: Religion in Colonial America* (New York: Oxford University Press, 2000). Representative figures of this "Christian America" approach included Jerry Falwell, Pat Robertson, D. James Kennedy, and Tim and Beverly LaHaye.

to evangelism. Eventually, as the twentieth century was brought to a close, many of these "evangelism first" churches began to emphasize social forms of ministry and outreach to those on the margins of society while remaining politically neutral.[35] There were yet others under the tent (clearly a minority) who perceived the mission in more distinctly intellectual terms, confronting the big ideas of late secular modernity.[36] This latter approach strongly emphasized an apologetic encounter with the increasing secularity and consumerism of late modern culture, and was largely independent of political loyalties.[37]

The more significant and subtle point is that modern American evangelicalism is not united by its political loyalties but by its collaboration across a diverse array of networks, denominations, and independent churches by virtue of what they have in common—namely, their primary loyalty to Jesus. This deep and broad coalition has transcended all the expectations of sectarian fragmentation given how many diverse theological traditions are represented in the networks.[38] This is an entirely different way to frame the question of the unity (and diversity) of the church than Protestants have historically done. Traditionally, the matter of church unity (or disunity) was

---

35. Representative of this large evangelical constituency was Bill Hybels and the Willow Creek network of churches, and also Rick Warren and the Saddleback network of churches.

36. Tim Keller and the ministry of Redeemer City to City, which he founded, is a clear example of this strategy. This last group, though much smaller, included a greater number of evangelical thought leaders, referring to the group of evangelicals with significant influence in scholarly circles both evangelical and non-evangelical. These are "academic evangelicals." One thinks of individuals as diverse as Mark Noll, Alvin Plantinga, Jim Wallis, Andy Crouch, and Miroslav Volf. See George Marsden, "A Renaissance of Christian Higher Education in the United States," in *Christian Higher Education: A Global Reconnaissance*, ed. Joel Carpenter, Perry Glanzer, and Nicholas Lantinga (Grand Rapids: Eerdmans 2014), 257–76.

37. The early phase (and influence) of Francis Schaeffer's work and the remarkable influence of C. S. Lewis on a wide swath of evangelicals mark out this side of the constituency through much of the second half of the twentieth century.

38. Mark Noll cites a comment from the eighteenth-century proto-evangelical evangelist George Whitefield when he was criticized by the Boston clergy for preaching in diverse kinds of churches. Whitefield responded that he saw regenerate souls among Baptists, Presbyterians, independents, Anglicans—all children of God, yet all born again in a different way of worship, and who can tell which is the most evangelical. Noll, "World Cup or World Series," in *Evangelicals: Who They Have Been, Are Now, and Could Be*, ed. Mark A. Noll, David W. Bebbington, and George M. Marsden (Grand Rapids: Eerdmans, 2020), 315.

framed around distinctive church polities, each attempting to articulate how multiple congregations are connected to each other. These polities focused on the question of ecclesial authority, whether that authority was understood hierarchically (Anglicanism), in a representative group of officers (Lutherans, Presbyterians), or in members of individual congregations (Congregationalists and Baptists). Each of these polities in turn wrestled with how the one and the many related across their own denomination's congregations. Are single congregations members of an association of churches (Congregational), integral parts of the federation of churches (Presbyterian), or local instances of one mystical church (Episcopal)?

The postwar neo-evangelical movement saw the distinctions of church polity as inconsequential to the question of church unity (or disunity). Both at the level of movement leadership and in ordinary evangelical church life, there was little concern with wider systemic issues of how congregations are connected (or not) to wider denominational structures. In the last fifty years, there has been an unprecedented explosion of churches that virtually hide their denominational connections, marketing instead their own cultural ethos and convictions. This has largely occurred inside the evangelical tent in contrast to mainline Protestantism, and surely there is little evidence of this within Roman Catholicism. The branding of churches by locale (e.g., Stone Creek Church) or culture (e.g., Renovation Church) has replaced the naming of churches with reference to their denominational connection.[39] Even as churches note their connections with other churches, the language of "network" often replaces that of "denomination." Networks of churches have much looser theological boundaries than denominations historically have had, and they tend to be focused on a common mission that binds their member churches together. Denominational affiliation still exists, and most

---

39. Christopher James, *Church Planting in Post-Christian Soil: Theology and Practice* (New York: Oxford University Press, 2018), describes the one hundred churches that have been planted in Seattle in the period 2000–2014. The vast majority "hide" their denominational affiliation (if they have one) in their church names in favor of highlighting their location in the city.

local evangelical-leaning churches still belong to a denomination.[40] But many of those churches no longer carry their primary identity in denominational terms. They have a sense of belonging in a very large house, called "evangelical," but they are not really sure where their own room is in the house.[41] They spend most of their time in the hallway rather than in any room belonging to a specific Protestant theological tradition. They are energized by conversations about Jesus with all the diverse parties that also reside in the house (for the most part), and they are mostly content to stay in the hallway talking. But they are wary of leaving generic Christianity for anything more specific and concrete. The blessing is that they have a sense that this is their house. The curse is that they don't have a sense of belonging to anything more specific and substantive.

DIVERSITY, DYSFUNCTION, AND THE LOCAL CONGREGATION

We have seen how evangelical churches and networks see church unity. How do ordinary church members think about it? Undoubtedly, their primary focus is the unity of their local congregation, which may on occasion extend briefly to consider the ways in which their local congregation collaborates with other congregations in their geographical space. This means the dysfunctions of local congregations remain deeply embedded in the minds of many church members that have firsthand experience of them. The "unity of the church" in these local contexts more nearly connotes relational unity rather than organizational unity with other churches or theological unity across a denominational

---

40. See Mark Thumma, "What God Makes Free Is Free Indeed: Nondenominational Church Identity and Its Networks of Support" (paper presented at the annual meeting of the Religious Research Association, 1999), http://www.hartfordinstitute.org/bookshelf/thumma_article5.html.

41. This metaphor comes from Michael Horton, who in turn cites C. S. Lewis as the originator of the metaphor—with a slightly different twist. See Michael S. Horton, "The Church After Evangelicalism," in Renewing the Evangelical Mission, ed. Richard Lints (Grand Rapids: Eerdmans, 2013), 134–60; C. S. Lewis, Mere Christianity (New York: Harper Collins, 2001 [original 1952]), xvi.

spectrum. By extension, the "diversity of the church" refers to the ways
people in a local congregation are different from each other.

Reflective of the postdenominational impulse in America (and
much of the West), church polity is peripheral to most pastors, lay
leaders, and surely the vast majority of church attenders. There is far
more pragmatic concern with congregational life than with the theological constructs of bishops or elders. People's sense of belonging to
a church may have little to do with belonging to a wider network of
similar churches or the particular ecclesial tradition of that congregation. Theological traditions rooted in the concrete institutions and
history of denominations matter far less than they did to previous
generations. Belonging to a church is belonging to a community of
neighbors, friends, and fellow believers. Pastors are seen as leaders
who hold a community together rather than serving a theological role
as a representative of a denominational tradition. Congregants likely
belong to a church because a friend initially invited them, and they
stay for a variety of other reasons—ranging from the depth of preaching, to the worship style, to the friendliness of the community, to the
children's programming. People are more likely to leave a church
because of church conflicts—either that they are directly involved
with or about which they have considerable knowledge—than disagreement with the denomination to which the congregation belongs.

Most of the letters of the New Testament were written into local
situations of conflict and dysfunction. The most significant of the
theological frameworks used to discuss these conflicts and dysfunctions comes from Paul's letters to the church at Rome (Romans 12)
and at Corinth (1 Corinthians 12). In those chapters, the apostle uses
the metaphor of a human body consisting of many parts that have significant differences but must learn to work together. "The eye cannot
say to the hand, 'I have no need of you,' nor again the head to the feet,
'I have no need of you'" (1 Cor 12:21).[42]

---

42. In the first half of the twentieth century, several church traditions actively sought to
restore the modern church to its earliest primitive shape, on the conviction that the primitive
church was organizationally more simple and therefore more harmonious and peaceful. See

To modern ears, these passages ring true, but often in the abstract. If one has experienced significant church conflict, it is difficult to understand how Paul's metaphor could be implemented concretely in a congregation. Members of a congregation do have different gifts and skill sets, but putting together the complicated puzzle of local church life with so many diverse pieces is difficult. The power dynamics in most local congregations are complex and often hidden from view.[43] Conflict is often held below the surface to preserve the appearance of being a "spiritual" community where everyone is supposed to get along. Studies suggest that nearly half of all pastors in their first five years cannot overcome the struggles of conflict in a congregation and leave the ministry.[44]

One unfortunate strategy to overcome the disunity and conflict in local congregations has been to create homogeneous churches that downplay the significance of difference.[45] However, even the most homogeneous churches have significant diversities. Members of a homogeneous church may all look alike on the outside (dress, style of worship, language, race, or ethnicity), but there remain many diverse temperaments; family backgrounds; occupations; and opinions about leadership, parenting, programming, and politics. There is no indication that conflict is any less present in congregations that may be described as homogeneous than in those congregations that look culturally diverse. Difference must be dealt with even in the most homogeneous-looking churches.

Richard T. Hughes, ed., *The American Quest for the Primitive Church* (Urbana: University of Illinois Press, 1988). A careful reading of the documents of the early church manifest anything but a harmonious set of local congregations.

43. See Andy Crouch, *Playing God: Redeeming the Gift of Power* (Downers Grove, IL: InterVarsity Press, 2013).

44. See Bob Burns, Tasha D. Chapman, and Donald C. Guthrie, *Resilient Ministry: What Pastors Told Us about Surviving and Thriving* (Downers Grove, IL: InterVarsity Press, 2013).

45. In an earlier generation, the church-growth movement suggested that churches grew most efficiently along racial, ethnic, or class lines. Accordingly, churches were not to cross those lines. But this was anathema to the New Testament church. See Larry W. Hurtado, *Why on Earth Did Anyone Become a Christian in the First Three Centuries?* (Milwaukee: Marquette University Press, 2016). Hurtado argues that the multiracial character of the early church was a fundamental commitment and without precedent in the ancient world.

Differences are more likely to be magnified the more intensely the community experiences its life together. Congregational ties vary greatly in intensity. The larger the congregation, the greater the tendency toward the anonymity of its congregants, and thus its ties are more nebulous and ambiguous. Conformity of belief, cultural habits, and leadership also factor into the equation. Conflicts within a congregation become more intense as the ties that bind the congregation are more significant.

Disagreements in congregations come in a variety of shapes and sizes. For example, there are classical confessional issues that define a church's theological identity. Across the ages, these matters have defined what is essential to the very being of the church and have appropriately been seen in terms of true or false. Was Jesus the God-man? Are there more gods than God? Is the Bible the authoritative Word of God? The church, both East and West, has traditionally claimed that its very nature and mission are determined by answers to these questions.

There are also a host of other theological issues that, while significant, have had less consensus across a diverse array of ecclesial traditions—matters such as whether infants should be baptized, whether the church should have bishops, and how the "days" of Genesis are best understood. These are matters of robust disagreement between and among churches, but they are less significant than those mentioned above even if on occasion they manifest themselves in the diversity of a local congregation.

Yet other matters pertaining to the habits of the church emerge from the cultural context in which churches reside: matters such as the appropriate musical instruments to be used in public worship, the style of leadership in the church, and the relation of the church to the cultural sphere. We might say these differences reside in a concentric circle yet further out than the differences mentioned in the previous paragraph. The tragic irony is that the further out these issues are on the concentric circle of importance, the more often they are the focus of conflict in the church. Local congregations are rarely torn apart over disputes about the classical confessions of the Christian faith. Far more frequently the conflicts emerge from different intuitions and interests as they pertain to the "style" issues in a local congregation or the mistrust of church leadership.[46]

A congregation is unlikely to disagree on issues of just-war theory or the deity of Christ, but they are likely to experience intense conflicts over issues such as worship, community life, and leadership. The "politics" of church life are often experienced as "us" versus "them," where the sides express deep disagreement, and tragically are played out behind the scenes.[47] Hidden from public view, these conflicts devolve so quickly that there is no easy resolution. Personality and style conflicts take on the appearance of fundamental theological differences.[48]

Families experience this dynamic in peculiar ways in our modern democratic culture as well. Conflicts of wills are interpreted as expressing core disagreements. Whether the matter is child-rearing, family budgets, or time management, disagreements are too often interpreted as having a "right" and a "wrong" side. These conflicts are especially challenging when they require one side to undergo fundamental change if the matter is to be settled. Harmony then appears possible only when one side loses. From the outside, family differences are frequently not life-and-death matters, but from inside the family dynamic, it is less obvious that the escalation of emotions attached to certain issues is inappropriate.

Congregational conflicts are not peculiar to the context of late modernity, yet there is a uniqueness to how modern democracies deal with conflict. The culture of most congregations subconsciously

---

46. Congregations can be torn apart by grave moral travesties, such as sexual abuse or embezzlement of funds. Most church scandals reported in the press fall in this latter category, though far more churches experience conflict created by the offensive actions of less moral gravity.

47. See Bob Burns, Tasha D. Chapman, and Donald Guthrie, *The Politics of Ministry: Navigating the Power Dynamics and Negotiating Interests* (Downers Grove, IL: InterVarsity Press, 2019).

48. See Peter Scazzero with Warren Bird, *The Emotionally Healthy Church: A Strategy for Discipleship that Actually Changes Lives* (Grand Rapids: Zondervan, 2015).

operates with a democratic polity—dismissing the complexity of power and authority while operating with naive assumptions about the interplay of temperaments and personal interests. A naturally introverted pastor favoring the privacy of the study while enjoying the public platform is often not prepared to deal with (or interested in) the relational complexities of diverse temperaments and strained relationships. Members on a church board, by contrast, often bring assumptions to bear on the pastor that they borrow from life outside the church.[49] The resultant battle of wills leads to such congregational messiness that even bystanders ask, "Where is the unity of the church?"[50] By virtue of its fundamental cultural commitments, democracy works best with a style of leadership from the middle, whose authority cannot be imposed from above and is not beholden to the interests of specific constituent groups.[51] However, most local congregations operate with an implicit (and sometimes explicit) hierarchical frame of leadership. Often the fundamental problem is that in churches we lead from the top when modern democratic culture yearns for leadership from the middle.

One of the significant lessons from recent leadership studies is that individuals with narcissistic tendencies often gravitate toward positions of leadership in our times, both because of their own inner sense of emptiness (to be filled by the appreciation of others) and because modern democracies incline so strongly toward narcissistic tendencies.[52] Democracy as a formal polity appears to give an equal

---

49. See Collin Hansen and Jeff Robinson, eds., *Fifteen Things Seminary Couldn't Teach Me* (Wheaton: Crossway, 2018).

50. Kenneth L. Swetland, *Facing Messy Stuff in the Church: Case Studies for Pastors and Congregations* (Grand Rapids: Kregel, 2005).

51. The telling title of a book for academic deans by Tammy Stone and Mary Coussons-Read, *Leading from the Middle: A Case-Study Approach to Academic Leadership for Associate and Assistant Deans*, ACE Series on Higher Education (Lanham, MD: Rowman & Littlefield, 2011), captures well the organizational dilemma of people in positions of leadership that are not at the top of the hierarchy in a university setting. In modern democracies, this is not peculiar to certain kinds of institutions but is endemic to the culture.

52. Tomas Chamorro-Premuzic, "Why Bad Guys Win at Work," *Harvard Business Review*, November 2, 2015, https://hbr.org/2015/11/why-bad-guys-win-at-work), writes, "An impressive

voice to all, but in reality every voice carries its own authority.[53] The temptation to read everyone else's experience through one's own is fertile ground for conflict. This narcissist tendency simply affirms this temptation outright rather than supposing it to be socially hidden.[54] In our narcissistic times, it is no surprise that the question of unity as it relates to the local congregation seems virtually intractable.

Congregations that begin by affirming the diversity of experience and intuition among its members and its leadership may be better protected from the narcissistic temptation. If the leadership question starts from the diversity end of the unity-diversity spectrum, there is a greater possibility that one's own experience will not be the sole interpretive lens through which events are understood. Diversity is the air that sustains modern democracies, but tragically it is the attribute least affirmed in ecclesial communities embedded in late modern democracies whose identity is hardwired always to think of (superficial) unity.

Showing Hospitality to Diversity

How then should we think of ecclesial divides that persist among our churches? We cannot permit the ecclesial square to grow in alienation and arbitrariness, nor can we naively suppose divisions will take care of themselves. Diverse churches in diverse denominations must begin to cultivate the desire to live together in, with, and through our differences. The animating vision of the gospel calls persons of diverse traditions to live together in truth and love, learning to talk with each

---

15-year longitudinal study found that individuals with psychopathic and narcissistic characteristics gravitated toward the top of the organizational hierarchy. ... This explains why bad guys often win—their success comes at a price, and the price is paid by the organization. ... And the more polluted or contaminated the environment—in a political sense—the more these parasitic personalities will thrive." See also Chuck DeGroat, *When Narcissism Comes to Church: Healing Your Community from Emotional and Spiritual Abuse* (Downers Grove, IL: InterVarsity Press, 2020); and Diane Langberg, *Redeeming Power: Understanding Authority and Abuse in the Church* (Grand Rapids: Brazos, 2020).

53. This is the core argument from the classic work by Nathan O. Hatch, *The Democratization of American Christianity* (New Haven: Yale University Press, 1991).

54. The surprising classic by Christopher Lasch, *The Culture of Narcissism* (New York: Norton, 1991), caught many observers off-guard because of Lasch's contention that narcissism was not simply a personality trait but a core value in late secular modernity.

other and slowly altering and deepening their traditions in response to that conversation.[55]

A principled and pluralistic ecclesial square, including that of the local congregation, is the only option available to us against oppression or anarchy. It is the option most suited to frame the unity of the church in a culture enamored of diversity.[56] This is both the genius of Protestantism and its greatest danger. Protestantism adapted easily to the emergence of modern democracies and was comfortable with the separation of church and state, where the politics of the nation-state were not the guarantor of the church's unity.[57] The modern democratic temper has proved to be the guarantor of the church's diversity. Methodists and Presbyterians and Pentecostals all found a home across the street from each other in America, as well as under the evangelical tent. But the danger of this "Protestant option" is the loss of a principled embrace of the church's mission. Pluralism without principle reduces to relativism. When differences are interpreted as inconsequential, the truthfulness of core confessional convictions also become inconsequential, and the church ceases to be a witness to the truth of the gospel.

Evangelical networks and congregations ought to engage with one another on the terms of the gospel rather than the terms of the conventional wisdom of a democratic polity or the natural conventions of secular versions of tolerance. They also must recognize that late modern democracy is the context in which God has placed the

---

55. Martin E. Marty uses similar language in articulating a framework for how the world's diverse religions ought to relate. See Marty, *When Faiths Collide*, Blackwell Manifestos (Oxford: Blackwell, 2005).

56. For the analogy to the wider public square, see James W. Skillen, *Recharging the American Experiment: Principled Pluralism for Genuine Civic Community* (Grand Rapids: Baker, 1994).

57. Paul Avis argues that the Reformation debates about ecclesial polity foreshadowed the diverse ways in which Christian churches came to grips with constitutional forms of governance. It would be a mistake to suggest, however, that ecclesial forms of democratic polity simply mirrored secular governance structures. They arose from the theological critique of ecclesial monarchianism. See Avis, *Beyond the Reformation? Authority, Primacy and Unity in the Conciliar Tradition* (Edinburgh: T&T Clark, 2006).

church in the West. Our differences will not be settled by appeal to a voting electorate, but neither can we assume that people work easily with older, hierarchical notions of authority. Church diversity makes sense inside the gospel mandate that many different members belong to the same body. Dealing with diversity therefore requires humility and wisdom. It requires vigilance against resentment and cynicism.[58] It requires a generosity of spirit and a depth of conviction. It requires churches to speak prophetically with the resources of their tradition while recognizing their own vested interests in those traditions.

Changing the ethos of our ecclesial identity as evangelicals may well require us to think of the commitment to our tradition less in terms of defeating an enemy and more in terms of showing hospitality to a stranger. Without a home (tradition), there is no place to invite the stranger into. A traditionless Christian is a person without a home. On the other hand, a tradition construed as a fortress is a most inhospitable place for strangers. A church based on the apostolic foundation will not sacrifice theological conviction for the sake of unity, nor will it use theological conviction as a club to be swung uncharitably at opponents.

We should take seriously the ideas of those with whom we disagree not primarily to overthrow them, but rather with the expectation that wisdom is found even among those who disagree with us.[59] If we invite the stranger into our tradition as a radical act of hospitality, we may in turn be invited into the stranger's tradition and taste some of its delicacies.[60] This requires churches not merely to be tolerant of each other but also to actively engage one another.[61] The conflicts

---

58. A penetrating analysis of the idolatry of cynicism is Dick Keyes, *Seeing through Cynicism: A Reconsideration of the Power of Suspicion* (Downers Grove, IL: InterVarsity Press, 2006).

59. In *When Faiths Collide*, Marty extends this suggestion at great length as a prophetic call to Christian churches to engage global diversity on distinctively Christian terms.

60. This is spelled out further in my "A Post-partisan Partisan Ecclesiology," in Lints, *Renewing the Evangelical Mission*, 161–88.

61. Cognizant of the liberal Protestant tendency toward tolerance as the best means of dealing with diversity, Karl Barth asked, "Was it a deliberate acceptance and initiation of the task when from the eighteenth century onwards the churches began to adopt the idea of mutual

of a fractured church are not healed by keeping emotional distance from those with whom we differ. Rather, healing comes when we invite the outsider into a conversation on the differences that have made a difference. This invitation to outsiders welcomes them into the wisdom of one's own tradition, while also recognizing that the sacred wisdom of the gospel is more expansive than one's tradition can fully capture.[62] This is a counterintuitive claim in the culture of late modern democracy, where our freedom is too often construed as a freedom from others and where we are encouraged to see our differences as disguised forms of division.[63]

The gospel is a strange form of hospitality, inviting outsiders into new choices and communities. The gospel is belonging, not to ourselves, but to the Triune God, and because of that belonging to others. If we are honest with our own inveterate loneliness, belonging to others can be very attractive. And if God hardwires us this way, it is little wonder that we feel relief when we no longer simply belong to ourselves.

The church should be a community where the "individual-as-chooser" never quite feels at home. The church is a place that infringes on choices, and eventually everyone feels like an outsider because they have bumped into people who make different choices than they do.[64] Pastors who do not recognize this in-built network

---

civility and tolerance? There is no need to ignore the advantageous results of that development, yet the serious criticism to which this mode of union is open cannot be ignored. The concept of toleration originates in political and philosophical principles which are not only alien but even opposed to the Gospel." Barth, *The Church and the Churches* (Grand Rapids: Eerdmans, 2005 [original 1936]), 34.

62. This account requires the "gospel" be further cashed out both concretely and theologically. This reminder comes powerfully in the words of the apostle Paul in Gal 1:6–9. See D. A. Carson and Timothy Keller, eds., *The Gospel as Center: Renewing Our Faith and Reforming Our Ministry Practices* (Wheaton: Crossway, 2012).

63. A very perceptive treatment of hospitality as a church-uniting strategy is Elizabeth Newman, *Untamed Hospitality: Welcoming God and Other Strangers* (Grand Rapids: Brazos, 2007).

64. Gary Babcock notes a common tragedy in many evangelical churches when he comments, "The exaggerated theology of the church purely as *congregatio fidelium*, understood as a gathered community of individual believers who have experienced individual conversion, is common in evangelical circles. Church is in this sense is the place where peoples' religious needs need to be met but a brief encounter with reality is in order. Amid the individualism

of potential frictions are ripe for burnout. Parishioners hoping to eventually find a church where everyone will choose as they do are bound to feel forever restless. It is countercultural to suppose God chooses us rather than we choose God. But if this is true, then the church does not exist because people choose to join it, but rather because God has chosen to gather his people into communities belonging to him.[65]

Churchly cocoons often leave us isolated from dissenting voices, while also (ironically) enabling us to privilege the relationships that matter the most. These are the two sides of democracy. Blessing and curse. After the fall, part of our experience is creation's reminder of how things are "supposed to be" and how things are "not the way it's supposed to be."[66] The ease of choices in late modernity is a terrific blessing. It frees us from the restraints of external powers and enslavements of stereotypes. However, the accompanying curse is the abundance of choices that often overwhelm our efforts to settle into a well-formed community. There is an eternal restlessness that works against forming loyalties to any community. It is a dangerous curse.

The wisdom of the gospel requires that we "bump into" the differences we have with each other, which in turn requires that these differences are made intelligible across our diverse cultural and social locations.[67] Being accountable to the gospel is a difficult labor, requir-

---

of so much of the contemporary church, people's religious needs are very often NOT met." Babcock, *The House Where God Lives: Renewing the Doctrine of the Church for Today* (Grand Rapids: Eerdmans, 2009), 169.

65. This is the heart of Michael S. Horton's claim that Protestant ecclesiology is covenantal rather than contractual, and that the great danger of churches bound together simply by voluntary choices is that individual choices will inevitably conflict with the divine choice that calls the church into being. See Horton, *People and Place: A Covenant Ecclesiology* (Louisville: Westminster John Knox, 2006).

66. This is the title of Cornelius Plantinga's depiction of sin in poignant and joyful terms (if that were possible): *Not the Way It's Supposed to Be: A Breviary of Sin* (Grand Rapids: Eerdmans, 1993).

67. Assuming that there are diverse ecclesial models present in the New Testament, Miroslav Volf writes, "The differentiation of various Christian traditions is not simply to be lamented as a scandal, but rather welcomed as a sign of the vitality of the Christian faith within multicultural, rapidly changing societies demanding diversification and flexibility." Volf, *After*

ing both humility and confidence. There can be little doubt that the gospel requires the hard work of reconciliation in the face of disagreements. We must be partisans of the gospel in such a way that it restrains the partisan commitments to ourselves. We must choose to limit our freedoms for the sake of the gospel, to be both partisans of the gospel and postpartisan toward ourselves. As I will argue in the final chapter, we need wisdom to know when to be partisan and when to be postpartisan. But first, we turn to the primary source of that wisdom—the Word written and living.

Our Likeness: The Church as the Image of the Trinity, Sacra Doctrina: Christian Theology for a Postmodern Age (Grand Rapids: Eerdmans, 1997), 21.

Not even the people of God in our epoch of redemptive history are called to create a holy culture, because Christians are called to go out into every culture with the gospel. We are a people, to be sure, but our peoplehood is spiritual. Culturally, we are Jew and Gentile, Greek and Roman, European and African.

—KEN MYERS, ALL GOD'S CHILDREN AND BLUE SUEDE SHOES

9

DIVERSE COMMUNITIES AND THE CONTEXTUALIZING OF DIVERSITY

THE ISSUE OF INTERPRETIVE PLURALISM

It is a common assumption in skeptical circles that the Scriptures of the Christian church do not articulate any essential unity that holds them together. The evidence for this assumption is that there are just too many different interpretations of the Bible to allow for any single belief system to emerge. There are too many diverse theological traditions to believe that any one of them could actually be true. It would be better to remain skeptical about the whole of Christianity than to be taken in by sectarian rendering.

A similar critique has been lodged against the Protestant traditions, which granted to every individual the right to read the Scriptures for themselves. This central conviction prompted many of the Reformation-era translations of the Bible into the vernacular, giving to individuals the opportunity to read the Bible in their native tongues. However, this also made it possible for the Bible to be interpreted in a thousand different ways—everyone was their own interpreter.[1] The consequence was a fragmenting of the Christian faith into many different traditions and the loss of a unified message. The modern

---

1. George Marsden, "Everyone One's own Interpreter? The Bible, Science and Authority in Mid-Nineteenth-Century America," in *The Bible in America: Essays in Cultural History*, ed. Nathan O. Hatch and Mark A. Noll (Oxford: Oxford University Press, 1982), 79–100.

commitment to the rights of individuals entailed that Christians could no longer believe in any single account of their faith—or so it seemed.

In light of these pressures, there has been an increased yearning inside the contemporary church for a move away from individual interpretations toward communal interpretations, where individual biases would be put aside and a greater consensus could emerge. If only greater respect was shown for the wider church community and less respect for our personal interpretive preferences, we would have a more consensual grasp of the biblical text—or so the sentiment goes. But the irony is that the postindividualist impulse has not led to any lessening of ecclesial fragmentation.[2] The privileging of communities over individuals has done little to mask intractable differences. A simple reaffirmation of the communal responsibilities of biblical interpreters is not likely to lessen the fragmentation either. Learning to live with the dialectic between unity and diversity and between communities and individuals is part of the wisdom of the gospel, but on this side of the grave there is no panacea to resolve all our differences. In what follows, I will consider this turn to community and the dilemma it creates for Christians in the modern era before tackling a wider theological response to the problem of diverse contextualizations of the gospel.

PRIVILEGING COMMUNITIES

Belonging to a community, or at least the appearance of belonging to a community, is important to most people today.[3] The picture of the lonely soul bowling alone is not something anyone wants to be saddled

---

2. In an earlier era, evangelical fragmentation concerned differences about baptism, the millennium, or divine election. See David F. Wright, "Scripture and Evangelical Diversity with Special Reference to the Baptismal Divide," in *A Pathway into Holy Scripture*, ed. Philip Satterthwaite and David F. Wright (Grand Rapids: Eerdmans, 1994), 257–76. The contemporary postpartisan fragmentation focuses on differences of cultural engagement, political orientation, or ethnic and gender issues. As an example, see Fernando Segovia, "Toward a Hermeneutic of the Diaspora: A Hermeneutic of Otherness and Engagement," in *Hispanic Christian Thought at the Dawn of the Twenty-First Century: Apuntes in Honor of Justo L. González*, ed. Alvin Padilla, Roberto Goizueta, and Eldin Villafañe (Nashville: Abingdon, 2005), 55–68.

3. Though different in their orientations, the MeToo movement and the Black Lives Matter movement work on the assumption that an individual's identity is tightly tied to a community

with.[4] We all want to belong to some group, even if we also want to hold lightly to the group's grip on us.

This turn to community may not be as thorough as the subjective turn in the era of the Enlightenment or the turn to language in early twentieth-century philosophical circles, but it has crept into popular culture at a much faster rate than its two earlier counterparts. The demise of the lonely, solitary self of modernity and the yearning for community in our time are breathtaking in their respective speeds.[5]

Communities at the beginning of the twenty-first century do not look much like the communities of tribe and clan and church of earlier times, nor in other parts of the globe. Communities of discourse today are more likely bound together by economic status, by leisure activities, by vocations, or by educational background—by common interests rather than by common traditions.[6] The media tend to interpret communities through a political lens, drawing on polling data interpreting the loyalties of a demographically defined group. The ties binding these sorts of communities together transcend personal connections. They inevitably are communities of abstraction, though the frequency of their use in the media exercises an inordinate pressure on those in that demographic.

Plenty of evidence shows that we are not nearly as communal as we would like to believe.[7] We still watch television in virtual isolation,

defining reality—gender or race, respectively.

4. Robert Putnam, *Bowling Alone: The Collapse and Revival of American Community* (New York: Simon & Schuster, 2001).

5. In evangelical theological circles, Stanley Grenz was a central figure in drawing attention to the significance of community for theological discussion. See Grenz, *Theology for the Community of God* (Nashville: Broadman & Holman, 1994); Grenz, *Created for Community: Connecting Christian Belief with Christian Living* (Grand Rapids: Baker, 1998); and Grenz, *The Social God and the Relational Self: A Trinitarian Theology of the Imago Dei* (Louisville: Westminster John Knox, 2001).

6. For the most influential sociological treatment of the paradoxes of community and individualism, see Robert Bellah et al., *Habits of the Heart: American Individualism and Commitment in American Life* (Berkeley: University of California Press, 1985). The notable exception here are local immigrant communities that sustain peculiar traditions in the midst of a secularizing culture that is no respecter of traditions.

7. George Rupp, "Communities of Collaboration: Shared Commitments/Common Tasks," in *On Community*, ed. Leroy S. Rouner, Boston University Studies in Philosophy and Religion (Notre Dame: University of Notre Dame Press, 1991), writes, "The prominence of the theme of

scan the internet by ourselves, and are fascinated by our own internal psychology. We may speak much about the praiseworthiness of community, but few are willing to count the costs of belonging to an actual living, breathing community. A colleague once remarked to me, "I love community. I just could never live in one." Like most of our sports heroes, we want to be wanted but would rather be free agents when it comes time for contract talks.

Why then do we talk so much more about community than we used to? And why is there a morally commendable tone attached to talk about community of the sort that used to be attached to talk about the individual? Why has the pendulum swung in the way it has, and what difference might it make for the way Scripture is lived out? Let me suggest three factors in this change of cultural ethos before spelling out the implications for an ecclesial identity of unity-in-diversity rooted in Scripture. The post-positivist turn in epistemology, the pervasiveness of globalization, and the technologies of democratization have combined to privilege the discourse of communities rather than individuals.

THE TURN TO COMMUNAL MODES
OF KNOWING AND INTERPRETING

Two generations ago, a host of conceptual battles were fought in the academy that moved the ideological playing field away from individually objective perceptions of reality toward context-dependent modes of understanding. Those context-dependent modes of understanding were construed in a variety of ways. Thomas Kuhn, a historian of science, pointed at the way in which socially constructed paradigms of research programs profoundly influence not only which questions are asked by natural scientists but also what count as appropriate answers. Science is as dependent on the assumptions of communities of scientists as it is on the hard evidence collected and analyzed by individual

---

community in contemporary literature and social commentary itself testifies to the deep sense of its lack in the consciousness of cultural elites in the modern West" (192).

scientists. The long-standing dogma of epistemic objectivism was stridently challenged by empiricist-leaning philosophers at midcentury as well.[8] Philosophers like W. V. O. Quine and Wilfrid Sellars jettisoned the language of objectivity and replaced it with the notion of weblike belief systems that have no individual points of correspondence with reality.[9] People hold beliefs because of socially reinforced mechanisms. The myth of the given, they argued, is a figment of the Enlightenment imagination.[10] Peter Berger and Thomas Luckmann in turn argued that reality is socially constructed rather than discovered by human inquiry.[11] Observation is as much socially approved interpretation as it is simple discovery of facts. Berger, in particular, was careful to highlight the relativist overtones implicit in the nascent sociology of knowledge, but in so doing he was hoping to relativize the relativizers.

THE TURN TO GLOBAL COMMUNITIES

There were also major changes in the global character of culture during the twentieth century, which influenced the turn to community at the outset of the twenty-first century. During the twentieth century, there was a sharp uptick in global economic activity. Unrelated to the shifts of conceptual paradigms, the economic boom of the postwar years brought a radical increase in international trade and with it a sharp increase in cross-cultural interactions. The globe was growing ever more intertwined as the consumer markets of North America and Western Europe spread their economic tentacles into parts heretofore unknown to them.[12] The globe grew smaller as diverse people groups

---

8. Richard Rorty rehearses this story at the beginning of his influential work *Philosophy and the Mirror of Nature* (Princeton: Princeton University Press, 1979).

9. See W. V. O. Quine, "Two Dogmas of Empiricism," in *From a Logical Point of View: Nine Logico-Philosophical Essays* (Cambridge, MA: Harvard University Press, 1953).

10. See Wilfrid Sellars, *Science, Perception and Reality* (London: Routledge and Kegan Paul, 1963).

11. See Peter Berger and Thomas Luckmann, *The Social Construction of Reality: A Treatise in the Sociology of Knowledge* (Garden City, NY: Anchor, 1966).

12. The phenomenon of globalization has not been experienced in uniform fashion across diverse cultural locations of the globe. There are multiple "globalizations" even as the pressure toward conformity to a single global reality grows stronger. See Peter L. Berger and Samuel

came into far more pervasive and persistent contact.[13] The loss of the limitations of geography ironically cemented an individual's identity within particular groups. The melting-pot mythology of American history seemed ill-suited to the era of the civil rights movement and second-wave feminism, massive new waves of immigration, and the demise of colonial sensibilities.[14] The realization was dawning that America's place in the globe was far more complex than previously supposed. Self-definition grew out of an encounter (and often against that encounter) with those who were culturally different. Identity politics was but a natural outcome of the forces of globalization. No one simply belonged to themselves. We were all part of a group over and against other groups.

The resulting fragmentation has also been made more complex by another axis of identity—namely, that of secularization. On that spectrum, communities find their identity by either moving toward a religious worldview or away from one. Those moving away from religious convictions or removed from any religious sensibilities altogether appear to be increasing in recent polling data in the West, while diminishing outside of the West. On that end of the identity axis, belief in God, or in heaven, or sin and salvation, is not denied; it is simply absent. This is especially notable among a large swath of the cultural elites in the West, where religion is viewed as simply irrelevant.

THE TURN TO TECHNOLOGICAL COMMUNITIES

A final part of the story is the democratizing technologies of the latter half of the twentieth century, most especially television and the internet. These technologies greatly increased the sense of power individuals possessed while freeing them from traditional constraints and

---

P. Huntington, eds., *Many Globalizations: Cultural Diversity in the Contemporary World* (New York: Oxford University Press, 2002).

13. See Mike Featherstone, ed., *Global Culture: Nationalism, Globalization and Modernity* (London: Sage, 1990).

14. See William R. Hutchison, *Religious Pluralism in America: The Contentious History of a Founding Ideal* (New Haven: Yale University Press, 2003), especially chapter 9, "Whose America Is It Anyway? The Sixties and Afterwards," 219–40.

traditional communities. The new technologies fueled commercial expansion, unleashing enormous pressures of conformity on consumers that implicitly pushed them into homogeneous communities with other like-minded consumers.[15] Data and information grew in unprecedented volume, carving out spaces for specialist communities of every imaginable kind.[16] An individual's sense of significance and security grew in proportion to belonging to one of these groups. As the mythology of heroic individualism weakened, the technology-driven consumer pressures created a new mythology: it is better to belong to a tribe with a brand than merely to oneself.[17] The explosion of social media in the last decade has only filled in that portrait.

Understanding these historical, cultural, and conceptual contexts is important if we want to discern the differences that make a difference. Paying attention to context and culture in the right way may enable us to hear more clearly how culture influences the understanding of contexts and, strangely, to be freed from its overly dominant role in our lives.

BIBLICAL MODES OF COMMUNITY

The Scriptures portray our identity in communal terms as well, but in strikingly different ways than in late secular modernity. Though Israel had a corporate identity as God's people, they had no sense of the individual autonomy so prevalent in late modern liberal democracies.

---

15. An early and prescient analysis of the character of the technological era is Jacques Ellul, *The Technological Society*, trans. John Wilkinson (New York: Knopf, 1964). See also Albert Borgmann, *Technology and the Character of Contemporary Life: A Philosophical Inquiry* (Chicago: University of Chicago Press, 1987), and Borgmann, *Power Failure: Christianity in the Culture of Technology* (Grand Rapids: Brazos, 2003).

16. See George Ritzer, *Explorations in the Sociology of Consumption: Fast Food, Credit Cards and Casinos* (London: Sage, 2001), and Gary Cross, *An All-Consuming Century: Why Commercialism Won in Modern America* (New York: Columbia University Press, 2002).

17. Suzanne Keller has argued that communities in technologically advanced contexts will continue to thrive because of the intrinsic yearnings of people for roots. In her thirty-year longitudinal study of a planned community in New Jersey, she concluded that the yearning for roots survived all the democratizing pressures of technology, though in very different social forms than traditional communities. See Keller, *Community: Pursuing the Dream, Living the Reality* (Princeton: Princeton University Press, 2003).

Those who have been reconciled to God in Christ belong to each other in peculiar premodern ways. In the New Testament, relationships in the people of God were defined by the uniqueness of the family to which one belonged, not according to inherited genes but by virtue of a common theological inheritance. The great treasure of the gospel defined their life together.[18] Belonging to each other was not signaled by wearing the same clothes or speaking the same language or living at similar addresses. Rather, it was by sharing the common gift of the gospel in contextually similar and different ways. It was belonging to a common story of creation and redemption, even while the story embraced many diverse communities and cultures.

One wrong-headed approach to the diversity of interpretations is to suppose that the conflict of interpretations should be accepted at face value because of the conviction that the Bible is simply a human book, parts of which will be helpful to some communities and other parts will be helpful to other communities. As argued earlier, the ambiguity of plural perspectives was a driving reason behind the Enlightenment project to abandon arguments from the Bible since there were so many diverse interpretations. Baptists and Anglicans and Presbyterians and Lutherans all had different ways to read and apply the Bible. From the vantage point of Rousseau or Voltaire, this implied that neither the Bible nor the diverse interpretations that arose from it could be trusted. For these Enlightenment figures, there must be a secular account of reality that is susceptible to generally accessible evidence and proof. That intuition continues to linger among many cultural elites even though secular renderings of reality are no less susceptible to diverse interpretations than religious ones.

In a strange irony, what was once viewed as a fundamental obstacle to believing the Bible (the diversity of interpretations) has become a strategy on the part of postmodern interpreters of retrieving the

---

18. See the powerful testimony of the Anglican archbishop of Uganda Henry Luke Orombi, "What Is Anglicanism?," *First Things* (August/September 2007), 23–28. He testifies to the theological inheritance of Ugandan Anglicans, which carved out a peace among warring tribes grafted onto the same tree of grace by the gospel of Jesus Christ.

Bible—at least the parts of the Bible that serve one's interests. Instead of seeing the diversity of interpretations as a problem, these newer interpreters simply embraced the conflict of interpretations, hoping that everyone could enjoy the parts of the Bible they liked while discarding the parts of the Bible they disliked. The ground for this strategy was, again, the assumption that the Bible was an ordinary human book, and different communities would find wisdom for their purposes in different parts of the Bible. Reducing the Bible to merely a human book allowed for it to be interpreted in diverse ways by diverse communities. Without a divine imprint, there was no need to reconcile the different interpretations. In many ways, this strategy anticipates that of liberal Protestants at mid-century, who attempted to tone down the supernatural elements of the Bible in order to make it more believable for "modern" ears. In both instances, denying the divine origin of the Bible made it more malleable for whatever purposes modern audiences could readily accept.

In the hands of late twentieth-century postmodern interpreters, the Bible came to be viewed as simply another member of the community of interpreters, displaying certain profound truths but also being corrected by the perspectives of marginalized communities. Scripture became malleable under pressure from diverse constituencies, which brought different perspectives and emphases to various parts of the Bible. The perspectives of the reader were as important as the perspective of the text. Readers influenced not only how the text was read but also what text was read as Scripture and how it fit into their lives.

All of this leads us to ask: Can diverse communal interpretations and applications of the Bible all be appropriate? Does the existence of diverse interpretive communities authorize those communities' peculiar ways of reading the Bible? And finally, how might the difference between interpretation and application affect the way we think about the diverse communities of interpreters? Those questions will be addressed in the next section.

Dramatic Diversity and
the Unity of Scripture

Reading the Bible well is not simply a matter of grasping the ways in which it describes the objective facts of history. Reading well is surely not less than this, but it is so much more. The Bible should be understood as creating a world of meaning and not merely describing facts. The language of Scripture is a framework of understanding in whose structure the interpreting community is perceived and interpreted.[19] The text of Scripture is not simply a set of descriptions of a world out there, but rather of a world to be inhabited, a story through which a community's lives are told. As a divine word, the canon of Scripture is not awaiting an interpretation but absorbs the ecclesial community into its reality.[20] We appreciate the power of Scripture yet further when we see that the power of its language is owing to the divine drama of redemption narrated on its pages.[21] This simple insight into the "drama-like" character of the Scriptures reflects the unfolding story.[22] God's revelation was not given at one time, nor in the form of a theological dictionary. The Bible, as Geerhardus Vos reminds us, is not a dogmatic treatise.[23] It is a book full of dramatic interest and comes complete with major and minor plots. It not only reveals God's redemptive purposes

19. This extends the argument from chapter 6 as it relates to the way in which Scripture itself is a model of unity and diversity.

20. This is language borrowed from Bruce Marshall, "Absorbing the World: Christianity and the Universe of Truths," in *Theology and Dialogue: Essays in Conversation with George Lindbeck*, ed. Bruce Marshall (Notre Dame: University of Notre Dame Press, 1990), 69–104.

21. Two conceptual claims linger in the background of this account. God is the sort of being who can speak and write, and God can speak and write in such a fashion that human writings are also his writings. For a defense of both claims, see Nicholas Wolterstorff, *Divine Discourse: Philosophical Reflections on the Claim that God Speaks* (Cambridge: Cambridge University Press, 1995).

22. More than any other modern author, Kevin J. Vanhoozer has teased out how important and complex and interesting this "simple" insight is. Far from squeezing the Scriptures into a single narrow mode, Vanhoozer has shown how rich and deep the Scriptures are if we follow this internal logic of the Scriptures themselves. His longest exposition of this can be found in *The Drama of Doctrine: A Canonical-Linguistic Approach to Christian Theology* (Louisville: Westminster John Knox, 2005).

23. See Geerhardus Vos, *Biblical Theology* (1948; repr., Grand Rapids: Eerdmans, 1985), 17.

but is a means of enacting those purposes as well.[24] It is historical narrative, wisdom literature, prophetic challenge, and apocalyptic visions all rolled up into one grand drama.[25]

The Scriptures have the characteristic parts of a drama: tension and vision, pain and hope, movement and consummation. This drama has real characters that develop and a God who discloses himself on the pages of history and occasionally speaks as one of the actors. There is a primary plot, which begins with creation, runs through the dysfunctions of the fall, and contains foreshadowings of redemption. This plot then reaches a surprising climactic intrusion of the Creator into the created order in the person of Jesus, who effects an astonishing re-creation and announces a final consummation of the entire created order as God intended. This unfolding plotline runs from Genesis to Revelation, and the entrance of the God-man into history marks out the "before" and "after" in dramatic and revolutionary terms.

There is an art to organizing the diverse materials of Scripture in a way that holds this great big story of redemption together. The sheer complexity of this epic story argues against reading the Bible in a narrowly uniform way. The organic unfolding of the message of the Bible frees us to read each passage or book of the Bible in the context of the entire passage and the entire Bible in the context of each passage.[26] The books of the Bible ought to be interpreted as inte-

---

24. John Murray reminded his readers, "Special revelation as deposited in Scripture is redemptive. It not only provides us with the history of God's redemptive accomplishments, not only does it interpret for us the meaning of these redemptive events; it is itself also an abiding and for us indispensable organ in the fulfilment of God's redemptive will." Murray, "Systematic Theology," in *Collected Writings of John Murray* (Carlisle, PA: Banner of Truth, 1982), 4:4. This article appeared originally as "Systematic Theology," *Westminster Theological Journal* 25, no. 2 (1963): 133–42, and "Systematic Theology: Second Article," *Westminster Theological Journal* 26, no. 1 (1963): 33–46.

25. Cf. Vanhoozer, *Drama of Doctrine*. See also Craig Bartholomew and Michael Goheen, *The Drama of Scripture: Finding Our Place in the Biblical Story* (Grand Rapids: Baker Academic, 2004), and Christopher J. H. Wright, *The Mission of God: Unlocking the Bible's Grand Narrative* (Downers Grove, IL: IVP Academic, 2018).

26. Susan Gillingham has argued against the claim that the Bible contains one story line on the grounds that not every book is self-consciously aware of its role in the story. See Gillingham,

grally connected to the whole of the drama of creation and re-creation (that is, redemption). The larger plotline "holds" the books together, though the meaning of any particular passage may not thereby be straightforward and simple. The story of the Bible is also the story that effectively retells our own narrative.

Major themes run the length of the whole Bible and provide distinct clues as to how the story unfolds.[27] These are woven into the fabric of the Scriptures by a master storyteller. When Jesus announced the coming of his kingdom, the first-century hearers may have heard echoes of David's kingship but wondered how Jesus could restore the monarchy in the midst of Roman rule. Jesus did not look the part of one who could overthrow the powers of a pagan empire spanning vast parts of the globe. He had a small band of followers. He spoke in parables and had no army. His kingship was not grounded in military might but in the reality that the Creator of the universe had entered his creation in the form of a servant. Jesus's kingdom redefined expectations about power and privilege. It would not be bounded by geography or culture or language. Its citizens would enter it by faith, not by sight. It was a kingdom not of this world but one that reoriented the story of everything in this world. The first would be last and the last would be first. Sin and death would be defeated by the humiliation of the king dying on a cross. Indeed, this was no ordinary kingdom, yet it continues to reach into every part of the globe to this day.

Other dominant themes across the whole length of Scripture include creation and re-creation, images and idols, mercy and justice, marriage and covenant, and temple and priesthood. Each of these

---

One Bible, Many Voices: Different Approaches to Biblical Studies (Grand Rapids: Eerdmans, 1999). In response, every book in Scripture does have a distinct sense of being party to the actual historical and covenantal relationship between Yahweh and his people Israel in the Old Testament and to the fulfillment of that relationship in the life, death, and resurrection story of Jesus in the New Testament.

27. D. A. Carson is the editor of a series of books, New Studies in Biblical Theology (Downers Grove, IL: InterVarsity Press), that tracks many of these themes across the entirety of the canon.

invites us into an alternate reality, reweaving the strands of a story of a new community together into a unity-in-diversity. When we see God asking Abraham to offer his son Isaac as a sacrifice in Genesis 22, it is not arbitrary to say it prepares us to see more clearly God himself offering up his son Jesus as a sacrifice. So it is that the community of followers of Jesus are called to sacrifice themselves for the good of others by means of which broken relationships might be reconciled. In the life, death, and resurrection of Jesus, God has done a brand-new work—but it is a work he prepared beforehand, and it is a work that continues to reinterpret our own lives.[28]

God revealed this message of salvation, redemption, and atonement progressively over many eras and embedded it as the story of many diverse individuals and institutions. This revelation was not delivered all at once as a classroom lecture; it unfolded over time. When the apostle Paul cites Genesis 15:6 in Romans 4:3 ("Abraham believed God, and it was counted to him as righteousness"), it is because the beginning of the story of God's gracious dealings with his people goes all the way back to Genesis and also because it is the same truth that interprets the life of Christians across the ages.

God speaks in and through the lives of individuals and communities across many different ages, not merely that he might be known in some abstract sense but that the relationship with humankind rent asunder by the tragedy of sin might be restored. In this sense God reveals the grand narrative of redemption, salvation, and atonement across a vast and diverse array of episodes and eras. Interpretive missteps occur either by paying too much attention to the trees and missing the forest or by imposing an alien or arbitrary forest on a set of trees. The way God has chosen to tell the story this way challenges us to see both the forest and the trees and to understand that this great big story of the gospel is also the story within which our lives make sense.

---

28. See N. T. Wright and Michael F. Bird, *The New Testament in Its World: An Introduction to the History, Literature, and Theology of the First Christians* (Grand Rapids: Zondervan, 2019).

The point to be underlined here is that biblical texts do not stand in isolation, only later to find their correlation and concatenation in the theological framework of the church.[29] The whole story of redemption, manifest in the themes running through the course of that story, serves as a clue to the unity-in-diversity to which each of us is invited.[30]

The Seeds of Cultural Pluralism
in a Singular Gospel

Viewing the canon as a divinely authorized drama allows us to view the history of diverse interpretations in a very different light. Far from capturing Scripture as it really is, the pluralized renderings of the biblical material often fail to capture the divine drama as it really is. In particular, they fail to capture the often complex relationship between creation and redemption as portrayed in the Scriptures.

When God created the world, the Scriptures record that God "spoke" it into being. The divine Word created the world, but more significantly, by the use of this metaphor the Scriptures communicate that the world was given meaning by his Word. The Word interprets the meaning of life and the destiny of history. The moral dimensions of the created order arise as reflection of the character of God. The active, creative Word of God is the language now in which the world "makes sense." There is a theological identity granted to the world by virtue of its being a "thing created." The world is contingent for its meaning and purpose on its Creator. God defines and interprets the world and repudiates alternative definitions and interpretations.

---

29. J. I. Packer writes, "Evangelicalism ought to allow the Bible to speak for itself in terms of its own interests, viewpoints, and emphases, in other words by a method that is thoroughly and consistently a posteriori." This would lead first to the organic relationship of themes across the Scriptures before settling on topics that have been organized systematically in retrospect. See Packer, "Infallible Scriptures and the Role of Hermeneutics," in *Scripture and Truth*, ed. D. A. Carson and John Woodbridge (Grand Rapids: Zondervan, 1983), 328.

30. Brevard Childs has forcefully argued against a "canon within a canon" on the grounds that the Scriptures grant identity to the church. This identity arises not from isolated passages but from the canon as a whole. The church's exegesis must therefore arise from this standpoint as well. See Childs, *The New Testament as Canon: An Introduction* (Philadelphia: Westminster, 1984).

As Genesis 2–3 unfolds, the moral fabric of the created order is torn asunder with humankind's refusal to center their identity in the divine character and command.[31] We cannot know why Adam and Eve rejected the divine norms, but we can know the consequences of that rejection.[32] Not only do humans bear responsibility for that rejection, but also human wisdom is now increasingly in sharp contrast to divine wisdom.

As a consequence of this disruption in the created moral order, the divine presence was removed and humankind experienced alienation from God in terms of unfulfilled desires. Their intrinsic yearning for significance and security did not cease, but they searched for alternative ways to satisfy the yearnings. Their restless wanderings became an enormous burden to be relieved at any cost. This search for significance is related in Genesis 11 in the Tower of Babel episode. This episode in the divine drama began with the collective yearnings of those on the plain of Shinar: "Come, let us build ourselves a city and a tower with its top in the heavens, and let us make a name for ourselves, lest we be dispersed over the face of the whole earth" (Gen 11:4). It was an attempt to build a tower that would reach to the heavens precisely because "heaven" was the only place a permanent home could be found and enduring significance and safety gained. The judgment on this human attempt to find an alternative significance ends

---

31. This does not settle the traditional controversy between natural-law theories of ethics and divine-command theories of ethics. One could still suppose on the above account that the Word of God, which defines good and evil, permeates the natural order—by which then good and evil are known. Likewise, nothing in the above account precludes a straightforward divine-command theory, which supposes that good and evil are themselves defined by the command of God. See John Hare, *God's Command*, Oxford Studies in Theological Ethics (New York: Oxford University Press, 2018). On the range of views regarding the divine-command theory of ethics, see Paul Helm, ed., *Divine Commands and Morality*, Oxford Readings in Philosophy (Oxford: Oxford University Press, 1981). See also Steve Wilkens, ed., *Christian Ethics: Four Views*, Spectrum Multiview Books (Downers Grove, IL: IVP Academic, 2017).

32. Henri Blocher rightly suggests that sin is "irrational" in the framework of creation. It does not "make sense." There is no "good reason" why humans sin. This is the mystery of the fall. See Blocher, *In the Beginning: The Opening Chapters of Genesis* (Downers Grove, IL: InterVarsity Press, 1984). On the "irrationality" of sin see also Cornelius Plantinga Jr., *Not the Way It's Supposed to Be: A Breviary of Sin* (Grand Rapids: Eerdmans, 1995).

not simply in the destruction of the tower but also in the scattering
of the peoples and a pluralizing of their language. In this early pre-Is-
raelite episode, cultural pluralism was part of the curse brought on
the people in consequence of the attempt to define their own significance. The diversity of languages was providentially brought about
to undermine their sense of security in their own accomplishments.
It would also serve proleptically as a sign of a future redemption in
which Christ would break down the walls that divide the nations.

This very same cultural pluralism was placed alongside the par-
ticularistic character in which the divine drama proceeded. The
promise given to Abraham in Genesis 12 and 15 is key in this regard.
Alongside the very command to separate himself from his family and
clan, Abram is promised the blessing bestowed would be a blessing
to all the nations. And here the pattern was established that God
would raise a remnant through which he would bring redemption to
the whole world. The divine exclusivism was precisely the method
through which a divine inclusivism would be instantiated. But the
order or direction of this pattern is most important. God was not
found in the richness and diversity of cultures in the first instance.
Rather, God disclosed his redemption through a particular people
(foreshadowing Jesus) by means of which the tearing of the human
community would be woven slowly back together. Uniformity was not
the intended result of this redemptive work, but rather a unity-in-diversity. Cultural pluralism would become the "carrier" of the radical
claim of the gospel that redemption would go even to the gentiles.

There was to be, for a time, a cultural unity in Israel to protect this
call to religious fidelity to the one and only true God, Yahweh. There
was a central location for the worship of God, expressing again the
prerogative of God to define worship. So too there was an (initial)
prohibition against the creation of a monarchy, rooted in the prohibition against creating a human king to replace the divine kingship.
Israel was to be distinctive in its separation and difference from the
surrounding cultures. This was a partial recovery of the original experience in Eden, but more so a typological anticipation of the final

fulfilled kingdom of God in which culture and worship would be one and in which there would be no discontinuity between the human and the holy.[33]

The divine drama progressed as it enacted the story of redemption. The climax of the drama was the first advent of Christ. In an ironic fulfillment of the anticipation of redemption, the followers of Jesus were no longer to be a sequestered ethnic group. The expansion of the gospel would break down the cultural boundaries that had previously limited the scope of God's reconciling work. The people of God were now to be found in all cultures, eating and drinking, enjoying music and art, and making tools with those who did not yet know the gospel.[34] The proclamation of the Christian message sought to break down the barriers between diverse cultures and rebuild bridges between communities formerly at enmity with each other. The dividing walls were to be broken down by the mercy of the gospel (see Eph 2). Now, even the gentiles and the Samaritans were to be full members of the redeemed community.[35]

In the original proclamation of the Christian message in Jerusalem, narrated in Acts 2, the curse of diverse languages was overcome, but not by destroying the diversity of cultures and languages. There at Pentecost, God typologically overcame the effect of the curse of Babel through the proclamation of the one gospel in diverse languages. The miracle of "tongues" in Acts 2 was the miracle of redemption itself—the beginnings of the restoration and reconciliation of diverse human communities to God and consequently the reconciling of these communities to each other.

---

33. See Meredith G. Kline, *Kingdom Prologue: Genesis Foundations for a Covenantal Worldview* (1981; repr., Eugene, OR: Wipf & Stock, 2006).

34. See Ken Myers, *All God's Children and Blue Suede Shoes: Christians and Popular Culture* (Wheaton: Crossway, 1989), for a suggestive treatment of a like-minded redemptive historical approach to culture.

35. It is not accidental that many of Jesus's parables place the Samaritan people in far better light than Jews of the first century would have placed them. The cultural divide between Jews and Samaritans ran deep into Israel's history, and yet this very tension becomes the context for the unfolding display of the Redeemer's mission.

This is the analogous situation we find ourselves in today. The drama of divine redemption continues to unfold in the outbreaking of divine mercy across the historical cultural divides. That drama is centered on the person and work of Christ, and this unifying center is also the very centrifugal force that pushes the gospel outward, across the length and breadth and width of the globe. The very exclusivity of the gospel in Christ is the foundation of its inclusive impulse.

However, the inclusive impulse cannot finally be reduced to a relativist impulse. The distinctiveness of the one man Jesus Christ prohibits equating the gospel with many diverse readings of that central truth. Culturally diverse applications of this gospel are appropriate, but not relativist renderings of the gospel. The universal makes sense in light of the particular. Therein lies the dialectic between unity and diversity in the divine drama.

Culturally Diverse Interpreters
of a Singular Gospel

The Bible poses an interaction of two diverse "ways-to-put-the-world-together"—ours and the Bible's. It is an interaction between the history of redemption and our own history. In this meeting as different communities of readers ask questions of the Scriptures, questions are being asked of them and they are forced to reckon with an alternative way-to-put-the-world-together.[36] This compels communities of readers to rethink many of their fundamental assumptions and ways of living, even communities who are situated in very diverse historical and cultural contexts. Reading the Scriptures in the company of differently situated readers may aid us in reckoning more fully with the Scripture's alternative way-to-put-the-world-together. Unfortunately, communities can also blunt the force of the Scriptures by equating the

---

36. Markus Bockmuehl writes of the confrontation between Scripture and its readers such that the reader is "the object as much as the subject of analysis and interpretation." See Bockmuehl, *Seeing the Word: Refocusing New Testament Study*, Studies in Theological Interpretation (Grand Rapids: Baker Academic, 2006), 147.

habits of their ordinary lives with the core values of Scripture. The taken-for-granted character of ordinary life often proves an impediment to hearing the Scriptures. From another angle, ordinary life may also bring fresh insights when it bumps into a different taken-for-granted ordinariness. Intentionally bumping into the diversity of taken-for-granted habits of different cultures may keep us from taking our own ordinary circumstances as normative.

Applying the Scriptures with a clear understanding of the contrasting as well as the overlapping values between the text and our cultural contexts is an urgent task. This requires not only a sufficiently rich reading of Scripture but also an understanding of how the Scripture gets expressed in an intelligible manner in diverse cultures, connecting it to the hopes and fears and errors of the people in a particular time and place. There is a pinch when a particular application (for example, organ music or Sunday school or leadership style) becomes entrenched as if it were the only reasonable one. At those times, the community of the saints is not always a communion of the saints, and the canon of Scripture too often gives way to innumerable canons within the canon implicitly justifying singular applications. Retreating into the safety of an ecclesial tradition or communal enclave may be a natural intuition, but safeguarding the identity of the church in this way undermines its connection to other churches that look very different in other cultural settings.

We overcome the exclusivist renderings of the application of Scripture when we fully wrestle with the idols that hover near a community's heart in our own cultural setting. This requires reading the Scripture not only in a community but against the community as well. Self criticism by a community is an important witness to the wider world, but biblical criticism of the community and its culture is a yet more powerful form of testimony. As Todd Billings notes, "All cultures have idols that resist God's transformation in the reading of Scripture; therefore a critique of culture is an important practice in receiving Scripture as God's word, discerning through Scripture the bounded character of the Spirit's work in Christ, which calls all cultures to continual conversion."[37]

It is clear that our experience as individuals gives rise to tensions and conflicts between our diverse settings. The experience of life as one living in Boston in the twenty-first century carries with it different perspectives from those who were living in Boston in the eighteenth century. New immigrants to Boston see life differently from those who have been in Boston for generations. Working in the high-rises downtown and working underground on the subway give two very different perspectives on the city. All Bostonians may root for the Red Sox, but the diverse cultures of Boston cannot all be squeezed into one homogeneous perspective. We must take seriously the differences that emerge from the finite realities of human nature and the manner in which lives are always situated in historically concrete contexts. There are also differences emerging from the diverse corruptions of cultures or communities.[38] Distinguishing between these two different kinds of differences is a notoriously difficult project. Conversation across diverse communities may shed light on both sides of the spectrum, but it is the Scriptures themselves that serve as the final court of appeal to distinguish the different sides. Applying the Scriptures to particular contexts requires the exposing of cultural idols as well

---

37. J. Todd Billings, *The Word of God for the People of God: An Entryway to the Theological Interpretation of Scripture* (Grand Rapids: Eerdmans, 2010), xv.

38. James K. A. Smith, *The Fall of Interpretation: Philosophical Foundations for a Creational Hermeneutic* (Downers Grove, IL: InterVarsity Press, 2000), and Merold Westphal, *Whose Community? Which Interpretation? Philosophical Hermeneutics for the Church*, The Church and Postmodern Culture (Grand Rapids: Baker Academic, 2009), both argue that evangelicals too strongly connect diverse appropriations of Scripture with the doctrine of sin. They take particular issue with the goal of interpretation as an objectively adequate non-context-dependent interpretation. However, both Smith and Westphal downplay the spectrum of differences between better and worse interpretations and thereby suggest that differences of appropriation are almost always owing to the peculiar perspective of the interpreter. But this belies the role truth plays in distinguishing better (or worse) appropriations. Anthony C. Thiselton has argued that classical foundationalism and epistemic objectivism are not necessary correlates of processes to determine truthfulness. Knowing the truth need not require objectivism any more than having a perspective requires sinfulness. See Thiselton, *The Hermeneutics of Doctrine* (Grand Rapids: Eerdmans, 2007), especially section 7.2, "Does a Communal, Contingent, Hermeneutical Approach Exclude Epistemology?," 126–34.

as appreciating the echoes of God's goodness. Communicating the power of the gospel requires both tasks.[39]

Contextualizing the Scripture is the project of translating the gospel into the language and conceptuality of a particular cultural context. It provides biblical answers to unique questions. To accomplish this contextualization, the richness and depth of the story line of the gospel must be expressed in ways that interpret and reinterpret the driving concerns of the context. This will not be successful apart from sensitivity to the peculiar language, values, and thought forms of the particular cultural context. Parts of the cultural narrative should be affirmed while also graciously exposing the mythologies grounded in other parts of the cultural narrative. Inevitably, different contextualizations should emerge in different contexts because of the diverse cultural locations into which the gospel goes. There is a unique, unrepeatable quality to each culture (and subculture) by virtue of the distinctive embodiment of persons in those historical and cultural contexts. On this side of paradise, every human experience will also be partially corrupted and intertwined with the socially constructed networks of brokenness in which their communities are located.[40] The fallen condition is individual and communal.[41] Appreciation for

---

39. Timothy Keller refers to this as the "missionary encounter" with one's own culture. In that encounter, there is a deep connection to the culture and a significant confrontation of that culture. In this regard, the church maintains its distinctiveness, serves and cares generously for all its neighbors, and calls people to repent and believe in compelling ways. See Keller, *How to Reach the West Again: Six Essential Elements of a Missionary Encounter* (New York: Redeemer City to City Press, 2020), 11.

40. Thiselton comments, "Many postmodern understandings of the human as corporately under bondage to forces of power beyond the control of the individual have more in common with biblical perspectives than the shallow liberal theological optimism that speaks only of the infinite value of an individual 'soul.'" Thiselton, *Hermeneutics of Doctrine*, 196. See also Thiselton, *Interpreting God and the Postmodern Self: On Meaning, Manipulation and Promise* (Edinburgh: T&T Clark, 1995). It should be added that evangelicals are no less optimistic than liberals when it comes to thinking about human nature.

41. The dialectic between systemic and individual corruptions may explain the sharp differences between recent theological communitarians (e.g., Stanley Hauerwas and Alasdair MacIntyre) and those who have defended individual human rights as a fundamental restraint on communal corruptions (e.g., Nicholas Wolterstorff and Jeffrey Stout). Reading both sides of the debate may temper individualistic tendencies among evangelicals and the unqualified embrace of communities on the other side. See Hauerwas, *A Community of Character: Toward*

diverse contextualizations must account for communities being differently embodied as well as differently dysfunctional.[42]

The history of music in the life of the church is an example of how we grapple with contextualization. Musical style is not simply a matter of taste, nor is it simply a matter of indifference. Music is a form of communication every bit as unique and important to a cultural setting as the spoken or written word. As there are genres of writing that communicate in unique ways, so there are musical genres that carry with them particular values intrinsic to the historical context from which they emerge. Hip-hop emerged as a music of protest in the midst of deep racial inequities of the 1980s.[43] Early folk was also the music of protest, but it emerged in the conflict of a generation gap in the post-World War II period.[44] As the historical contexts changed and consumer pressures were applied, both genres mutated. Churches were largely hesitant to embrace either genre because they had originated outside of the church, and also because of the way in which their adoption into consumer markets lessened their prophetic voice. Unfortunately, many churches held on to a populist genre of music that originated at the turn of the nineteenth into the twentieth century. The result was not only the loss of a prophetic edge in music but also the loss of a compelling musical language to communicate with American culture in the latter half of the twentieth century.

---

a *Constructive Christian Social Ethic* (Notre Dame: University of Notre Dame Press, 1981), and Hauerwas, *In Good Company: The Church as Polis* (Notre Dame: University of Notre Dame Press, 1995). See also Nicholas Wolterstorff, *Justice: Rights and Wrongs* (Princeton: Princeton University Press, 2008), and Jeffrey Stout, *Democracy and Tradition* (Princeton: Princeton University Press, 2004).

42. David Kelsey, *Eccentric Existence: A Theological Anthropology* (Louisville: Westminster John Knox, 2009), is a massive attempt at reckoning with human identity as essentially embodied without losing the distinctively theological character of personhood as both sacred and fallen.

43. On the general history of hip-hop, see Emmett G. Price, *Hip Hop Culture* (Santa Barbara: ABC-CLIO Press, 2006). The best treatment of hip-hop in the context of the church is Emmett G. Price, ed., *The Black Church and Hip Hop Culture: Toward Bridging the Generational Divide* (Lanham, MD: Scarecrow, 2011).

44. On the history of folk, see William Roy, *Reds, Whites, and Blues: Social Movements, Folk Music, and Race in the United States* (Princeton: Princeton University Press, 2013).

There were those, to be sure, who thought differently. Though it seemed radical at the time, the Jesus music exemplified by Larry Norman now looks almost tame by virtue of the revolution it produced. In the early 1960s, Norman and others in the Jesus music movement expressed the countercultural desire to speak to a new generation in the musical language of that generation—a move that was viewed with disdain by the older generation.[45] It was Norman's contention that music must not only speak to a culture but often against a culture—in this instance, against the culture of affluence that flooded America after World War II and too often domesticated the gospel. It was the language of revolution expressed by early rock that had not yet been overly commercialized, though it eventually was captured by the very economic forces against which it was arrayed in the first place. In the beginning of the 1960s, the new Jesus music sought to wage a protest against the religious status quo.[46] This did not emerge from any particular exegesis of biblical passages, but rather by looking at the cultural situation and thinking how to appropriately and prophetically apply the gospel to the nascent baby-boomer generation. The loudest criticism of the movement was that it had simply adopted the values of the new boomer culture. The mistake in that criticism was to suppose that "older" music simply floated free of a particular cultural context. Diverse cultural settings require different frames of reference to apply the gospel in a compelling and prophetic manner.

To take another example, applying the gospel in a small town and in a large urban setting in late modernity should look very different. The idols will vary across these diverse settings, as do the taken-for-granted cultural values of those settings. The temptations peculiar to small-town life are very different from the temptations peculiar

---

45. Norman's well-known song "Why Should the Devil Have All the Good Music?" spoke volumes about his intentions.

46. For a brief historical account of Jesus rock and its commercial stepchild, contemporary Christian Music (CCM), see Paul Baker, *Contemporary Christian Music: Where It Came from, What It Is, and Where It's Going* (Wheaton: Crossway, 1985).

to large cities.[47] Power brokers are present in both situations, but cultural power is exercised in very different ways. Money and ideas are the vehicles through which significance is interpreted in a large city. In a small town, hierarchies often exist by virtue of personal and family relationships. Politics is associated with people. In large cities, politics is facilitated through the media. The church is in great peril if it simply attempts to apply the gospel in one setting as if it were the same as the other. Churches need to wrestle with the habits, customs, and dominant values of their own cultural context, understanding how the gospel both challenges those values and overlaps with them.[48]

As a final example of diverse contextualizations, Christianity grew in the late Roman Empire not by virtue of any cultural privileges it possessed. It grew because it cared for people in ways that ordinary citizens of the empire did not, and because of its distinctive sexual ethic. In the memorable phrase of the second-century Epistle to Diognetus, Christians "shared their food not their bed."[49] In the empire, slaves and others lower on the social ladder were at the sexual disposal of their masters and any others higher up the social ladder. The Christian conviction about sexual chastity outside of marriage was radical in its protection of human dignity for all those lower on the social ladder—most especially for those on the very lowest rungs. The respect for those considered worthless by the empire in the manifest generosity of material resources and also in the protection of sexual relations from abuse signaled a distinctive cultural witness in the face of Roman habits and customs.[50]

47. The contrasts are stark and important. On the nature of cities, see Stephen T. Um and Justin Buzzard, *Why Cities Matter: To God, the Culture, and the Church* (Wheaton: Crossway, 2013). On small towns, see Stephen Witmer, *A Big Gospel in Small Places: Why Ministry in Forgotten Communities Matter* (Downers Grove, IL: InterVarsity Press, 2019).

48. Mass media as well as social media can appear to flatten different cultural contexts by appearing to transcend the limits of space and place. It would be wrong, however, to suppose that were true. They have exercised a profound influence, but they have not excised the concreteness of human existence.

49. Cited by Larry W. Hurtado, *Destroyer of the Gods: Early Christian Distinctiveness in the Roman World* (Waco: Baylor University Press, 2017), 153.

50. See Hurtado, *Destroyer of the Gods*, and Rodney Stark, *The Triumph of Christianity* (San Francisco: HarperOne, 2011).

The cultural pressure today is for churches to land on one side or the other of those early Christian forms of contextualized compassion. This divide appears as an unbridgeable chasm. Either one upholds the dignity of human life from conception and a "traditional" sexual ethic, or one supposes that racial/ethnic inequities matter and poverty alleviation is a priority.[51] Affirming only one side of this divide causes contemporary churches to become captive to one side of a political agenda and abandon their compelling and prophetic stance to the full breadth of late modernity. By doing so, churches grant to the wider culture the authority to set the terms of its encounter with Christianity, and thus lose their distinctiveness. Crossing this divide within the framework of the gospel would be both cultural and countercultural at the same time.

The unfortunate dichotomy between reading the Bible in support of a pro-life position or in support of racial equity has forced two different interpretive matrices on Scripture. The political lens has wrongly become the interpretive lens for reading Scripture. The concern for life is pervasive across the canon, as are the concerns for the multicultural shape of mission in the New Testament. The reality is that these two political intuitions both belong to Scripture, even though the political polarization of our time appears to require a stark choice between them. The lurking idol of our time is equating loyalty to the gospel with loyalty to a political party. While a community can never simply be removed from the political sphere, it is imperative not to be defined by the regnant political categories.

Recognition of political differences with regard to race, gender, and ethnicity or to a moral framework for life and sexuality does not entail that those concerns always be tribal in character. They can serve to undermine the arrogance of cultural structures that do not recognize their own idolatries. In the 1960s, the civil rights movement cast grave doubt on the notion of an objective American perspective that could speak for all and represent every citizen. As America learned

---

51. See Keller, *How to Reach the West*, 23–27.

painfully through the struggle, not all perspectives are created equal and not all Americans experience life in equal ways.[52] In that same era and as a result of second-wave feminism, we learned to appreciate the fact that a women's experience is not in all respects identical to a man's experience. Gender makes a difference, though it is not always clear what that difference is.[53]

Inhabiting the World
Created by the Word

Christians across the ages have continued to read the Bible long after they first became acquainted with it. There is always more to learn, and more of the Scriptures in which to be embedded. The church has insisted that its theological goal is to inhabit the narrative of redemption as revealed in the canon, not merely to understand it. Why else continue to read the Scriptures day after day and year after year?

Christian communities assume that, by consistently and persistently paying attention to the Scriptures, additional discernment is always possible.[54] There is always the hope of a richer immersion in the narrative of redemption and greater absorption into the wisdom of the gospel. It is an ordinary practice that communities read the Scriptures together, in part to guard against the eccentricities of private interpretations and in part to encourage the whole of the community to be absorbed into the whole of the gospel.

The wisdom of Scripture resides in the gospel itself, which means the Scriptures ought to interpret the Scriptures, by means of which the community of readers is interpreted. What may have seemed confounding and confusing initially may become wise and provocative

---

52. An especially valuable treatment of the civil rights movement as a distinctive theological movement can be found in Charles Marsh, "The Civil Rights Movement as Theological Drama—Interpretation and Application," *Modern Theology* 18, no. 2 (April 2002): 231–50.

53. See my *Progressive and Conservative Religious Ideologies: The Tumultuous Decade of the 1960s* (London: Routledge, 2010), chapter 5.

54. Wolterstorff, *Divine Discourse*, uses the language of "first hermeneutic" to reference the church's ongoing public reading of Scripture.

over time. It becomes wise and provocative not because the Scriptures have changed, but because readers change in their understanding of themselves in relation to the Scriptures. Luther's dictum that we should read the Scripture in the first instance as our adversary reminds us that the Scripture is in an important respect the ultimate "other." It stands against us and challenges our normal assumptions about life.[55] In utterly unexpected ways, it also invites us into its world and manifests a strange hospitality to strangers.

The Scriptures are a life-giving Word, and in this sense the church comes to know the Scriptures by living them. It is likely that diverse parts of the redemptive drama will affect diverse readers in diverse manners. And over this diversity of responses the text cannot exercise temporal control. Different communities will read the Scriptures in different ways for a host of different reasons. This descriptive diversity lays no normative claim on the church until there is an explanatory account of the differences that matter and the differences that do not matter. Noticing that the Scriptures are read in diverse ways by diverse peoples may amount to no more than that diverse people read in diverse ways.

The gospel requires that we "bump into" the differences we have with each other, which in turn requires that these differences are made intelligible across our diverse cultural and social locations. Being accountable to others is difficult, requiring both humility and confidence. If reconciliation is at the heart of the gospel, it ought to be reflected in the ways different gospel communities deal with each other across their divisions. A chief challenge facing deeply polarized ecclesial communities is to read the Scriptures "with one another" and "against each other."[56]

---

55. This Lutheran sentiment is summarized and captured well by Gerhard Ebeling, *Introduction to a Theological Theory of Language* (London: Collins, 1963), 17.

56. See Gay Byron, "Biblical Interpretation as an Act of Community Accountability," *Union Seminary Quarterly Review* 56, nos. 1-2 (2002): 55-58. Byron's central concern is the African American community of scholars, which has often been excluded from the academic guild of biblical interpreters.

As we are now well aware, the resurgence of Christianity outside of the West has revitalized diverse notions of mission and evangelism.[57] Attached to that awareness has been the (slower) realization that Christianity is translatable across a virtually infinite set of cultural contexts.[58] This theological translatability entails that biblical interpretation likewise not be confined to any single set of culturally defined parameters. The task of reading the Bible across cultural boundaries is intrinsic to the gospel. The accompanying danger of reading the Scriptures in overly particularized ways is inevitable to some extent, but this danger should not prevent the church from engaging the task of reading the Scriptures across diverse communities.[59] Getting outside our cultural cocoons of partisanship is likely to give us deeper and richer applications.[60] There is no mechanical way to determine which differences make a difference until we enter into the conversation with diverse communities and allow those conversations to instruct us about the differences that make a difference.

Showing genuine theological hospitality to the other may not settle the conflicts of our public ecclesial square, but it will more nearly reflect the gospel we confess at the heart of that ecclesial square.[61] Failure to listen to communities outside our own provides a false sense of security. For good and ill, we must recognize that messiness

---

57. The early work of Lesslie Newbigin was a particularly pungent theological call to recast the nature of mission from a "sending to foreign shores" notion to an "embedded *missio dei* in every culture" notion. See Newbigin, *The Household of God* (New York: Friendship Press, 1954), and Newbigin, *Trinitarian Faith and Today's Mission* (Richmond, VA: John Knox Press, 1964).

58. See Timothy C. Tennent, *Theology in the Context of World Christianity: How the Global Church Is Influencing the Way We Think about and Discuss Theology* (Grand Rapids: Zondervan, 2007).

59. Darrell L. Guder has written of the need for the "continuing conversion" of the church in its cross-cultural interactions. All cultural translations of the gospel bear some imprint of their social location and stand in need of correction and are only corrected as the gospel bumps up against translations from other social locations. See Guder, *The Continuing Conversion of the Church*, The Gospel and Our Culture (Grand Rapids: Eerdmans, 2002).

60. I borrow this phrase from David Brooks, "Getting Obama Right," *New York Times*, March 12, 2010, https://www.nytimes.com/2010/03/12/opinion/12brooks.html.

61. I am borrowing several clues from Martin E. Marty, *When Faiths Collide*, Blackwell Manifestos (Oxford: Blackwell, 2005), though applying the hospitality of the gospel to the interpretive square rather than to the wider global religious square, as Marty does.

in the ecclesial square is inescapable. Privileging communities above individuals or individuals above communities will not resolve this messiness. It is not a realistic option to suppose fundamental interpretive conflicts are going to be solved anytime soon, but we must never give up the yearning to be reconciled across our conflicts. We must learn to live as faithful readers with and through our diverse applications. Learning to live faithfully is a task accomplished by wisdom—and we will explore the nature of wisdom in the final chapter.

Our ancestors portrayed the world as a drama, not merely a place with objects. The constituent elements of the drama were order and chaos and not material things. Order is where events are predictable and cooperative. Chaos is where the unexpected happens that you cannot control. How do I ensure order rather than chaos? was the primary question of life.

—JORDAN PETERSON, 12 RULES FOR LIFE

10

THE WISDOM OF DIVERSITY AND THE DIVERSITY OF WISDOM

WISDOM IN AN AGE OF DIVERSITY

In this book I have been trying to understand the great diversity of differences surrounding us in this present time, to recognize the conceptual resources to think more faithfully about unity, and finally to ponder the ways of navigating life through a thickly pluralized and polarized age. There are no clear and fixed rules to deal with the complex of differences in which our lives are embedded. No set of laws could ever exhaust the diverse circumstances confronting us. Yet we are morally responsible agents called to live out our faith amid so much diversity. Thus discernment is required to know which differences make a difference, and why they make a difference. It obligates us to recognize the patterns of our cultural moment and the circumstances in which we find ourselves. It also asks us to bring to bear more than merely pragmatic intuitions that arise from our own temperaments and backgrounds. A framework of wisdom that reaches deep into the nature of the created order and the fundamental character of the Creator-creature relationship is crucial to navigating the surrounding diversities—both how they contribute to a richer unity and how they undermine aspirations for unity.

The variables we need to take into account as disagreements come to the fore in our polarized age are almost too overwhelming to catalog. Discerning the level of social trust in a particular situation is a skill not easily taught since there are too many factors involved. This means that information about the multitude of factors will never be sufficient to determine the proper course of action. Knowing central facts of the situation is important, but more is needed. That "more" is what the Bible and most cultures have referred to as wisdom. It is not the same as knowledge or information, nor is it simply the same as common sense. It is surely not to be equated with modern notions of IQ. What then is it?

The Nature of Wisdom

Wisdom begins with the realization that God has made the world with certain patterns and that our flourishing rests in embracing those patterns and resisting the lure of running contrary to those patterns. Wisdom acquiesces to the fact that we humans are not God. As the book of Proverbs reminds us, wisdom begins with the fear of the Lord. It is God who distinguishes right from wrong and declares that humans created in the image of God have an intrinsic dignity and worth as responsible moral agents. Wise people do not try to remake the world in their image but accept being made in the image of God, as are all their diverse neighbors. This first fact of wisdom accepts the fundamental goodness of the created order in which life is lived out because of the goodness of the God who made it.[1]

The second fact of wisdom is the recognition that the world is not the way it is supposed to be. What may seem to be a conflict between these two "facts of wisdom" is actually part of the perplexing nature of wisdom itself. It is able to distinguish between the goodness of the created order and the brokenness of the created order, neither naively accepting the brokenness nor becoming cynical about the loss of goodness in the world. Wisdom is able to cut the gordian knot between the intrinsic goodness of the created order and

---

1. Two very helpful introductions to the nature of wisdom in the Bible are Craig G. Bartholomew and Ryan P. O'Dowd, *Old Testament Wisdom Literature: A Theological Introduction* (Downers Grove, IL: IVP Academic, 2011), and Tremper Longman III, *The Fear of the Lord Is Wisdom: A Theological Introduction to Wisdom in Israel* (Grand Rapids: Baker Academic, 2017).

the interwoven brokenness of that very same created order. Parents must make this distinction all the time, teaching their children the "protective restrictions" of freedom, treating them with dignity and compassion and with realistic discipline when their children's moral dysfunctions manifest themselves. Parental wisdom does not choose between love and correction.

A third fact of wisdom is that it is at home in diverse environments because it is by nature sensitive to the diversity of circumstances. Wisdom is at home in the sea of diversity because wisdom discerns the differences that make a difference across diverse contexts.[2] It does not flatten out reality by presuming that every situation is the same and that the same method of social interaction will be appropriate in every diverse setting. A wise person easily pivots as circumstances change. When the apostle Paul asserts that he has become all things to all people (1 Cor 9:22), he is simply affirming that he has learned to approach different people in different ways. Wisdom sees through the diversity of circumstances not by virtue of a universal law but by the simple nature of diversity. Evangelism that assumes everyone is curious about God in the same way will fail. Marriages that assume that husbands and wives think out of the same intuitions are headed for ruin. Wisdom is that ability to step into these situations and recognize and appreciate the differences.

The writer of Proverbs supposes that sometimes it is important to answer fools (26:5) and sometimes it is important not to answer fools (26:4). Knowing when to answer and when not to answer is a matter of wisdom. In Proverbs 26, the difference relates to the expectation of outcomes. If we are tempted by the foolishness of the fool, then wisdom suggests we refrain from answering. If, on the other hand, we discern the fool may come to understand the folly of his or her ways, wisdom suggests we provide a genuine response. When is it

---

2. Cf. Tremper Longman III, *How to Read Proverbs* (Downers Grove, IL: InterVarsity Press, 2002): "Wisdom, then is not a matter of memorizing proverbs and applying them mechanically and absolutely. Wisdom is knowing the right circumstance to apply the right principle to the right person" (56).

wise to answer a fool and when is it not? No list of rules could ever completely exhaust the proper circumstances by which we might distinguish the cases. At the heart of circumstantial wisdom is the relational intelligence requisite to understand the character of the person with whom we are dealing.

A theological illustration may help expand the point. It is not an uncommon claim in the history of Protestant theological reflection to affirm that pride is the root of all sin.[3] However, many in a congregation do not primarily suffer under the pretense of pride and hubris. In their hearts, prideful assertion is not what undermines their relationship to the living God or to those around them. Their own self-identity may tend in the opposite direction—toward insecurity and insignificance rather than the will to power.[4] Wisdom understands that character flaws are different for different people. Painting human dysfunctions with one large brush leads inevitably to simplistic solutions. Cornelius Plantinga has written, "Sin is conceptually messy."[5] There is not one deadly sin, but at least seven of them, and even that classic set of categories does not fully capture the many faces of our dysfunctions and brokenness.[6] Wisdom demands that we treat human dysfunctions with all the conceptual complexity to which human experience testifies, and to which the biblical record gives ample testimony.

---

3. This is the central way in which Reinhold Niebuhr characterizes sin in *The Nature and Destiny of Man: A Christian Interpretation* (Louisville: Westminster John Knox, 1996 [original 1941]).

4. This was actually the claim being made by several feminists in the 1960s. One of those voices, Valerie Saiving wrote, "The temptations of woman as woman are not the same as the temptations of man as man, and the specifically feminine forms of sin ... have a quality which can never be encompassed by such terms as 'pride' and 'will to power.' They are better suggested by such terms as triviality, distractibility, and diffuseness; lack of an organizing center or focus; dependence on others for one's self-definition; tolerance at the expense of standards of excellence ... in short, underdevelopment or negation of the Self." Saiving, "The Human Situation: A Feminine View," *Journal of Religion* 40, no. 2 (1960): 108–9.

5. Cornelius Plantinga Jr., *Not the Way It's Supposed to Be: A Breviary of Sin* (Grand Rapids: Eerdmans, 1995), 12.

6. See Rebecca Konyndyk DeYoung, *Glittering Vices: A New Look at the Seven Deadly Sins and Their Remedies*, 2nd ed. (Grand Rapids: Brazos, 2020).

A fourth fact about wisdom is that it is a learned habit, but there is no mechanical means to acquire it. Wisdom is not simply a means of self-improvement, as if one could by sheer willpower learn how to be wise. Ben Franklin's famous list of self-improvement principles carried with it much wisdom in regard to interpersonal relationships (for example, talking rather than listening too much, seeking truth for its own sake as opposed to defeating your opponent in argument, not telling long and pointless stories, not ridiculing those with whom you disagree), but lacked the complexity of knowing how these principles become woven into one's character.[7] Franklin's principles often focus on influencing others for one's own benefit, which is contrary to wisdom as it is described in Scripture. Biblical wisdom is not interested in self-promotion but in the flourishing of the relationships in which one is embedded. Wisdom is confidently humble and able to glean insights from a variety of diverse sources. Wisdom resists listening only to those who reinforce one's own opinions. It takes seriously the opinions of those who disagree. By this a wise person places the well-being of others ahead of his or her own self-interest. A wise person is also open to correction and yearns for deeper knowledge. Wisdom is not so much possessed as a goal for which one aims. Wisdom comes from the influence of wise people and resists the influence of foolishness. This entails that one be able to distinguish between wisdom and foolishness to begin with. As the book of Proverbs suggests, you need wisdom to understand wisdom (4:7). It is also important to realize that wise persons are sometimes foolish and foolish persons are sometimes wise.

A final fact about wisdom is captured in the old adage about truth: "If you want someone to know the truth, tell them the truth. If you want someone to live that truth, tell them a story." We all live our lives in the midst of our memories of the past, inside the "stories" we tell ourselves. In this regard, our memories are a selective retelling of the story of our

---

7. See Walter Isaacson, *Benjamin Franklin: An American Life* (New York: Simon & Schuster, 2003).

lives. There is an inevitable linking of the past to the present in our minds. Sometimes it is done consciously, but often it is done below the surface of our consciousness. Memories are the means by which we are embedded in a story, and as with any novel, certain events are emphasized more than others. Those points of emphasis illustrate the patterns through which we interpret the present realities. Some "tell" the stories of their lives through the crises or tragedies of their past. Others remember their best achievements and the accolades awarded them. None of us recall the same events in exactly the same way. Our peculiar memories are not simply chosen by a conscious decision on our part. The patterns of our memories never entirely match up to the reality of the past, nor do they adequately interpret how others experienced those same events. As a result, wisdom calls us to be humble about our memories and to temper the confidence they appear to give to us about the significance of past events. Wisdom helps us place those memories into larger contexts because it recognizes our own self-perceptions, though appropriate, are not always fully aligned to reality. Listening to the stories of others well requires us to accept them for what they are and challenge them for what they are not—and we should come to expect that of others as they listen to our stories.

The history of American histories is fascinating in just this regard. Our collective memories have ebbed and flowed across the centuries. Images are formed in one era that change significantly in later eras. We tell the story of "America" differently in different periods of American history. James Madison has long been pictured as a virtuous founding father whose intellect was a large influence on the shape of the new republic. In recent decades, though, historians have also come to judge Madison as lacking in courage and integrity in times of war—especially the very unpopular war of 1812.[8] The presidency

---

8. Cf. Michael Beschloss, *Presidents of War: The Epic Story, from 1807 to Modern Times* (New York: Crown, 2018), and Noah Feldman, *The Three Lives of James Madison: Genius, Partisan, President* (New York: Random House, 2017).

of Ulysses S. Grant has also undergone significant revision in recent decades. The historical memory of Grant in the era of Jim Crow was of a failed presidency fraught with internal corruption and a constant losing battle with alcoholism. While acknowledging the realities of corrupt staff and an ongoing struggle against alcohol, contemporary historians have painted a larger and greatly revised picture of Grant that includes major civil rights legislation and a determined battle against racism in the aftermath of the Civil War.[9] Histories of the Vietnam War have emphasized the disastrous decisions that led to the horrible outcomes of the war, but that story has been much more fully told with the release of the audio tapes of Lyndon Johnson. The tapes tell a different story of Johnson's advisors than was known previously, and Robert McNamara in particular.[10] We now know Johnson was ambivalent about the war from the beginning, while his advisors strongly pushed him into war. With each of these presidents, the stories of their successes and failures have been significantly revised as historians have uncovered more of the circumstances of their presidencies. The stories changed even as they retained many of their earlier elements.

Wisdom discerns when a fuller story is needed to fill out the account, though often other limitations restrict our access to the facts of the larger story. Stepping back (or up) to the thirty-thousand-foot level, the story of creation, fall, redemption, and consummation has been told for us as the primary plotline of eternity. We do not have all the "facts" of the story, but the Great Storyteller has given us the patterns in which that story is to be interpreted and in which our own lives fit. Wisdom, as the Proverbs remind us, begins with the fear/respect of the Lord. The Bible is a story of human persons embedded in an account of the good life and eternal life. It is when we make our peace with those patterns of the good life that our deepest satisfactions

---

9. Chernow, *Grant*.

10. Michael Beschloss, *Reaching for Glory: Lyndon Johnson's Secret White House Tapes, 1964–1965* (New York: Simon & Schuster, 2001).

are illuminated and our tragic behaviors are placed into a more adequate moral framework—both one of justice and of undeserved mercy
and forgiveness. It is also when we come to understand and embrace
the reality that we are living on the plane of eternity that we will come
to see the dignity of others rooted in that same eternity.[11]

The Wisdom and Foolishness
of Group Identities

The world of late modern democracy works with a multitude of stereotypes arising from the enormous social complexity of our times.
But persons are never reducible simply to their group identities—
whether as Asian Americans, religious liberals, or conservative
Republicans. These group identities do matter but should never be
viewed as exhaustive. Persons are far too complex to be captured by
any single group to which they belong, whether that belonging is voluntary or by the reality of one's birth. The right of free association in
a democracy captures the instinct that the groups to which we belong
may well change over time, and any one of them does not fully illuminate one's broader identity. There are some groups so large they
could not possibly do justice to individual identities within the group.
Large group identities such as "evangelicals" or "fans of college foot-
ball" may express one variable in a person's preferences, but these
tendencies must be described at such a generic level as to downplay
how different its members are in their relationship to the group itself.

So it is with other kinds of judgments made of people. Stereotyping
others has been a significant part of the exclusion narrative detailed in
chapter 2. Stereotyping is part and parcel of a fallen world. Classifying
individuals on the basis of a group identity runs against the grain
of democratic individualism. The claim of "equal dignity for all"
means that everyone is to be treated with dignity as an individual.
However, the rise of modern sociological treatments of group patterns

---

11. Cf. Leon Kass, *The Beginning of Wisdom: A Commentary on Genesis* (New York: The
Free Press, 2003).

has brought with it the tendency to treat individuals as intrinsically belonging to groups, all of which have unique, sociologically defined tendencies. Political analysts divide groups by voting blocs—"white suburban women vote this way," "evangelicals on average voted this way in the last three elections," "people under the age of thirty-five voted this way." At the macro level these sorts of statistical analyses have merit. But at the micro level, they lead to stereotypes—namely, interpreting people's actions on the basis of their group's political voting record. Experts in data analytics help companies selling consumer goods know what kinds of marketing appeals to their target consumer audience. Dividing people into consumer groups helps companies spend their marketing dollars more efficiently. It also forms stereotypes of those very same consumer groups, and blurs the difference between group behavior and individual identity. Church planters will often study the demographic patterns of the intended population. While collecting data and recognizing patterns of ordinary behavior and beliefs can help frame an effective means of understanding the general area, it can also lead to the formation of neighborhood stereotypes unless one is mindful that group identity is not equivalent to individual identity. Unique individuals can be easily lost in large group social identities.

Resisting the move from group identity to individual identity ought not entail that one's group identity is considered insignificant or unimportant. The complex of voices speaking into any individual's identity is too vast to suppose that an individual's habits and thoughts are solely determined by an attachment to a single group or community. The sheer diversity of late modernity ought to make us leery of overdetermining the ties between group and individual identity, without giving up the intuition that groups exercise an enormous influence on our lived experience. These wider associations help to shape what we take to be normal and natural.

How then could we possibly account for large sociologically relevant patterns of group identity while still treating individuals as responsible moral agents in their own right? Wisdom. Wisdom is able to take both ends of this spectrum into account simultaneously. As preachers target their message to the congregation as a whole because of the patterns they have discovered in the congregation, so they must also develop ways of communicating that treat individual congregants as individuals. There is no single mechanical way to develop this skill, but failing to do so will prove relationally disastrous to a preacher. The blessing in this is to reckon more carefully with the ways in which individuals are profoundly relational, profoundly influenced by their peer group, and also unique individuals with their own identity in the sea of diversity.

THE NEIGHBORLY PRACTICE OF WISDOM

Part of the task of the church is making the case that the church's mission actually contributes to the flourishing of the wider culture in this very respect. While not supposing the church is free from corruption, its mission is to be a witness to the dignity of every human life, to the inevitable brokenness of every human life, and to the surprising mercy of God that is to be reflected in the intentional work of reconciliation of those at enmity with each other. Evangelical churches have failed to make this a significant goal in the last several generations, and desperately need to confront their negligence in not caring for the diverse contexts in which God has put them. Striving to be good, honest, and gracious neighbors ought to be part of the church's task in every age, but especially in our polarized democracy. Not only will this open doors for witness, but the logic of the gospel requires it. This is the logic that puts the well-being of others ahead of our own well-being.

This is captured in the parable of the good Samaritan (Luke 10:25–34). In this story, Jesus reminds the religious lawyer that his neighbor is anyone and everyone whom he finds in need, and is surely not limited to those who offer him social benefits by their association. The parable is startling because it overturns the accepted stereotypes then operative in the Middle East. The Samaritans would have been considered cultural outcasts by comparison to the pharisee in the story. Yet as the story unfolds, it is the Samaritan who extends mercy to the one lying injured on the side of the road—a stranger who likely would have otherwise hated the Samaritan. All the while, the allegedly virtuous Pharisee passes by the injured stranger, caring more for his own comforts than the needs of the other. Being careful not simply to put ourselves in the place of the Samaritan, the deeper meaning of the parable is that God has come to us as the Samaritan came to the stranger— expressing mercy in the most surprising of circumstances.[12] This is neighborliness as the gospel spells it out. It does not require us to be heroes but servants. The hero is known for self-assertion in the face of great odds. The servant is known for self-sacrifice to help others.[13]

WISDOM FOR OUR CULTURAL MOMENT

We should continue to ask why certain differences have come to the front of our cultural consciousness. Understanding the historical contexts of the differences that have garnered our attention is a first step in dealing constructively with them. This understanding provides a means to evaluate the significance of the differences against the context of other times and places. Racial divides have been part of the American experience for four centuries. We should not suppose these can simply be ignored or that they affect everyone in the same way. They are deeply ingrained in our historical narrative, virtually ubiquitous in contemporary culture, and maddeningly complex. Recognizing that a unique historical narrative has framed race relations also helps to resist the notion that these racial divides are a permanent part of the created order. The absence of these racial divides in other times and other places provides guidance for overcoming the tragedies of our own history. It is not an option simply to accept these divisions at face value or to suppose that they do not undermine the biblical commitment of universal human dignity. How we treat each other across racial divides goes a long way toward illustrating how we understand the God who created this diversity.

---

12. See Timothy Keller, *Generous Justice: How God's Grace Makes Us Just* (New York: Penguin, 2012).

13. Elizabeth Newman, *Untamed Hospitality: Welcoming God and Other Strangers* (Grand Rapids: Brazos, 2007).

The exclusion narrative by which our culture understands the tragic history of race relations in American history has also been used by some to defend a new sexual morality. Sex outside of marriage was long considered immoral not because those engaged in it lacked human dignity, but because the action itself was understood within a larger moral framework. The freedom from any moral framework other than one's own self-determination has unfortunately led to the claim that the older sexual ethic was itself oppressive and discriminatory.

We should remember that on a secular rendering of morality, there can be no absolute or universal moral values, which means that there would be no secular moral basis to claim anything is wrong with cultural forms of oppression to begin with. It is only within a moral framework of universal human dignity arising from a transcendent source that cultural forms of oppression can be accurately diagnosed. And even then, wisdom is required to determine the difference between disagreement and disparagement. In a democracy that trumpets freedom from external controls, the discrimination narrative has too easily become all-encompassing to account for any and all differences.[14] Disagreement happens for multiple reasons, and moral disagreement is not equivalent to disparaging those with whom one disagrees. Disparaging others manifests a disregard for the intrinsic dignity of human life. Discerning the difference between disagreement, disparagement, and discrimination is critically important in a time like ours.

Wisdom and the Church

If wisdom is required in the public square, how much more so in the ecclesial square. The gospel is the very form of sacred wisdom appropriate to dealing with ecclesial diversity. It is the gospel for which the church exists and through which the church is to act. It is

---

14. See Robin DiAngelo, *White Fragility: Why It Is So Difficulty for White People to Talk about Racism* (Boston: Beacon, 2018). While directly confronting the conflicts over race relations, DiAngelo unfortunately interprets all racial conflicts along the oppression-discrimination spectrum and supposes only a win/lose scenario. In so doing, she greatly oversimplifies the conflicts and limits the actual possibilities of genuine improvement.

as a consequence of the gospel that the "dividing wall of hostility" is broken down in Christ (Eph 2:14).[15] He is our "peace" in whom the many are fit into one body and with whom the many diverse members are to contribute.[16]

The way we deal with diversity inside the church ought to be squarely rooted in the logic of the gospel. The reconciling work of the gospel contains impulses that take seriously the corruption in the hearts of individuals and the lives of communities. The gospel restrains temptations toward self-righteousness found in the abuse of authority as well as the independence from all authority. Inside the wisdom of the gospel, the democratic impulse ought to serve as a restraint on the self-righteous ethos that too often attends those in authority. And in reverse, inhabiting the gospel ought to temper the uninhibited choosing of individuals for themselves unleashed by the democratic impulse.

Inside the church, democratic impulses beg for a theological account of individuals and the communities in which they are bound together. Democracy as a theologically interpreted category, rather than a political or economic category, demands a wider narrative. There are no such things as bare democracies. Democracy intuitively distrusts the concentration of power, but often sidelines substantive discussion of the common good because of the diversity of convictions it protects. In the church, the common good is the communal orientation toward the living God. There may be a host of other goods the church protects, but it is the central good of its covenant with the living God that ought to make it always vigilant against the abuse of human authority and the autonomy of an unfettered human will, both

---

15. Lesslie Newbigin writes, "There is no place at which mankind can receive the gift of unity except the mercy-seat which God has provided. We can only be made one at the point where our sins are forgiven and we are therefore enabled to forgive one another." Newbigin, *Is Christ Divided?: A Plea for Christian Unity in a Revolutionary Age* (Grand Rapids: Eerdmans 1961), 9.

16. See Eph 2:11–16; 4:1–16. In chapter 2, Paul writes of the "two becoming one," and in chapter 4, he writes of the body being held together by its many joints.

of which are fully capable of revisioning the merciful covenant God has established through Jesus.

The first ecumenical council in Acts 15 manifested theological checks and balances inherent in the gospel in order that the gentiles would not be excluded. However one construes the structures of authority in the Jerusalem Council, it is clear that theologically informed democratic impulses were operative in the deliberations of the council. Diverse voices were given a platform to process the complicated issues surrounding the relationship of Jewish Christians and gentile converts. There was a profound loyalty to the gospel, which in turn generated a generous spirit towards the gentile unbelievers.[17]

The gospel communities that emerged from the Jerusalem Council embraced diverse tribes, races, and cultures, all because Christ was the peace who had broken down the dividing wall of hostility in his death and resurrection.[18] The gospel is expressed in the church as the reconciliation of estranged parties because they belong to the same Lord. At the heart of the gospel is not the overcoming of diversity but the reconciling impulse in dealing with "strangers."[19] Reconciliation is the goal because of the prior experience of reconciliation with God in and through the gospel. Reconciliation does not obliterate the differences between strangers. In the divine-human experience of reconciliation, the two parties retain their differences. God is still God, and we are still creatures after reconciliation has been effected by the gospel. As a result of the gospel, we learn to interpret those differences charitably. So it is with reconciliation that takes place within the church. The estranged parties retain many of the differences after

17. Lesslie Newbigin makes this point most powerfully in his *Foolishness to the Greeks* (Grand Rapids: Eerdmans, 1986).

18. This is one of the central claims in Hans Boersma, *Violence, Hospitality, and the Cross: Reappropriating the Atonement Tradition* (Grand Rapids: Baker Academic, 2005).

19. Michael S. Horton, *Covenant and Salvation: Union with Christ* (Louisville: Westminster John Knox, 2007), makes this same point with regard to Christians being united to Christ. Salvation does not "merge" identities but rather reconciles estranged parties. See especially chapter 9, "Covenant Participation: Meeting a Stranger."

reconciliation, though the differences no longer serve as fundamental obstacles to a renewed relationship.

Much of human experience within the church in our times expresses a very large "but." Far too many people experience the church not as a place of reconciliation but as a place of conflict. Its profession of the gospel and the reality of the contrary make the church especially liable to the criticism of hypocrisy—by outsiders and insiders. The answer to this criticism is to abandon the utopianism that underlies it. The gospel is not a story about the church's perfectibility and especially not the appearance of perfection. It is a misunderstanding of the very character of the gospel that leads to this criticism. This misunderstanding works on the assumption that, by God's help, the church and those within it somehow lose their moral deficiencies. This erroneous assumption leads to the expectation that when the church manifests dysfunctions and brokenness, we should be surprised and cynical. This legalist heresy supposes that God demands (near perfect) obedience to a law as a prerequisite of being acceptable. But the grace of the gospel is not grounded in obedience, and when the church (unfortunately) succumbs to the legalist heresy, it should rightly be criticized for losing sight of the gospel.

Navigating the mysterious tension between the free, unmerited grace of the gospel and the life of those forgiven by that grace requires a sacred wisdom. It is reflected not in a new kind of self-righteousness but in the humble, self-denying act of reaching out to those who are different and from whom one might be estranged. This is the heart of the sacred wisdom of the gospel as it pertains to the issue of diversity and disagreement inside of the church. The manner in which the church deals with diversity inside its own membership is often reflective of its understanding (or misunderstanding) of the gospel. That is to say, the gospel itself contains the seeds of wisdom in dealing with internal diversity. It is theological wisdom precisely in the sense that it arises from the work and character of God in the gospel.

The peculiar wisdom the church is called to possess is by virtue of the Scripture that serves as its constitution. This is not a wisdom common to the wider culture, though on some occasions it will surely overlap with the common wisdom of a culture. Insofar as the Scriptures give no explicit instructions regarding theories of politics or economics or aesthetics, the church should be careful of speaking authoritatively into these areas. The Scriptures do speak of general concerns about economic equity and justice and beauty, which surely should guide the church's voice in any wider cultural conversation. But the church is not constituted as a political entity or an economic organization and will lose its prophetic role in the culture if it too readily equates its voice with a specialist understanding of politics or economics or art. The church will likely have specialists in its midst, and they should be encouraged to speak into the pressing issues of the day out of their specialty knowledge. Discerning the difference between individual members speaking out of their specialties and the church speaking from its own embrace of the Scriptures is both important and difficult. Wisdom in this area navigates the fine line between individual responsibilities in and to the culture and the communal responsibilities of the church in and to the culture.

THE UNEXPECTED VICTORY OF WISDOM

The ancient wisdom of Scripture may seem problematic at first glance because it affirms that the world in which we live is both good and broken. Life is full of uncertainties, and to the human eye it is unpredictable. Biblical wisdom encourages us to adjust to the ambiguities of life, and in this regard it seeks to draw us into the mysteries of life and faith.

The wisdom of Scripture reminds us not to accept the mythologies of our times too readily. Wealth is more often a snare than a blessing. Humility makes us more stable than pride. The tongue (and Twitter) is to be used judiciously. A faithful marriage is more satisfying than a momentary experience of sex outside of marriage (online or in person). Possessing political power is both a great responsibility and a terrible danger.

These brief proverbs are discussion starters leading into a more careful consideration of central myths that the human heart embraces in every age, though the context and circumstances of those myths will vary greatly from age to age and from culture to culture. These bits of wisdom are not intended as a set of rules to follow but rather as guides to help to navigate the vagaries of life. The navigation system works by calling attention to the need for a moral center that sees through the myths we humans create to validate ourselves and our insecurities.

In our era of intense pluralization, there is a great need for a navigation system able to discern why certain differences appear to matter more than other differences. It is also important to learn to recognize other kinds of difference that are overlooked but play a significant, if hidden, role in our disagreements. As we have seen, the long and tragic history of race relations in America continues to echo loudly in our time through the complexities of our racial experiences today. Individual temperaments are not determined by race or culture, but wisdom would strongly suggest they play a significant role in the way our cultural conflicts are played out locally and nationally.

In our time of identity ambiguities, there is an inevitable search and yearning for a stable place to situate oneself. The search for those places of stability and security in the midst of so many diverse options creates openings for the dominant myths of our time to gain credence. In a consumer world, wealth possession (rather than wealth creation) is seen as a buffer against the vicissitudes of life. In a technological time, we treat our gadgets as security blankets. In a time of polarized politics, hatred for our opponents on the other end of the spectrum grants solidarity with those on our end of the spectrum. In a time of deep uncertainties, new forms of authoritarianism can give the illusion of providing order in the midst of chaos.

In each of these areas, wisdom leads us to a more realistic understanding of the way God has made us, and also the ways in which our dysfunctions are manifest. It is too easy for most of us to see someone else's brokenness. It is incredibly difficult to have a realistic understanding of our own flaws. Navigating differences with the people we cross paths with (or those we choose not to cross paths with) must begin in the first instance with a realistic diagnosis of our own hearts and souls. Until then, jokes told at someone else's expense will not bother us. Until then, we will treat gossip as entirely appropriate. Until then, we will not reckon with our own words impulsively spoken in anger. A deep, introspective dive, though often instructive, may not always be required for this sort of wisdom. There is no one, preordained way that a realistic diagnosis must take place—but it must take place for wisdom to emerge as the doorway into fruitfully dealing with our differences.

If you ask yourself, Who are the wisest persons I know?, it is likely they will not all fit the same profile. They are likely older. They are likely to have experienced significant suffering, which resulted in their examining the meaning of life. They are not ordinarily the smartest people, nor the wealthiest people, nor the most powerful people. They may be simple farmers or artists or novelists or elementary-school-teachers or nurses or coaches. When surveys show that 90 percent of Americans believe they are above average (whatever that might mean), wisdom must be acknowledged as a rare commodity in our time. When we bump into wisdom, our hearts are strangely warmed.

When we look into our hearts with honesty, wisdom calls forth hope and not despair. We gain wisdom when we abandon hope in ourselves and learn the habits of being interwoven with others, and especially being accepted by the Lord of the universe because of this strange reality we call grace. God's strange design of justice being interwoven with mercy is the template by which our world works best. Clinging to both is crucial to expressing a wise witness to a watching world. Speaking of sin without grace leads to despair and legalism. Speaking of grace without sin leads to naivete and license.[20]

---

20. Cornelius Plantinga writes poignantly, "To speak of sin by itself, to speak of it apart from the realities of creation and grace, is to forget the resolve of God. God wants shalom and will pay any price to get it back. Human sin is stubborn, but not as stubborn as the grace of God. ... But to speak of grace without sin is surely no better. To do this is to trivialize the cross of Jesus Christ, ... to cheapen the grace of God that always comes to us with blood on it. In short, for the Christian church to ignore, euphemize, or otherwise mute the lethal reality of sin is to cut the nerve of the gospel. For the sober truth is that without full disclosure on sin, the gospel of grace becomes impertinent, unnecessary, and finally uninteresting." Plantinga, *Not the Way It's Supposed to Be*, 199.

I close, in part, where I began—in that small village in southern Zimbabwe. It was a world of differences—of traditions, of worship, of culture, of race, of socioeconomic status—and yet there was something that transcended all of those differences. We experienced it in a very short and compressed time frame—but it was clear to those of us who experienced it. The differences were real and were very much a part of the conversation during our time in the village. We did not share a common language, but we shared a common humanity as well as a common faith. Had we stayed in the village longer, undoubtedly some of the differences may have become more significant. However, it was the glimpse of a unity-in-diversity that moved all of us deep in our souls.

Many of our experiences of difference do not carry such a strong hint of underlying unity. The brokenness of the created order and of our own hearts is often too big an obstacle to see underneath the surface. It is wisdom that sees through the brokenness and the differences to an underlying unity while also not minimizing them. Wisdom discerns the differences that enrich the unity and the differences that undermine the unity.

This sort of wisdom is aspirational in nature. It will never fully be realized on this side of the grave. We await the day when every tongue, tribe, and nation will worship together in the throne room of heaven. I am not sure what that worship will look like—will it be closer to my style or more Zimbabwean? What I do know is this—that heavenly experience will not wipe away our differences, but neither will we experience those differences as disruptive to the way in which the Creator has reconciled all things to himself. May the small glimpses we get of that final realization of our unity-in-difference motivate us to work for it on this side of the grave and yearn for it on the other.

ACKNOWLEDGMENTS

U nity and difference in the life of the church is the primary focus of this book. Its origins lie in a previous work of mine on the explosive and surprising decade of the 1960s. That decade exploded the mythology of a settled American cultural unity and set in motion fierce culture wars over the direction of the country. It brought to the fore deep differences that had previously simmered below the surface. Into this strange new world, the church rethought its mission. It was no longer simply a carrier of a unified Christian culture, but now was a marginal voice in a time when religious faith seemed increasingly irrelevant.

In my own reflections, the work of Lesslie Newbigin (1909–1998) gained special prominence. The former English bishop reminded the West as far back as the 1970s that the church now resided in a missionary context and must learn to speak the gospel in a new language. Alongside Newbigin, the work of Peter Berger illustrated that this post-religious world was also a world of pluralism and deep polarities. In light of this, how would the church not only learn a new language but also learn how to live faithfully into its calling of being a community of unity-in-difference?

I am grateful for friends and colleagues who have generously given of their time and energy to read the manuscript in whole or in part as it morphed into its final form. Kevin Vanhoozer, George Marsden, Darryl Hart, Ben Sasse, Jim Singleton, Sean McDonough, Steve Crocco, Drew Martin, Nathan Dicks, and Graham Cole are to be thanked in particular. I have had the privilege the last several years of working with Redeemer City to City in New York City. It is a ministry of deep collaboration across the five boroughs bringing together churches across a wide denominational spectrum for the purpose of learning to speak "Newbigin's new language." Its intellectual inspiration and founder, Tim Keller, has been a genuine servant leader in the movement to see gospel-shaped churches work together. I am grateful for his friendship and for his willingness to experiment with new ways to train pastors in a place like New York City.

I am also grateful to Todd Hains and the folks at Lexham Press for taking on this project, which, though relevant in this era of polarization, is also a project with significant minefields surrounding it. And many thanks to Elliot Ritzema, my editor at Lexham, for making both the prose and the argument of the book much more clear than it would have been without his deft touch.

After thirty-five years on the faculty of Gordon-Conwell Theological Seminary, the last ten as the chief academic officer, I am thankful for the experience of unusual unity-in-diversity across those years. At times the diverse voices pulled in the same direction, and other times not so much. Learning to appreciate those realities was not always easy, but it was an important learning lab for thinking through what makes communities healthy or not. Preparing pastors to step into churches facing the same set of questions only amplified these concerns. To colleagues across more than three decades I owe a deep debt of gratitude.

Though the focus of the book is largely on the unique community of the church, it is undoubtedly true that friends and family were the communities that most strongly shaped how I think about unity and difference. Long-time friends Brannin and Tanya, from a different generation, living and ministering on a different coast, with vastly different backgrounds, nonetheless share a strong sense of being invested in the same mission of the gospel. I am deeply thankful for their commitment to me and to this project, which I have dedicated to them.

Kate, Sarah, Lucas, and now Nathan (Ward and Henry) and Emily have encouraged and challenged my assumptions about how families deal with differences while sharing core values. They have made sure there is always a gracious edge even if we do not see eye to eye. They have laughed when I take these issues too seriously, reminding me that our common humanity means there is always something to enjoy if you look in the right places. They also remind me what a special gift God has given me in my best friend, life partner, and the one who has taught me more about unity-in-difference than a thousand books on the subject possibly could. Ann has made sure this project was finally completed because she knew the book was but a simple reminder that God has made us to be a difference-in-unity, and that the reminder is never a substitute for the real thing.

SUBJECT INDEX